ARNOLD FOUNDATION STUDIES

NEW SERIES: VII

ARNOLD FOUNDATION STUDIES

The Arnold Foundation of Southern Methodist University was established in 1924 with an endowment from Mrs. Ora Nixon Arnold of Houston to assist in training young men for leadership in public affairs and to stimulate a greater interest in general in the problems of citizenship.

From 1933 to 1943, the Foundation issued its Studies quarterly; in 1950 the New Series was initiated, to consist of somewhat longer monographs which are to appear at irregular intervals.

New Series

Edgar Quinet

A STUDY IN FRENCH PATRIOTISM

RICHARD HOWARD POWERS

Arnold Foundation Studies VII

DALLAS: SOUTHERN METHODIST UNIVERSITY PRESS

LIBRARY OF CONGRESS CATALOG CARD NUMBER: 57-9693

PRINTED IN THE UNITED STATES OF AMERICA AT DALLAS, TEXAS

To
Walter L. Dorn

Acknowledgments

I WISH TO EXPRESS my gratitude to M. Georges Duveau for his encouragement, aid, and advice when I was beginning this study; to D. L. Demorest who read the manuscript and made many important and helpful suggestions; and particularly to Walter L. Dorn who suggested and directed its preparation, and who gave me his time and counsel without stint. I wish also to express my gratitude to the staff of the *Bibliothèque nationale* for their courtesy and assistance.

RICHARD HOWARD POWERS

Southern Methodist University
Dallas, Texas

Contents

Introduction

AS IT HAS BEEN SAID of the French that no other nationality (save, perhaps, the English) possesses a common consciousness more deeply rooted or more stubbornly enduring, so it has been said of Edgar Quinet that in all of French literature there exists no other author whose books teach the fatherland with a more persuasive force. A publicist, a philosopher, a poet, and a historian, Quinet was a patriot first.

Edgar Quinet was born at Bourg en Bresse in the department of Ain on February 17, 1803; he died at Versailles on March 27, 1875. The aftermath of Austerlitz was his earliest memory, Sedan the realization of a prophecy frequently repeated. For the French patriot the contrast between these events was a painful one. The reality which found its most shocking material expression in the debacle of 1870, but which had confronted France since 1815, was the decline of national political influence. For many a patriot no other hurt could have engendered the distress which accompanied this ever more apparent fact. Heine, indeed, attributed the restlessness and impatience, so marked in the period between these dates, to the suspicion of Frenchmen generally that the twilight of their greatness was upon them.

Certainly, things had gone miserably wrong; but was Waterloo accidental and transitory, or was it conclusive? After the Grand Monarch, the Enlightenment, the Revolution, the Empire, had the curtain fallen? Quinet, at least, could never accept the pronouncement of Providence at Waterloo as final; he believed only that it could be explained. Error brought to light could be corrected. At first, however, the suspicion that France suffered more than a temporary military defeat in 1815 did not seem really convincing. For many the full implication of Waterloo did not become apparent until after July, 1830, and not persuasive until after February, 1848. Only after 1830 did Quinet the patriot emerge, and it was after

1848 that he turned all of his attention to explaining the reason
for failure in the past and to outlining the only hope for the
future.

The prejudice which damns, that which would honor; the half-
truth based upon careless investigation; the evaluation rooted in
limited understanding or partial familiarity; these have characterized much of the historical commentary on Edgar Quinet. There
have been good reasons for this, as well as notable exceptions to it.
First, he was an impassioned spokesman on one side of a debate
which continues to divide many Frenchmen into bitter factions. Few
historians, whatever their nationality, rise above that battle in
describing it. Secondly, Quinet was prolific; nearly half a century
separated his first from his last major work, and during the interval
his thought went through a rather complex development.

In all of his mature work the man gave evidence of being an
intense patriot; there has been no disagreement here. Love of fatherland in France has never been so much a monopoly of party, however, that Quinet may be said to be very adequately characterized
when he has been charged with that passion. His place was in the
Revolutionary tradition. In so saying one approaches unfirm but
more solid ground. A leading spokesman of that tradition, Gambetta, said, in March 1875, that Quinet was "one of the fathers of
contemporary democracy, one of those who has done the most, by
the spoken and written word and by his actions, to assure this
democracy which surrounds me."

The funeral orator was echoed at the time of the centennial
commemoration of Quinet's birth, by a spokesman who typically
refused the adjective "French" to Catholic France when he wrote of
Quinet's influence: "Since 1870 one may say that French thought
is permeated by his influence. We live amidst his thought; we live
by it."

Adrian Dansette suggests that Quinet's thought seems banal to
his mid-twentieth-century compatriots precisely because during the
Third Republic it penetrated everywhere. And, in spite of a deepen-
ing ignorance of what he wrote, the place assigned to Quinet by
friends of Revolutionary France remains a large one. Roger Soltau
epitomizes the viewpoint of this school in his interpretation of
Quinet's role:

To spend twenty years in exile, to have the courage to stay out voluntarily, not to return as long as despotism was on the throne, to have had enough disciples in France to establish the Republic of 1870, all this meant something akin, not to political thought but to religious fervor....

...Michelet and Quinet did a great work in their college pulpit, and their so-called "lectures" were a real factor in the great *élan* of 1848 and in the formation of the ideal which has been the inspiration of generation after generation of the rank and file...of French Radicalism....

What was the nature of this religious fervor? Charles-Louis Chassin was a devotee. For him Quinet was the prophet who had never forgotten for a single instant what he had felt, experienced, and understood as a boy: the debasement and soiling of the fatherland in 1814 and 1815. The sinister flames of the campfires of the foreign invaders were always before his eyes. In all of Edgar Quinet's political and literary works Chassin found those flames kept alive. Fervor was not all, there was dogma as well: Chassin learned from Quinet that man's sole hope lay in the re-establishment of the hegemony of the French spirit. The necessary first step in the reconquest of her destined role was for France to efface every material and spiritual consequence of 1814 and 1815.

Sainte-Beuve, like others who made similar comment, enjoyed repeating that, in spite of his flashes of prophetic sight, Quinet was one of those poor souls who could never quite disentangle their thought. Gabriel Monod replied that Quinet was neither confused nor befuddled, but that he saw things too large—he inherited from French classicism the habit of expressing ideas in the most general terms possible. Monod believed that Quinet, and all the reformers of the early 1840's, saw in a religious reform the condition and the necessary point of departure for social reform. A religious renovation, a democratic revolution, or at least evolution, and reassumption by France of the democratic apostleship which she had assumed by the Revolution were, Monod thought, the essential elements of Quinet's teaching and his writing during all of his life.

The frequently clever and arresting synthesis of Emile Faguet allows one to forgive, partially at least, the accident that elements in the factual record are disturbing to his generalizations. Faguet

had both shrewd and untrue things to say about Quinet. An exclusive preoccupation with religion made Quinet seem to him an
anachronism, "profoundly marked by the seal of the past." Therefore, only a religious revival could bring about a renewal of interest
in his work. Another half-century has seen but little in the way of
a renewal of such curiosity, and Quinet has remained possibly the
most neglected figure among those who played an equally important
role in nineteenth-century French thought, or in events. But, if
Quinet was anachronistic, he was not so in his preoccupation. He
had much contemporary company. Faguet himself devoted much
attention to similarly minded men.

Presuming that the eighteenth century was destructive of
authority and uncreative in its accomplishment, Faguet placed
De Maistre, Bonald, Lamennais, Ballanche, and Cousin in the
category of those who strove, in various fashions, to restore authority. Saint-Simon, Fourier, Comte, and Quinet, equally moved by
the conviction that humanity required a moral purpose, strove to
replace the authority which had crumbled. Faguet saw in Quinet
a Protestant De Maistre, less the wit, having none; or a Protestant
Bonald, without the logic, being less than sure in this regard.
De Maistre's wit and Bonald's logic are both sectarian prejudice
rather than a universal conviction. But Quinet was a spokesman
for intolerance.

Faguet reached the conclusion that although a religious revival
would bring a resurrection of Quinet's thought, and would make
him appear to have been a prophet, in the meantime his influence
had contributed to the making of a France which was antireligious.
In finding Quinet's thought banal rather than anachronistic, Adrian
Dansette would reduce it to a Protestantism without dogma or
ecclesiastical organization which, lacking the power to suppress
Catholicism, ultimately aimed at separating the Catholic Church
from the State in France. This is equivalent to saying that "anticlerical" embraces the essence of Quinet, a judgment that is close kin
to Faguet's conclusion that his influence was to help make France
antireligious. Both are essentially Catholic judgments, and are based
upon Catholic definition.

We associate with the eighteenth century the diffusion of confidence in a new Heavenly City. Because he possessed reason and a

free will man was perfectible; the study of past mistakes and the observance of the natural laws by which they were punished made their repetition avoidable. Thus knowledge had a mundanely useful application: life here below could be made a progressively more pleasant experience. The presumption upon which this optimism was based was that natural man was good. The conservative (the epithet is used broadly to name the individual who believed that the irrational factor was decisive in activating man, a creature whom evil dominated) never ceased to point to the horror and the tragedy which he was certain had been the logical result of these vanities, or, for the orthodox, these heresies. The liberal (the individual optimistic about the nature of man), on the other hand, cried out that once necessary institutions and environment had been created, enabling man's reasonableness to find expression and to give it authority, all would then soon be well, or much better.

Edgar Quinet grew out of the eighteenth century. Heir to the faith that man could fashion a world near to the image of his ideal, he saw that the event, experience, seemed to deny that inheritance again and again. Believing in the attainability of Fraternity, that key of the liberal arch, he observed the domination of an unalloyed bourgeois materialism and the insidious growth of a bitterly class-conscious proletariat. The development of his thought is in part the record of his adjustment of received theory to what seemed to be experimental fact.

Under the impetus of great scientific advancement faith in man's capacity for almost unlimited progress reached dizzy heights as the nineteenth century progressed. Lovejoy writes of "those disastrous illusions of man about himself which were . . . so characteristic of the century . . . and against which our own age has, scarcely less disastrously, revolted." Of that disastrous revolt nothing can be said here, but Quinet is an early and instructive example of it.

Possibly the men of one age are essentially no more self-sufficient than those of another, but certainly the conscious need or desire for some transcendental faith was a marked characteristic of Quinet's early environment. As a youth Quinet sought a firmer philosophical or religious base for the optimism he had inherited. The year 1830 was one of crisis and disillusion which narrowed his horizons. Humanity gave way to France as Quinet's first preoccupa-

tion, briefly after 1830, then finally in the 1840's. When he turned
his attention to the social regeneration of France his particular
interest as an instructive example begins.

The consensus is that Quinet made a significant contribution to
the formation of the French-democratic-liberal tradition. This volume relates Quinet to French liberalism, and also covers that part
of his thought which was less widely shared by those of his con-
temporaries who were in general associated with him. The events
of Quinet's life are closely followed up to the Revolution of 1848,
and special consideration is given to that part of his later work which
grew out of the failure of that revolution to bring about anything
but a new reaction.

After 1851 Quinet came to believe that the greatest misfortune
in the history of France had been the failure of the Reformation
to triumph there as it had in countries which became Protestant.
The reason for his conviction was that the French spirit, having
failed to break the bonds of an obscurantist religion in the sixteenth
century, had been buried two centuries deeper in the Catholic tradition. The last quarter-century of his life was devoted to presenting
this message, in one guise or another, and pleading for the policies
which might save the future. On one hand courage permitted him
to retain a noble hope; on the other he found logic too demanding.
The faith he found for himself he wished to impose upon all
Frenchmen. The study of history in the light of his own experience
taught him the necessity for intolerance. An examination of that
experience may explain why.[1]

Edgar Quinet

A STUDY IN FRENCH PATRIOTISM

1. Early Environment

THE QUINET FAMILY settled in Bresse sometime before that area passed from Savoy to France in 1601. Edgar's immediate forebears were cultivated bourgeoisie of moderate fortune. His paternal ancestors had been magistrates in Lyon and Bourg, his grandfather the mayor of the latter city in 1791. The boy's mother came from a French-speaking Swiss Calvinist family; her father had been mayor of Versoix, her natal village.

Edgar's father, Jerome Quinet, served with the Republican armies as a War Commissary. In spite of his hatred for Napoleon his tour of duty continued into the Empire, and he was with the Army of the Rhine until 1807. In the spring of that year the Quinet family established itself in the country near Bourg, at Certines, a property which had been in the family for some three centuries. Jerome Quinet, who later evidenced little sympathy for his romantically minded and undependable son, left Edgar's early upbringing to the mother, while he himself pursued the solitary study of mathematics. The mother dominated the boy's early development.

After he had attended the *collèges* at Bourg and Lyon, Edgar was sent to Paris to study law. Now seventeen, he was averse to any of the occupations which might have assured a livelihood, but was nevertheless placed in the home of wealthy relatives in the expectation that he would eventually be launched in a business career. Such a plan was the result of a family compromise. The father had hoped that Edgar would prepare himself for an army career. Serving under the white flag is said to have seemed impossible to the boy, and an introduction into the banking world was the adjustment reached. The son soon withdrew from his part of the bargain.

Within a year Edgar had deserted his patrons, but continued to live in Paris on a more or less meager allowance from his father, ostensibly in order that he might continue his law studies. Family connections provided him with entrance into the fashionable bour-

3

geois world, and he steadily enlarged the number of acquaintance-
ships which he had formed in intellectual and literary circles. In
February, 1823, the month of his twentieth birthday, he had printed
at his own expense his first published literary creation, a pamphlet-
length satire aimed at the current Catholic idealization of the
Middle Ages.[1]

Quinet was a boy and became a man in Restoration France.
In time his lot fell with that party for whom the return of the Bourbons had been the darkest hour in the life of the nation; in time he
became possibly the most passionate spokesman for those who made
that interpretation part of a tradition. One need not accept, and one
can go far in repudiating, the portrait which the mature Quinet
drew of his own youth; what is more important is that what he
later depicted as having been his own personal experience had been
a common one. He appropriated it when he wished to reach an
audience which would be moved by the recital of an experience
they had themselves deeply felt.

Musset projects a countryside covered by slow-moving pale
black-robed phantoms. Seeming strangers knocked upon the doors
of dwellings. Still trembling with a fear which had seized them,
now a generation ago, these phantoms presented the inhabitants
with great parchment documents. With these creased and tattered
records they dispossessed the unfortunate usurpers. One was astonished that a single corpse had been able to attract so many vultures.
This was France after Waterloo, Restoration France, "one of the
most striking reversals of modern history."

From Saint Helena Napoleon pronounced that the Battle of
Waterloo had been as fatal to the liberties of Europe as the Battle
of Philippi had been to those of Rome; and Quinet one day wrote
that "the Revolution surrendered its sword in 1815."[2] The Revolution, which, as Victor Hugo expressed it, is in the service of mankind, is a battle perpetually waged for what is just, perpetually won
for what is true. Justice is the essence of man; truth the essence
of God.

For France defeat was not all: a nation was shamed. Foreign
occupation gave force and a durable violence to this sentiment of
shame; foreign uniforms clothed brutal masters, permanent pil-
lagers.[3] Quinet recalled, at least, that as a youth he had found a

historical parallel in Tacitus: the fall of another empire, the invasion of other barbarians. The Prussian of 1815 was the clearly distinguishable descendant of the brutal tribal warrior of a previous millennium.[4]

Throne and altar joined in sharing the first fruits of Waterloo. Musset wrote that in that unhappy hour youth observed and listened, thinking always "the shadow of Caesar would debark at Cannes and breathe life into the still form; but the silence was uninterrupted, the only banner aloft, the pale lilies." When youths spoke of glory, of ambition, of hope, of love, of life a single dinning response was the answer: "Become priests." Stendhal's Julien Sorel memorized the New Testament in Latin, then De Maistre's *Du Pape*. He believed in one as little as in the other, but in the early days of the Restoration ceased to speak of Napoleon and announced his intention to become a priest. Laughing like Mephistopheles he told himself: "Well enough, I know how to choose the uniform of my century.... How many are not the cardinals of meaner birth than myself who have ruled."

The theoretical role of the divine right monarch, that of being "a full-dress political image of God," was, writes Jacques Maritain, "a royal privilege which became rather detrimental to God in the sequel."[5] Divine right monarchy was not restored to France in 1815, but if clericalism means the utilization of the spiritual power for the benefit of the temporal power the Restoration offered the exemplary image of such a regime. There were 80,000 paschal communions in Paris in 1815, 20,000 in 1830. France *"vomissait le cléricalisme"* in July, 1830;[6] one may say, the sequel. The act consistent with the word was the ideal Quinet wished to instil in all men, but he could not fail to note that the very sincerity of the passions of the Restoration had been a cause for its weakness. Few governments had, he thought, put so much good faith and frankness into their hatreds; but in fighting the new age openly the regime had been as far as possible from the political spirit that finally prevailed. The Restoration never learned that by according men the shadow the substance could be taken from them. When the people had wished to deceive themselves they had not been permitted to do so.[7]

The nobility of the *ancien régime* returned to France after twenty-two years of exile, having forgotten nothing; so, at least, has their frame of mind frequently been described. This judgment is too simple, writes Adrian Dansette. They had forgotten the philosophical prejudices of the eighteenth-century Enlightenment; they had learned religion, at least religion as it had been understood by believers under the *ancien régime*. The France to which they returned to rule was, except for the peasantry, predominantly irreligious. At the beginning of the Restoration even youth was abandoned to the influence of parents and teachers hostile to Catholicism. A report prepared by the young Lacordaire showed that of the 7 or 8 per cent who had partaken of paschal communions at the time of their entrance, but 1 per cent of those leaving the royal *collèges* at Paris had retained their faith. At St. Cyr cadets who attended communion in uniform risked provoking duels with their comrades for so dishonoring the school.

Seventy of the ninety bishops appointed during the fifteen-year reign of Louis XVIII and Charles X were of noble birth; the clergy they headed were almost exclusively royalists. The political standard was the religious one. The Bishop of Troyes expressed the nearly unanimous opinion of the upper clergy in affirming the principle that there existed an eternal contract between throne and altar, one of which could not exist without the other. Nationalism, so bruised and sensitive before a regime installed and protected by the victorious enemy, could respond in only one fashion toward the altar bound and delivered to that throne. The issue, however, was a deeper one.

The French Revolution, wrote Renan, was the first attempt on the part of humanity to take over its own reins and direct itself. Here we need not examine the claim to originality; the faith of Revolutionary France in man's reason, in science, and thus in progress was its essential characteristic. In 1815 the Vatican ordered the prohibition of illumination by gas and of vaccination for smallpox within the Papal territories. During the Church attack upon the University the clerical organ *Mémorial Catholique* launched a furious offensive against the theories which prevailed in the philosophy courses at that institution: here the student heard of the indefinite perfectibility of the human spirit, whereas religion teaches one to shudder at the consciousness of our degraded nature. The cleavage extended to the bowels of the earth.

Success in two matters embodying the Church viewpoint serves to clarify the implacable enmity of the Catholic and Revolutionary traditions. The law of sacrilege, providing for the death penalty, was promulgated on April 20, 1825. In its principal dispositions the law was never applied, though through no fault of the authors of the law. Taking the lives, in the name of the absolute right of truth, of those who committed sacrilege, Bonald insisted, did no more than send the criminals before their natural judge. Not so well remembered is the strong protest of another prominent Catholic, Lamennais, that the law was atheistic because it did not protect Catholicism exclusively. Dansette concludes that the law did have one victim: the regime which had the madness to assume responsibility for it. The other Ultra victory particularly to be noted was the victory over the University. Attacks, vigorously led by Lamennais and Chateaubriand, ended in success for the Church when, in February, 1821, the University monopoly was broken and secondary education placed under the surveillance of the clergy. At the end of the Restoration two-thirds of the professors of philosophy within the secondary system were priests.

It was the king of England to whom, after God, Louis XVIII owed his throne. The Ultras looked to Wellington to assist them in replacing that too moderate monarch with the future Charles X, and pleaded with the Allies not to withdraw the occupying troops whose presence was necessary to the success of their plots. Hatred for England was as old as French national feeling, and now the intensification of the one accompanied the intensification of the other.

A definition of a nation well suited to the conception of France held by men of the Revolution is that of Renan: "To have common glories in the past, a common will in the present; to have done great things together; to wish to do greater. . . . In the past, an inheritance of glories and regrets; in the future, one and the same program to carry out." The common glory in the past was the Revolution. The common will in the present was to reverse the temporary defeats of 1814 and 1815. As for the future this statement, although of later date, expressed a general feeling always large in the Revolutionary viewpoint. At the College of France, in February, 1844, the Polish poet Mickiewicz damned the error of those who in France concerned themselves with utopian schemes of material betterment, or primarily with French social problems. The time was not yet for the sword to be exchanged for the plowshare. No, the armies, the fleet, the arsenals of France belonged to humanity. On them reposed the possibility of true progress.[8]

Baneful gift, that crown received without intermediary from the hands of Blücher and of Wellington; Wellington whom Chateaubriand then called "our new Turenne." That crown signified civilization's sorrow. This association of France with civilization was referred to by Soltau as "that identification of the destinies of political France with democracy and civilization, which has led to such a crippling of the French mind."[9]

The judgment was too stern; if it was meant to characterize the French mind, rather than the French mind as represented by the dogmatism of the Church and the official Revolution, it was false. But how just it is as a description of particular phenomena! Whereas during the Restoration men like Armand Carrel thought in terms of France heading a warrior democracy, formed into a Holy Alliance against monarchy, the Bourbons made their own use of French armies. Intervention in Spain in 1822 was termed by Quinet the giving of aid to the "crucifixion of a nation." The blood of a nation divinely appointed to lead humanity forward and onward into light was perversely spent in the cause of darkness.[10]

Although intense nationalism and anti-Catholicism are conspicuously absent in his correspondence and other writings which date from the Restoration, the autobiography of Quinet's first twenty years, written in 1857, in which he projected backward many of his later attitudes, is an important record. He evoked 1815 in these terms. One night and the world seemed overturned; what had been virtue became crime. Condemnation did not stop at things: first the master of his school, a former captain of the dragoons, was proscribed; then the police overran his parents' house, displacing objects even in the boy's room, searching for Baudot, a former member of the Convention and a frequent visitor of his family. In the change of temperament of a whole nation, each person was forced of necessity to give a new direction to his thought, to destroy his past education, to create for himself another nature; it seemed to the boy as if in a moment not only the climate, but the atmosphere in which men lived had been changed. Even the benefits intermixed in the deluge of misfortune angered and irritated youth.[11]

If the nation may be said to have accepted the Restoration as an imposition of the peace treaty, "without passion, with indifference and resignation," priests, nobles, and the wealthy bourgeoisie thought and felt in a different manner. For them the Restoration was the beginning of a revenge to be taken "for old humiliations and a long period of defeats."[12] Within a matter of months the bourgeoisie had been disillusioned by the regime they had welcomed; but for the nation in a larger sense it was the execution of Ney, the massacre of Protestants in the Midi, the public butchering of a live eagle by a hysterical royalist mob at Carcassone that inflamed hatred in French hearts.

Quinet would have it that similar incidents affected his own development. The trial, conviction, and execution of one of the most popular men in his department, for having plotted "the assassination of all nobles and all wealthy proprietors of the department," in having gone over to Napoleon during the Hundred Days, marked the commencement of his hatred for the Bourbons. Also, it had revived his Bonapartism.

On the eve of Napoleon's arrival in Paris on his return from Elba, the grandfather of Ernest Renan told his wife to rise early the following morning and look toward the steeple of the village church. When morning came the tricolor was flying there. Twenty times risking their necks the grandfather and several other "patriots" had raised the "national flag" during the night. When several months later the Bourbon flag replaced it the grandfather went out of his mind.[13] If more able to bear his sorrow, Ernest's father shared these feelings, a patriotic attitude which came to be associated with the name Napoleon.

The author who wrote that there is no force in history more powerful than sentiment will rouse as much debate as consent; he used understatement when he added that defeat at Waterloo strengthened the sentiment of France for Napoleon.[14] The Quinet household was but an example. The implacable hatred of Jerome Quinet for the Emperor was only disarmed when fortune changed, when the disaster was consummated; then came the day when he could be heard to defend the traitor of the *18 Brumaire,* of the

Concordat, of the coronation at Notre Dame. The mortal hatred of Edgar's mother for the tyrant who had exiled Mme de Staël did not halt tears she shed, "for *him* as well as for France," when disaster struck. The legend grew, for better or worse the nature of Napoleon suffered distortion; the projection and the original differed much. The offspring later reminded Marx of that section of the Napoleonic code which forbade investigation into the question of paternity.

Quinet made an important contribution to that legend during the July Monarchy, which history revenged. The reaction he recorded as having been his upon the death of Napoleon has been said to describe "the feeling with which the news ... was generally received in France."[15] This amounts to legend becoming part of the history of a legend. In his measured confession of error Quinet recalled that during the seven years of exile the name of Napoleon had daily descended into silence, almost into forgetfulness. Then death suddenly revived forever the hero's empire over men's minds. This, Quinet wrote, had been his own experience. Mme de Staël, for whom his admiration had been so great, caused him to doubt, but in 1821 the hero prevailed. Between 1815 and 1821 he made no positive choice between liberty and Napoleon; he did not believe he must sacrifice one to the other, but as liberty was a growing preoccupation Napoleon faded from his mind. Then the formidable news of 1821 caused a new eruption of enthusiasm. The hero returned to haunt his intelligence, no longer as his emperor, but as a specter which death had almost entirely transformed.

Quinet now saw in him a being entirely different from that which the world had known:

That ideology which he had disdained, henceforth he must serve it, because he was now no more than an idea ... He himself had ended by being conquered by those notions of liberty and justice. What greater demonstration of their truth, of their power! He had wished to crush them, but had himself been forced to submit. Was this not proof that they were invincible.[16]

An irreconcilable accommodation was made between a cult for liberty and one for Napoleon. Quinet and others did not go to Napoleon, Napoleon returned to them. It had been well understood, so he believed, that the reconciliation took place in the clouds, with a phantom, not a monarch who had escaped from the tomb.

When Quinet looked back and then wrote in these terms in 1857 he was in exile and a republican, immensely proud of his consistency in thought and action. The close union of Bonapartists and Republicans had been a feature of the Left opposition during the Restoration. One of the most promising of later Republican leaders, Armand Carrel, permitted himself to take up the thesis of Napoleon's liberalism. As a liberal and a friend of the people the Emperor was celebrated in a hundred songs.[17]

December 3, 1851, which found Hugo, like Quinet, crushed by the monster both had done their share to create, revealed the former compelled to write, in his vain appeal to the army that it resist the coup d'état: "This man says that his name is Bonaparte. He lies, for Bonaparte is a word which means glory. This man says that his name is Napoleon. He lies, for Napoleon is a word which means genius."[18]

Almost at once Proudhon, after this event, showed the way to the Left in re-evaluating the legendary Napoleon, by writing that the series of battles which had brought trophies, at so much cost in treasure and in blood, could be reduced to a military trilogy, "of which the first act is Aboukir, the second Trafalgar, the last Water-loo."[19] The time came when Quinet characterized Napoleon as the "great Italian who had made use of the arm of France," as damning a pronouncement as he could make, in a work which was his con-tribution to what by then would be a growing republican-inspired anti-Napoleon literature.[20] Hugo must have felt in that early Decem-ber of 1851 the time was too short to explain, to re-educate.

The enemies of reaction had glorified what the Restoration had proscribed. At hand seemed a mighty weapon; somewhat care-lessly it was chosen. Wellington was the new Turenne of the most lionized and eloquent of Catholic lay spokesmen; the Englishman Burke was author of reaction's bible. A complacent government turned its back as heroes of France were torn from their graves to have their remains dragged through filth, to be dumped into rivers; a Catholic clergy incited and fed the flames of a searing national humiliation—a bitterly intensified anticlericalism and the cult of Napoleon were natural avenues for discontent to take. Intense patriotism, the cult of the strong man, the military hero, the constant appeal to the authority of national interest—how false it is to associate these exclusively with those who wish to preserve the status quo, or with the political Right. Under the Restoration, as under the July Monarchy, the democratic tradition in France clothed its demand for social change in a jingo nationalism, in an attack upon peaceful foreign policy, upon cosmopolitanism, and upon a Church headed by a "foreign" Pope.

Assessment of the Napoleonic legend should include Heine's commentary. In May, 1840, Lamartine rose in the Chamber of Deputies to speak against the government on the question of returning Napoleon's remains to France. He spoke with eloquence and with all the semblance of reason, expressing his lack of admiration for those who had for official doctrine liberty, legality, and progress and who now took the sword and despotism for their symbol. The oration aroused the warm enthusiasm of the extreme Right, a faction by then antipathetic to the poet-politician. Heine found the speech disagreeable, in spite of the truth it contained; for the speaker's mental reservations were dishonorable and the truth was spoken in the interest of falsehood. Although it was a thousand times true that Napoleon had been the enemy of freedom, and that his glorification was a dangerous example, it was not this tyrant, not the hero of the *18 Brumaire,* not the thunder-god covetous of glory, whom Frenchmen wished to honor in memorial ceremony.

No, he is the man who represents young France against old Europe... in his person the French people had been victorious, in his person debased, in his person they honor and celebrate themselves—and every Frenchman feels this. This is the person whose glorification is debated. Thus one forgets the dark side of the deceased and pays him homage, *quand même;* the Chamber commits a grave error through its untimely higgling. The speech of Lamartine was a masterstroke, full of perfidious blossoms whose delicate poison addles many of the weak minded; but its lack of honor is but poorly masked by lovely phrases, and the Ministry may be pleased rather than disturbed that its enemies have so clumsily betrayed their anti-national feelings.[21]

The perpetuators of the legend may be put in no better light than this.

The expression "the two Frances" has come into such general usage, and the interpretation which it represents has been so warped and bent by recent application, that it may be restated here. Renan is indirectly responsible for the term, having said upon one occasion that "in the womb of our country, as in Rebecca's, two people are struggling to be born, each of which wants to smother the other." Paul Seippel, in 1905, took this as text for a study of the "eternal dualism between the France of the Church and the France of the Revolution," and noted the extraordinary likeness between the two opponents—twins really. "Each believes in a 'moral unity' of France which he identifies with his own creed, and which he seeks to impose by means fair and foul...neither in fact really believes in liberty at all, but is at heart a dogmatic authoritarian."

Soltau accepted the interpretation and concluded that the root cause of this dualism was

...the policy of religious unity typified in the revocation of the Edict of Nantes, the identification of all religion with Catholic orthodoxy of the strictest kind, and of the Church with political despotism; so that no political or social emancipation became possible without war against the Church, dogma being met with dogma, persecution with intolerance, one vision of unity with another. In all this turmoil there was no room for freedom.[22]

The difficulty here is that not *the* two Frances, but *two of the* Frances are meant, a very different matter. Not only is it impossible to place many a French figure in either camp, but certainly the essential nature of French life is not accurately mirrored by such a stereotype. In all of the turmoil, there has rather been room in France for greater intellectual freedom than possibly anywhere else. On the other hand the interpretation may serve as a valuable guide when applied to two of the dominant political forces in modern France, and it has real relevance when restricted to them.

Revolutionary France was hardly represented in the Chamber of Deputies during the Restoration. At that time, it should be remembered, there were ten million taxpayers in France; less than one-tenth of these were electors and frequently only one-half of these exercised their franchise. The Doctrinaires, headed by Guizot and Royer-Collard, and the Liberals, most ably and most generously represented by Constant, formed an official opposition to the policies of the returned Bourbons. The Doctrinaires had welcomed the returning monarchy but were soon dissatisfied with the result; though important, the special area which they were willing to regard as the legitimate accomplishment of the Revolution was small. England before the first Reform Bill, with somewhat more of royal prerogative, was their ideal. The Liberals are to be differentiated from the Doctrinaires only in degree; they were monarchists of strong conviction. Louis Blanc believed that under the Restoration the policy of both was adequately summed up in the slogan "enslave the monarchy without destroying it."[23]

A constitutional monarchy based on a highly restricted property suffrage, or, one may say, the Charter put into practice, was their common program. The outward forms of the Restoration with a change in personnel, this was the desire of both groups. The July Revolution became their victory when they were able to capture it from the quite different forces which had overturned Charles X. However, even if the choice of a Guizot would have been swift indeed had he been confronted with the alternative of either Robespierre or Charles X, only with injustice may such a man be forced into either of "the two Frances." And political control in France has consistently rested with the interests men like Guizot have served.

The Republicans were an almost silent group under the Restoration, representing a sentiment more than a party, but holding views which corresponded most closely to those still prevailing among a large part of the French middle class. During the last ten years of the Empire the government had put much effort into erasing the Republic from memory. The word became synonymous with the Terror. Success in establishing this association is often credited to the regime upon the basis of Quinet's account of his own experience. As a boy, coming into contact with a work which retold those recent years he was unable to understand the references to "Girondins," "Jacobins," and "Montagnards." "A single word had replaced all of the others, the Terror, a word which no one defined for me. I would have needed a dictionary for each line; to such a degree the language of the Revolution had promptly ceased to be a living language."[24]

Silenced by the Restoration, "the other France," that of the

Revolution, retained control over the mind of the bourgeoisie, which remained vaguely republican, strongly anticlerical, and patriotic. Quinet went through a development which, as an example, does its bit to justify the charge which Seippel and Soltau have made.

2. *The Importance of Mme de Staël*

BENEDETTO CROCE concluded that modern liberalism could, without hesitation, be called a "religion." Taine, the product of another Catholic environment, described the philosophy of the eighteenth century as a system in which Reason replaced God, and intolerance matched intolerance. Dogmas, fanatics, inquisitors, and martyrs, and the ambition to reshape man in the form of a preconceived type were a part of the new as well as the old faith.

In Restoration France the political standard was the religious one. Liberalism faced Catholicism. Both religions did demand the whole man, separation of public from private life being as forbidden by one as by the other. Mme de Staël had placed Germany and France at the opposite extremes of the moral chain—Germany considering ideas as the source of all material impressions. But, in spite of her philosophic idealism, she could not fail to note one French virtue. Whereas among Germans there seemed to be no connection between thought and action, in France one was hardly ever concerned with abstract ideas except in their connection to practical matters. Here we truly have the vaunted French logic, that aspect of the French classical spirit which in Taine's eyes was a French form of insanity.

These matters have a relationship to Quinet's early development which will become increasingly apparent. As a young man Quinet gave a natural and unquestioning allegiance to the political heritage of 1789. But that this should have solved all questions of faith and religion escaped him. He suffered from doubt, and sought certainty.

Individualism, or the right of private judgment and the inviolability of the human personality, was one of the precepts of the Enlightenment. A reaction against individualism, both in its democratic and liberal manifestations, was among the strongest and most persistent currents in the intellectual history of nineteenth-century

16

France. Important in this reaction was a group of men possessed with the idea that individualism as a principle had caused the disappearance of the spiritual power. Believing that this force was necessary to men, they saw the task to be the restoration of Catholicism, or the creation of a new faith. Quinet was among those who believed a new faith to be necessary.

The crucial question is whether or not the Enlightenment deserves the frequent charge that it was primarily negative in its accomplishment. For the present it need only be stated that the young Quinet became closely associated with a group dominated by the view that it was, and that his early thought was profoundly influenced by this interpretation. Referring to the leaders of the previous century he wrote, in 1825, "They destroyed everything (and I am very satisfied that this is so) with their persiflage. Now it is necessary to construct, there is a need for convictions, for affections, and for the sentiment of liberty and humanity."[1]

Mme de Staël imposed her opinions and her ideals with respect to Germany on many Frenchmen, particularly upon those who were not obstinately bound to the tradition of the eighteenth century, and who were curious about new tendencies. What is meant by "eighteenth century" here is the materialism which seemed the necessary logical consequence of its philosophic determinism, the aspect against which Quinet revolted.

According to Mme de Staël the increasing influence which she observed of a mocking skepticism was but the natural outcome of a philosophy which attributed all of our ideas to our sensations. Passing from the critique of a philosophy which believed only in what could be proved as a fact or a calculation, she arrived at Kant. His theory of the sublime, which he made consist in moral liberty in conflict with nature or destiny, satisfied her. The power of destiny and the immensity of nature were in infinite opposition to the miserable dependence of mortal creatures. However, a spark of sacred fire in the human breast triumphed over a physical universe subject to necessity and natural law. It sufficed that this spark exist to resist all the material forces of the world. The proper resolution of the question of free will was the pivotal concern. Mme de Staël asked what was more important than for man to know that he is responsible for his actions and in what relationship the power of his will stands with respect to the circumstances which influence or control it. What would be our conscience if only our habits gave birth to it, if it were nothing but the product of colors, sounds, and odors?

Faith seemed logical in the face of such a depressing hypothesis; and the logic of Mme de Staël reduced itself to this: so bleak a thought must be rejected, its reverse embraced. Natural and immutable laws were projected out of faith, laws within the understanding of the conscience, if not the reason, of the commonality of men, which permitted the application of the Gospel precept: judge the prophets by their works. That maxim could then serve as a guide among philosophies: all that tended toward immorality was but a sophism. She concluded that this life had meaning and value only if the religious education of humanity were the goal, if it served to prepare us for a higher destiny, by the free choice of virtue here on earth. Metaphysics, social institutions, the arts, the sciences, all ought to be appreciated in relationship to the moral perfectibility of man. Moral perfection was the touchstone which was given to the ignorant and the learned alike.[2]

The difficulty posed to the eighteenth century by its identification of man with nature, both being the necessary product of natural law, has been stressed frequently. Seemingly this identification threatened to eliminate purpose from the world and lead to the inescapable conclusion that "whatever is is right." Carl Becker believed that there thus arose the necessity to separate society from nature once more, and he wrote: "It is well known that such separation was effected by Rousseau: 'man is born free but is everywhere in chains;' 'naturally good it is society which corrupts him,' so ran the famous formula of the new dualism."[3]

In her search for an authority which would sanction a distinction necessary to life itself, through the medium of German philosophy, Mme de Staël returned Rousseau to France. The Rousseau of *Emile:*

Conscience! Conscience! divine instinct; immortal and celestial voice; sure guide of a being ignorant and limited, but intelligent and free; infallible judge of good and evil.... Without you I feel nothing within myself which raises me above beasts but the wretched privilege to be confused in error, with the aid of an understanding without rule, and a reason without principle.

In Paris during the last years of the reign of Louis XVIII, Quinet was deeply concerned with the connection between abstract ideas and practical matters. But religious faith, not a political philosophy, was his own practical need. Charléty, seeking an adequate yet brief means of contrasting the spirit of the Restoration with that of the July Monarchy, noted that under Louis Philippe "the impassioned word, oratorical, flamboyant, or even solemnly apostolic replaces the measured, academic and doctrinaire distinction of the preceding age."[4]

This historian believed that it sufficed to bring together the names of a Royer-Collard or a Benjamin Constant and those of a Michelet or a Quinet to make minute comparisons unnecessary. As a young man Quinet sought a sanction for the characteristics he later embodied.

At the close of his life he recalled the despair which had hung over the youth of his generation:

We advanced in life enveloped in heavy mists. You say: "Deliberate obscurity; the affectation of misunderstood genius." No, all was not voluntary in that despair of the intelligence. We sought the light, and it was refused us because, badly oriented, we sought it where it could not appear to the human spirit.[5]

Quinet recognized himself in Werther. Like Goethe's hero he knew the desolation and discouragement of a young man confronted by a society in which his place was not marked in advance. In order to maintain the semi-independent status which his separate establishment in Paris permitted him to enjoy during the years between 1820 and 1825, Quinet needed to deceive his father as to both his inclinations and his ambition. To do him full justice, it is quite possible he deceived himself concerning his ability to satisfy parental wishes. Only his mother understood the breadth of his dreams; and even she expected, if she did not demand, that he prepare himself for some respectable place in society. The young man found it impossible to devote himself seriously to any such purpose. He was erratic, at least in pursuing the goals staked out for him by others. However, if improvident, he was not necessarily inconstant. There is one interpretation of the Romantic ideal which suggests that the first and great commandment is: "Be yourself, which is to say, be unique!" Quinet found strength, if not light or peace, in this precept.

Croce gave Mme de Staël the credit for beginning in France the doctrinal development of modern liberalism. Prepared for this role by her study of German speculative thought, she added the requisite political element to that base. This woman was most important among those from whom Quinet sought guidance. The sources of her inspiration were much the same as those of Victor Cousin, whose personal encouragement was to be of importance to Quinet. For Cousin too "the eighteenth century was the age of criticism and destruction, the nineteenth ought to be that of intelligent reconstruction." The challenge was the need to build a new edifice with the "debris," to find a more profound analysis which could serve the future.[6]

Quinet's enthusiasm for Mme de Staël was instilled by his mother, who as a young woman had met her famous compatriot. When a boy, hearing his mother defend her exiled heroine from the ridicule in fashion under the Empire among those who took their cue from Bonaparte, he "but half understood that language, the impression, however, was that which a harp might have had on me; without being able to say why, I was moved, it was as if scales had fallen from my eyes."[7]

Later, in 1820, standing between two centuries, he and others of his generation were torn between two persons: Chateaubriand and Mme de Staël. As different from one another as he, at least, could imagine: one was Catholic, one was Protestant; one turned toward the Middle Ages, the other to the uncertain future. Quinet wrote that he was confused by their almost diametrical opposition, after the first promise that their very brilliance and separation from the common herd would give him the inspiration and light he sought. And Quinet recalled that, if her answer to his searching was never quite complete, never altogether satisfying, it was to Mme de Staël that his allegiance had gone.

In fact it was only much later that Quinet became conscious of this "diametrical opposition." He entered into the literary world of Paris just at the time when the followers of Mme de Staël and Chateaubriand were becoming reconciled. And when he first laid eyes on Chateaubriand Quinet wrote: "I must not postpone a moment letting you know of the most profound joy which I have perhaps ever felt. I have seen Chateaubriand...." It did not matter at all that in appearance Chateaubriand was in the ranks of the enemy in religion and politics.[8] In time it came to matter very much.

Chateaubriand noted that whereas Mme de Staël saw "perfectibility" everywhere, his own "folly" was to see Jesus Christ. But he knew as well as she that morality was the base of society, that if materialistic determinism were true there could be no real virtue or vice, and consequently no morality. Relative and changing laws could not serve to support morality, by its nature "absolute and inalterable."[9] Thus it was more than their brilliance which brought Mme de Staël and Chateaubriand together.

Mme de Staël was, to be sure, a more direct influence upon Quinet's development. She and Benjamin Constant are often thought to reflect their French-Swiss origin by their permanent concern with the civil and political implication of religious faith. Through his mother Quinet was closely connected with the same tradition.

In 1820, when one of his professors at Lyon gave only lukewarm and qualified approval to Mme de Staël's De l'Allemagne, Quinet wrote to his parent that this fact was enough to discourage him with the age in which he lived. Soon thereafter he was looking forward to taking up the study of German, a desire inspired by this work. The intention was long postponed, and in February, 1824, he reported to Mme Quinet that a friend was being very kind in lending him English translations of German works which were unknown in France. This kind friend "loved Mme de Staël passionately"; upon this basis, Quinet wrote, he always "measured" his men.

During these same years Edgar became acquainted with and enamored of Rousseau. In 1857 Quinet related that his mother had kept the works of Jean-Jacques from him as a boy, because of their possible effect upon his naturally overheated imagination. This may have been the case, but in 1821 he was rereading the Confessions. When two years later he made a summer visit to Switzerland he showed a detailed familiarity with Rousseau's work, as well as a consuming admiration for it.[10] De l'Allemagne, and particularly the chapter on "enthusiasm," was, however, Quinet's bible during these years, and the most decisive intellectual influence of his early life.

During the first twenty years of the nineteenth century German philosophy and letters appeared as the great initiator. The Empire had marked a period of relative intellectual sterility in France, and its close saw develop a wave of enthusiasm for the German accomplishment. The great impetus to this movement was Mme de Staël's *De l'Allemagne.* The Empire had hindered the spread and cut off the development of Rousseau's thought in France; but in Germany Herder, Goethe, Schiller, and German romantics following Herder gave new direction and new results to that inspiration. Then with the fall of Napoleon, "as after the giving way of a dam, the new German world of thought, often muddied, streamed into a French literary and philosophical world parched by the Empire, and gave back richly what we had once received."[11]

"Enthusiasm" was the name Mme de Staël gave to the non-rational. She introduced the chapter of *De l'Allemagne* devoted to it with the confession that these pages in many ways summed up the whole work. The German people's enthusiasm was not only their distinctive trait, but also the means by which the human spirit moved forward; with it, and only so, life could be dedicated to that which was invisible, and to interests which had no immediate action upon our well-being.

Mme de Staël's conviction that skepticism was but a natural result of philosophic materialism (that philosophy according to which to hold an opinion was but a delicate manner of indicating interest) we know. She found that the eighteenth century had been quite correct to consider morality founded upon interest to be a consequence of a metaphysical system which attributed all ideas to sensations; for if there be nothing in the soul but that which sensations have put there, the agreeable and the disagreeable ought then to be the sole motive of our actions. Helvétius and Diderot, in this tradition, had explained even the devotion of martyrs by self-love. The other error had been that of Leibnitz, who had founded his system purely on reason; whereas, to reason about the liberty of man was but a step from doubt that such liberty is real. Put your hand upon your conscience and you *cannot* doubt that liberty.

The philosophical idealism of Mme de Staël, which she found in Rousseau and in Kant, by its nature refuted a morality founded upon interest. Making the life of the soul all that mattered rooted our actions in the exercise of our will and in the practice of virtue. Individuals are virtuous when they sacrifice their particular interest to the general interest; governments are bound by a similar code, for all true principles are absolute, since if two and two are not always four the most profound algebraic calculations become absurd. Mme de Staël was a Protestant Christian moralist, but both her Christianity and her moralism were steeped in the idealism so characteristic of German thought after the turn of the century.

As a disciple of the conservative Montesquieu, her individualism foreshadowed that bourgeois liberalism which in the nineteenth century became a fortress against radical democracy. Against this timorous liberalism Quinet was to represent a reaction. However doubtful the authenticity of her liberalism, her views on religion foreshadowed those of Quinet. The philosophic spirit, her true religion, could by its nature never, she felt, become an affair of the masses of any nation. Thus, like most intellectual aristocrats of her day, she thought that a positive religion was necessary for the people. Although her philosophic outlook placed the full responsibility for conduct in the free choice of the sovereign individual person, she was convinced that only traditional political and religious institutions could provide the necessary sanctions for public-spirited behavior in the masses. It is not surprising therefore that her argument should culminate in an advocacy of a state religion. She never pardoned Napoleon the Concordat, but despite the protestations of her *Considérations,* his fault was much less that he recognized a state religion than that he had recognized Catholicism as that religion. There could, indeed, be no more effective weapon against Catholicism, which she execrated, than to establish Protestantism as the state religion. "Then the State would have in its hands all of the influence of a cult which it supports, and that power which is always exercised by the interpreters of religious ideas would be the support of republican government."[12] To equate this with individualism, liberty, and idealism may well seem utterly impossible, but it foreshadowed the mature Quinet.

The most striking feature of Quinet's letters to his mother down to 1830 is the absence of any suggestion of his later passionate patriotism. Nor is there any evidence that he aligned himself with those elements with whom he later became identified. So long as his idol was Mme de Staël, this cannot be surprising. "Anti-French, anglophile, so is *Corinne;* and Corinne is Mme de Staël completely and absolutely."[13] This is unjust, but it is the interpretation of all those who greatly admired Quinet the patriot.

Quinet's most loved book, *De l'Allemagne,* lavished exaggerated paeans of praise on Germany and England, and was written with the purpose, in part at least, of undermining the influence of French culture abroad. It had been published at a moment when France stood all but alone against a coalition headed and sustained by the nation which shared her enthusiasm. When one recalls the place Waterloo held in Quinet's interpretation of world history it is astonishing to find his idol writing, less than four months after that event, of her beloved England:

One has seen her, as a knight armed for the defense of the social order, preserve Europe during ten years of anarchy, and during ten others of despotism. Her happy constitution was, at the beginning of the Revolution, the goal of the hopes and efforts of the French; my soul has remained there where theirs then was.[14]

That Mme de Staël during the Hundred Days was tempted to rally to Napoleon, "out of love for France and liberty," was as little known to Quinet as was the fact of her enthusiasm for Napoleon on the occasion of the *18 Brumaire.*

The admiration of the eighteenth-century *philosophes* for English liberty, for the English constitution, for English customs, was nearly unanimous. Mme de Staël in this only followed Necker, and it was thus a part of her cult for her father as well. The Quinet who visited England in the spring of 1825 reported back to France the type of impression to be expected from a person greatly under Mme de Staël's influence. He wrote, "I breathe more freely than in France," and then, in his first letter upon returning to Paris, "It is the first time in my life that everything joined to favor my desires; when nothing was contrary to my illusions. Days of enchantment! land of liberty!" London was more "truly magnificent" than Paris.[15]

It was scarcely in character for a French patriot to speak in this fashion of the country of Pitt and Wellington. For a democratic republican, French or not, English liberty was a very dim torch, indeed, in 1825. The truth is that the young Quinet was neither patriot nor democrat. Two years later he traveled to Heidelberg, to find "that all things combined to make him happy where he was." He added that, excepting a recent visit with his mother in the country, there had been but two previous occasions in his life when he had been happy, in England and in Switzerland.

Faguet did his countrymen the disservice of terming the eighteenth century the least French of all literary centuries, reaching this conclusion because of the degree to which its principal figures were cosmopolitan in outlook. It has been said of Mme de Staël, of Swiss parentage, with a Swedish husband (not, however, her most important loyalty), that England was the country of her choice, Germany that of her thought, and France that of her birth and of her friends, but that the country of her "soul" was the society of great and distinguished men of all lands.[16] Nothing could be more foreign to the expressed views of the mature Quinet than this division of loyalties; few attitudes came in for more bitter attack from him than did "cosmopolitanism." But, before 1830, his views and attitudes may be more easily fitted into the tradition here represented by Mme de Staël than into any other. For those who have preferred his mature opinion no blame has been attached to youthful error, so emphatically repudiated in the age of wisdom.

Quinet's Protestant tendencies have been a matter of some debate, the typical conclusion being that his "religious philosophy always retained a strong Protestant coloring." If one means by Protestant the Savoyard faith the judgment may stand. But in 1825 Quinet was a nominal Catholic, and, surprisingly, anti-Catholicism is little apparent in his thinking. We will find that as late as 1838 he had not finally or irrevocably broken with the Catholic Church. His mother, to whom the conventions and the proprieties were so important, in spite of her own apparently sincere Calvinism, saw to it that as a boy Quinet entered into the Church of his most respectable countrymen. As a young man in Paris, if his letters to his mother are to be trusted in this regard, he did frequently attend Protestant services. In the spring of 1822 he reported that he did so every Sunday. A year earlier he had written, " I prefer to pray to God in your church; when there I feel less unworthy of you."

Almost all that Mme de Staël had to say was borrowed, Rousseau and Kant being the creditors to whom she owed her finery, but this did not immediately concern the youthful Quinet. He knew her *De l'Allemagne* better than he knew any other book, and his admiration for the work was profound and enthusiastic. In those parts of it from which we have just drawn is to be found the philosophical foundation of much of his early work. Bossuet will explain some of the modifications or differences in emphasis of the young eclectic, Herder and Vico the rest.

3. German Interlude

THE EPHEMERAL CHARACTER of human destiny is most apparent in the aftermath of war or revolution. The prospect that human history is without purpose or meaning obtrudes upon the consciousness of reflective persons. More ordinary men are then apt to conclude, as Herder did, that a philosophy of history is true because some philosophy of history is necessary for peace of mind. Without this certainty Herder believed that "all events upon the world scene become merely mist.... How frightful is the aspect to see in revolutions but ruin upon ruin—continual beginnings without end; the endless shifting of fate, without lasting purpose."[1] History, "wenn Vernunft sie nicht aufklärt, wenn Sittlichkeit sie nicht ordnet," was but angry chaos.

Quinet related that he was turned to the study of primitive epochs by the barbarism in which all of his generation in France had been enveloped. The collapse of a world had been his first education. He interested himself in history, searching for analogies in the past, and in this fashion a subject which previously he had found unbearable became a living thing. History was a main preoccupation of liberal romanticism in France, and Quinet had this example clearly before him. He recalled, however, that before knowing German philosophy at first hand, before knowing Vico, he had "by instinct become engaged in an analogous path... without guide, without counsellor... launched in the metaphysics of history."[2]

In 1823 he worked on a group of essays. He intended to entitle these combined studies *Institutions politiques dans leurs rapports avec la Religion. Le Juif errant* had made little impression anywhere. Undismayed Quinet set himself to this larger task. More than ambition demanded that he make haste. Jerome Quinet was impatient with the youth's seeming dalliance. Mother and son were in league in keeping up the pretense that Edgar was devoting his main energies to the study of law, and the authorship of *Le Juif errant* was kept secret from the patron who made it possible. Not that even Mme Quinet was encouraging. She dreamed of a more worldly success for her son than the most talented writer could expect to enjoy. Only by some prodigious accomplishment did it seem possible that these obstacles could be overcome. But the young man soon sensed that the essays of 1823, as well as his yet more ambitious *Histoire de la Personalité humaine,* written in 1824, were beyond his forces. It was this realization which decided him to undertake the translation of Herder. Thus he might enter upon the scene more modestly, but still make a useful and necessary contribution.

The historical works of Guizot and Thierry both came to his notice at this time, and perhaps did something to make Quinet doubt his own readiness to treat subjects such as he had undertaken. In more ways than one he was not so without guide and example as he later suggested. He knew eighteenth-century thought, having been nourished on it. That century had conceived history, not as the recital of a succession of facts, but as the analysis of the evolution of customs and ideas. Early in 1823 Quinet, "occupied with history," had been reading Robertson and Hume, in French translation. He had found the latter of particular interest, because in his history of England one could observe "the march and progress of liberty in representative government" through the "continual succession of revolutions."[3]

The unpublished essays, written between the publication of *Le Juif errant,* early in 1823, and his *Introduction à la Philosophie de l'Histoire,* published in 1827, allow certain conclusions to be drawn as to Quinet's conceptions before his meeting with Cousin. In December, 1826, Quinet left France to reside at Heidelberg. He remained in Germany until December, 1829. Here he continued his studies and became a friend of Creutzer. That his early mysticism was not purely the influence of that experience, as has been presumed; that his 1828 *Origines des Dieux* did not result solely from the confusion on the part of an impressionable youth caught up in the giddy atmosphere of obscurantist Heidelberg, is suggested by his 1823 "Préliminaires":

...the philosophical examination of nature has led to the discovery, in each leaf of the forest, on each stalk of grass in the field, of a world which also has its valleys, its rivers, its plants and trees, its inhabitants with different origins and customs. Besides, on that slip of grass there is room for hate and vengeance, as well as wars. There is place for death; that is to say that nothing lacks there in order to give a representation of real fidelity of that vast and animated scene which man observes....

Submitted in this to the same laws, the moral world presents the same phenomena. Here the universe is represented in the individual; the individual in the universe; and when all identifies the existence of the nation with the existence of the individual, I admire a marvelous dawn, which habit and prejudice have prevented our seeing; I admire it, I do not explain it. But that by that astonishing concordance the great should be instructed by the small; that particular applications depend in their turn upon the generality of things, so that to whatever side one may turn there is a lesson for peoples or for the individual; that there is neither grandeur nor smallness for Him from whom every moral law emanates, and before whom the point and the sphere are one, the shepherd and the assembly of tribes. A moderate [*tiède*] reproduction, a unity so perfect in all of those objects to which understanding applies itself, at least aids me to conceive how the supreme intelligence contemplates in a glance, fine and prolonged, all truths; how one is explained by the other, exists, the one in the other; or rather how a single truth, existing eternally, eternally immutable, is eternally the source of all others.[4]

The 1828 work is said to be "inspired by the pantheism with which the Teutonic soul then seemed intoxicated," but Heidelberg cannot be blamed. During several years Quinet experienced an almost feverish attraction for the thought he embodied in this 1823 essay. The spirit of Herder's *Auch eine Philosophie der Geschichte* has been described as a "sentimental-teleologische Naturempfindung, die Mensch, Natur und Gott in eimem heilig-schönen Zusammenhang brachte."[5] To the impetuous and unstable French youth this aspect of German philosophy seemed a foretoken of tranquillity. In a later essay Quinet stressed above all else the "serenity" of Herder. Before his decision to translate the *Ideen zur Philosophie der Geschichte der Menschheit* this quality of German thought was important in leading him to such an undertaking. Mme de Staël had turned his eyes toward Germany; then, apart from predilection, there was the possibly decisive factor that she and Benjamin Constant encouraged Quinet in the belief that the role of interpreter of German thought for the French audience was waiting to be filled.

The late years of the Restoration were marked by a general religious, as well as Catholic, revival. The thought of men like Constant and Cousin represents an increased preoccupation with religious matters which was very noticeable outside the Church. In 1824, when the youthful Quinet was groping for answers to questions which seemed all-important, and was already strongly attracted to what he knew of German developments, Benjamin Constant published the first volume of *De la Religion.*[6]

Faith in progress was the universal which brought together representatives of most of the intellectual currents outside the Church during the first half of the nineteenth century. *De la Religion,* which was much influenced by Creutzer, Quinet's future master at Heidelberg, is instructive for the insight it gives into the contemporary treatment of the problem. The work was the most ambitious Constant ever undertook, and he devoted more than a quarter-century to writing it. A philosophical idealism, which was all but identical with that of Mme de Staël, served in this work to support the author's contention that religious forms must be progressive. The five volumes may be regarded as an elaborate effort to bring history to the support of this conviction.

As it was apparent to him that a faculty must exist separating man from beasts, Constant believed it only logical that this characteristic (the religious sentiment) should be the "fundamental law of his nature." The form, or the manner in which this sentiment found outward expression, could be of infinite variety; indeed, only its presence was constant and universal. What mortals believed and hoped could always be found "within the circumference of their understanding." Positive religions, however, had a stationary and dogmatic character which refused to follow the intelligence in its discoveries, or even the soul and the emotions, which every day rendered more pure and delicate. For Constant the history of all positive religions was thus that of a struggle between an established faith and the intelligence which outworn dogma wounded, between the sentiment and the form which no longer satisfied it. The human race had no more cherished or precious principle to defend than that of progress, nor had any been defended at the price of higher sacrifice. Henceforth, he believed, if one wished to render to religion the only homage worthy of it, and to support it upon the only foundation which could be solid and unshakable, progress must be made its principle as well.

In the 1820's this represented, almost primarily, an attack upon the Catholic Church. But Constant professed to be a Christian, preferring Protestantism to all other Christian communions. Place had then to be found for revelation: "Yes, without doubt, there is revelation, but that revelation is universal, it is permanent, it has its source in the human heart."

One may say that the young Quinet accepted all but the conclusion that Catholicism could not change, and that on this score he was no more than uncertain. Constant, like many non-Catholics, feeling that the absence of the religious sentiment was simply impossible, felt also that that which was outworn would without doubt pass away. So much for Catholicism. On the other hand "a mysterious agitation, a desire to believe, a hunger for hope was manifest everywhere." German idealism, in essence a modernized and secularized Christianity, which was at once mystical and moralistic, was only one example he could see of this, one of the manners in which a human need was being met.

Quinet greatly admired Constant. The brief and merely polite note by which the latter acknowledged receipt of Edgar's *Le Juif errant* was a treasured possession of the younger man. In 1827 he sent the first volume of his Herder translation to Constant with a letter which expressed his sincere and warm veneration for the longtime friend of Mme de Staël. However, in view of Quinet's much closer association with Cousin the latter's criticism of Constant's work is worth noting.

In the final volume of *De la Religion* Constant stated that his hostile critics had done him the service to point out that his manner of viewing religion "was identical in its essentials" with that of Cousin. But Cousin coldly repudiated the notion that his and Constant's viewpoints were identical in their essentials, and his reason for doing so casts light upon Quinet's attitude. Philosophy might suffice for an elite, but the people required a cult. For this reason

Cousin disapproved of Constant's disrespectful treatment of Catholicism.[7]

That in 1950 a prominent Catholic spokesman, Jacques Maritain, should have written that the "progress of moral conscience is
indeed the most unquestionable instance of progress in humanity"
is understandable. In the early nineteenth century the ideas of
progress and perfectibility seemed too great a threat to Catholic
articles of faith to permit their acceptance in any form whatsoever.
The transformation or the end of Christianity was a thing much
discussed, and the idea of progress had a close relationship to this
discussion. After mid-century, even, the Catholic position remained
that progress was "the religion of those who had abandoned the
Christian faith."

Cousin, however, was not alone in hoping that a Catholic transformation might take place. Ballanche is frequently named with
De Maistre and Bonald as a member of a trio which led the
theocratic reaction against the thought of the previous century,
even when credited with humanizing the principles of his colleagues.
Heine once remarked that Ballanche wrote books which everyone
praised and no one read; he is still not read. Ballanche helps to
explain, in part, why Quinet, and possibly Michelet, not to speak
of a number of the romantic school who parted with Catholicism
after 1830, did not break with the Church earlier. He deserves to
represent a "liberal" Catholicism far different in its nature from
the political party which took the name. A modernized Catholicism
to fit his philosophy would have been very near the religion Quinet
later wished to establish.

Ballanche was another who honored the memory of Mme de
Staël. It was his announced purpose to give expression to the profound religious idea which God had given his era the mission to
accomplish: the organization of a new social order. Before contrasting the views of Ballanche it is important to remember that
De Maistre despised the people, and even more he despised the
individual; as the Pope was the Church, so the Monarch was the
State. Everything that concentrated the nation satisfied him; the
aristocracy and democracy dispersed it, thus they were errors. His
Christianity condoned injustice in relegating justice to the world of
eternity. If for no other reason divine right kings were put on earth

to punish man, to make this life a vale of tears that he might earn the right to pass into a better world. As for government, the king was responsible to the Church, the depository of truth, and the Church was the Pope.

Ballanche discovered Vico during his visit to Italy with Mme Récamier in 1823 and 1824. Whether his interest in the eighteenth-century Italian preceded that of Michelet is unimportant here. Apparently they discovered him independently. Vico had been translated into German in 1822, and it was probably this translation which brought him to the attention of Victor Cousin, who in turn suggested to Michelet that he undertake a French translation.

At least in part influenced by Vico, Ballanche arrived at a philosophy of history according to which progress was providential and Christian. According to this synthesis societies, when they grew old, could find salvation only by entering into and accepting the rising spirit of the new age. Clovis, for example, had bowed his head to Christian law as the only means of self-preservation for his dynasty. For the nineteenth century the issue was clear: Ballanche declared that without a fundamental readjustment of Christianity to new concepts its doom was sealed. Himself frequently numbered among the theocrats, he wrote that religion was compromised by those religious persons who insisted that only the Middle Ages had been truly "Catholic"; that theocracy was compatible, even, with religion; and that man should remain chained, submissive to an authoritarian institution. Humanity had progressed beyond such necessities.[8] He foresaw that geological evidence was on the verge of permitting the rather definite conclusion that life on this earth had gone through an evolutionary process; this was when his purported colleague, Bonald, proved the existence of God by beginning with the premise that evolution was too insane and filthy a notion to take into consideration at all.[9]

Ballanche frequently divorced himself from De Maistre, with specific references to that "prophet of the past." Upon the latter's death he wrote that, now face to face with eternal truth, De Maistre must recognize that his dreams had been "sterile and without power." Faith could work prodigious miracles, but could not change the present into the past.[10] In response to De Maistre's unconcern that evil be rewarded by success, and that efforts at virtue fail here below, in the belief that a future life would repair the balance, Ballanche wrote: "I would dare name this form of justification impious." Such a doctrine attenuated in measure as the moral sentiment of humanity became more perfect. Here Ballanche was farther removed from orthodoxy than was Cousin, who proved the existence of Heaven by referring to the evident fact that on earth virtue did not *always* find its just reward. In the face of a philosophy which would have denied participation in their government to the people, Ballanche admired Fénelon for having favored such participation. But since Fénelon times had changed. Participation of the people in the governing power no longer sufficed. Society, once instituted, marched forward to its independence, and in the present state of ideas and opinions (1827) the time was at hand when the emancipation should be expressed by control, by the people itself being the governing power.[11]

Present in this work, if never openly stated, was the concept that Christianity had left the Church, and that, for all its errors, the Revolution was in fact its modern expression. Ballanche spoke of 1815. It had required, shamefully enough, the presence of all of the armies of Europe to induce France to give just recognition to Jeanne d'Arc. A people felt the need for territorial unity, for the unity of language and of traditions; when violently suppressed this spirit must one day burst its bonds. Moral unity gave to each people its personality and its genius.

Quinet knew Ballanche well. Never did he note for the record the strange and striking similarities in their thought. There is no absolute certainty that he read this particular work, though he sent *Orphée* to his mother in 1830. Supercilious with regard to the volume, he added that Ballanche was an excellent fellow for whom he had a strong affection. Ballanche has been discussed here in order to indicate that a sincere and devout Catholic need not, in 1827, despite appearances, have foreseen the *Syllabus of Modern Errors*. Nor did he need to have been Ultramontane in outlook, or to have seen sacrosanct dogma in the pronouncements of De Maistre and Bonald. Thus one has what is possibly a partial explanation of why Quinet did not attack the Church until the time when the picture was fully developed for him, and also when his own views had become fixed.

Quinet began work on a study of Bossuet in 1823, and completed it at the end of 1826. He described Bossuet's effort and accomplishment:

...he attempts finally to concentrate into a single absolute principle the entire chain of phenomena which he has just traced in such vivid colors. Not only the character, but the law of metaphysics is predicted. If God had appeared with authority in the sphere of the individual's life, in the history of human kind, in the spectacle of the physical universe, he will not be less present in the conscience and the reason of man. As he has broken empires and worlds with his hand, he would not leave a less profound impression upon *les faits intérieurs....*

On this document there is a notation in Quinet's hand that he reread this essay in 1845, and again in 1850, both times deciding that it could not be published without review. In this essay he wrote that Bossuet, in his *Histoire universelle,* had established the unity and the purpose of humanity's efforts in this world. The history of humanity was the history of Providence speaking through man's conscience.[12] At this level of abstraction Bossuet was not incompatible with the philosophic idealism of Mme de Staël, Constant, and Cousin—rather the reverse. But Quinet gave to this view an emphasis which made it the fundamental characteristic of his outlook. Bossuet was the person most frequently referred to in his private notes, during all of his life, and the author he most frequently reread.

With his usual insistence upon his own originality, Quinet related that he read Bossuet in 1823, examining him in his different aspects, "with regard to the principles which I had just formed on the metaphysics of history." He found these views justified and confirmed. Quinet sought a single and absolute principle, but the limitation of Bossuet's orthodoxy stifled the young romantic. The principle, secularized and modernized, appeared to him across the Rhine.

Constant made recent German thought on religious matters of particular importance among the manifestations he noted of a revived sentiment. Creutzer and Goerres were especially pointed out. It was, Constant felt, unfortunate that their thought had not gained in France anything like the audience which it had been accorded in the rest of Europe, and he hoped that his own work would do something to rectify this situation. When the first volume of his work appeared Quinet had just begun, or began soon after, his translation of Herder.

This was the first French translation of Herder's *Ideen zur Geschichte der Menschhheit*. From the time of this undertaking in 1824 until 1830 Quinet was an enthusiastic spokesman for the new German ideas. Until immediately after the July Revolution his closest associations were with those in France who were a part of this movement. Of these Victor Cousin was most important. Enthusiasm for Cousin was virtually unanimous among young liberals during the last years of the Restoration. Quinet was introduced to him some months after undertaking the Herder translation. The translation and Quinet's introductory essay, *Introduction à la Philosophie de l'Histoire de l'Humanité*, were begun in late 1824, although the *Introduction* was probably not finished until the summer of 1826, the complete translation not till the end of 1827.[13]

A publisher's agreement to pay six hundred francs upon the delivery of each of the Herder volumes in translation, the first of which Quinet promised would be ready in one month, made possible the young man's visit to England for the first two weeks of April, 1825. With this windfall seemingly assured Quinet left for London, in part because he hoped to improve his faulty command of English. He also intended to correct errors in his translation of the first volume, a draft of which he had completed.

When he had returned to Paris and was at work on the *Introduction,* difficulties arose with the publisher and the understanding was broken. Then, early in May, a few days before his first meeting with Cousin, Quinet obtained an audience with Degérando, with whom he had previously exchanged several letters, in the hope of gaining the active support of the older man in his Herder enterprise. Degérando and Charles de Villiers had been of immeasurable assistance to Mme de Staël in her preparation of *De l'Allemagne.* She had been in correspondence with both after 1802, knew De Villier's *Philosophie de Kant* (1801); she had also made use of Degérando's *Histoire comparée des systèmes de Philosophie* (3 vols., 1804), one of the first French works to make use of German developments.

The boyish enthusiast, ambitious and unknown, not unnaturally thought of Degérando as a person who might use his influence to aid in making the Herder project a success. At their first meeting the older man gave encouragement, remarking that Quinet had undertaken a work to which he himself had hoped to turn in his old age. He placed his library at Quinet's disposal and mentioned that a close friend, Camille Jourdan, was "infatuated with Herder." How Degérando responded to the fact that his visitor did not know the German language is not recorded. He did promise to give the youth all of the aid within his power, and offered to write a notice to be printed at the head of the work so that, as the delighted young man informed his mother, "my name will be accompanied and protected by a name illustrious in the moral sciences." Then, without Degérando taking an active part in either development, Quinet found a new publisher, and was introduced to Cousin. His confidence was bolstered and he promptly lost all desire to have his translation appear under the protection of an established name. Not that his contacts with Degérando became less frequent. Partly under his auspices Quinet became a member of a group of Germanophiles who, in July, 1825, had in mind a *Revue germanique,* the purpose of which was to have been to acquaint the French public with German letters. Degérando, Stapfer (the translator of Goethe and the former tutor of Guizot), and Cousin were among the prospective editors. Quinet was promised the opportunity to participate, but the review never appeared, that of 1827 with the same title being a different enterprise. As the youth progressed with the translation of Herder he was in frequent touch with Degérando, and, it is to be presumed, received his assistance. Typically, Quinet remembered that he had not been assisted. Degérando had read the translation as it progressed, but "for his pleasure, for he made no observation at all." Not knowing German Quinet translated from an English translation, although even his English was uncertain. This seems to have been a matter of little moment.

Victor Cousin did little more than give Quinet further impetus along a road already entered upon, but the importance of the encouragement he gave to the younger man is not to be discounted. Levraut, the director of a Strasbourg publishing firm, almost simultaneously contracted to publish the Herder translation and intro-

duced the young romantic to Cousin. The meeting took place only a
few days after Cousin's return to Paris following a six-month sojourn
in a German prison.

For Quinet it was love at first sight; very shortly he was writing
to his mother that "liaison" was the only word which properly
described his relationship with Cousin. After the first meeting he
wrote: "A man with whom one is in sympathy stirs you like the
sight of the sea or of a beautiful night." If the personal magnetism
of Cousin was enormous, Quinet's response was extravagant, and for
several months unremittent. That summer he made a practice of
walking through the Luxembourg Gardens, along a route which
permitted him, at one point, to catch a glimpse of Cousin's window.
But a person as little prey to immoderation as Ernest Renan recalled
the "incomparable life which the conversation of Cousin exhaled,"
and the Cousin Renan knew had lost something of his enthusiasm,
for he was twenty years older than the sage of thirty-three who cap-
tivated Quinet.

Cousin gave freely of his encouragement and of his time, was
enthusiastic and uncritical. In July Quinet read the beginning pages
of his *Introduction,* by now nearly one hundred pages in manuscript,
before a gathering at Cousin's home. He had hardly begun before
the master interrupted with delighted cries of "C'est beau! C'est
parfait!" Cousin's idealism, fervor, and optimism, his impressive and
dramatic manner, account, in so far as Quinet's own personality
does not, for the passionate episode. Later Quinet was repelled by
Cousin's theatrical emotionalism. One may presume that in 1825
just this trait dazzled him. As for Cousin's thought, this seemed to
Quinet scarcely different from that of Mme de Staël. Thus Cousin
seemed a re-enforcement of an old faith. The philosopher was the
first to admit this similarity, and pointed to Mme de Staël and
Chateaubriand as foremost among the literary representatives of
his doctrines.

Cousin believed that the time of exclusive theories was past, and
confidently set for himself the task of conciliating all systems, taking
from each that which the "facts" justified. He too represented the
reaction against eighteenth-century materialism, which his authority
gave the permanent label *sensualism.* Not that he disavowed a more
basic and more general characteristic of Enlightenment thought—

not at all. He believed that nothing which lacked the property of universality was worthy of the slightest attention. Because of his faith in *le sens commun* he felt justified in making the claim of being Catholic, "though more Christian."[14]

Faguet concluded that of all the men who made the effort to establish a new spiritual power during the years between 1820 and 1850 Cousin was the least of the failures. Certainly Cousin was most practical—or, in other terms, he demanded least of the faithful. Boas wrote:

> Cousin seems to have seen his goal from the very start.... It was a political goal. His task was to found a philosophy which would be non-Catholic and non-atheist, which would provide for liberalism but not for republicanism.... He was eminently fitted to give philosophical expression to the rule of Louis-Philippe.[15]

Possibly this does not mirror the true nature of Louis-Philippe's reign, and it should be noted that the greatest enthusiasm for Cousin existed before his elevation in 1830; but his philosophy is well characterized.

In the eloquence of the Savoyard vicar Cousin saw "the most sane as well as the greatest production of the eighteenth century." A different sort of religion was required by the people. Without religion, philosophy addressed itself to but a small mass of humanity, and thus ran the risk of being without great effectiveness for the manners and the life of those who made up the greater part of the nation. On the other hand, Cousin believed that without philosophy the most pure religion could not escape superstition, and thus saw the intellectual elite leave its fold. When this occurred, as the eighteenth century clearly showed, bit by bit skepticism spread downward to the masses. Thus the alliance of true religion and true philosophy was at once natural and necessary; natural because of the common fund of truth both recognized, and necessary for the better service of humanity.[16] Very similar to Mme de Staël's, Cousin's outlook was more obviously related to that which found crass expression in Napoleon's frequent remarks on the usefulness of religious superstition, a type of remark indeed frequent in governing circles during the July Monarchy. We will not, until after many years, find Quinet on this road, but before 1830 the implications of this aspect of Cousin's thought were not particularly in evidence. During the Restoration Cousin represented a strong reaction against the materialism involved in the doctrines of the previous century, against what he termed *une doctrine désolante*. A defense against skepticism was what he offered, and what Quinet sought. Cousin's intellectual and political opportunism was obscured for Quinet by his own sincerity.

Quinet, in later life, could state, with more justice than has usually been granted, that Cousin "taught me neither an idea nor a fact; I owe him nothing."[17] None the less, Cousin encouraged and supported Quinet in his studies, and in his nascent ambition to become the interpreter for France of German philosophy. Exactly how decisive this was is impossible to say, but its importance is not to be doubted, and the charge that Quinet was ungrateful is justified.

Michelet knew Cousin before he met Quinet. It is probable that Cousin brought the two younger men together as early as May, 1825. They had certainly met before February 11, 1826, the day of the first meeting of a philosophical society, a group brought together by Cousin. The membership was made up of Cousin, Jourdan, Guignat, and Poret who made a bimonthly report on ancient philosophy; and Michelet, Quinet, and Jules Simon who took modern philosophy as their province. The close friendship between Quinet and Michelet dated from this time, an intimacy which was not disturbed until December, 1851. Michelet, in later life, was as disposed as was Quinet to discount the importance of his early relationship with Cousin. If Michelet, who was five years Quinet's senior, was never quite so overwhelmed by Cousin's personality, he did have the youthful ambition to write like him some day.

An emotional crisis, occasioned by developments in a relationship between Quinet and a young married woman, resulted in his decision to leave France temporarily. Cousin and friends at Strasbourg recommended Heidelberg as a retreat from temptation, and in December, 1826, Quinet crossed the Rhine. Creutzer drew him to Heidelberg, and he carried a letter of introduction from Cousin to the German scholar. Quinet remained in Germany for slightly more than two years, except for periodic visits to France. At Heidelberg he came to know well both Creutzer and Schlosser. The young man's ambition to become an interpreter of German thought and culture for the French public was intensified, and he now determined to make this his career. The distasteful matter of earning a livelihood pressed itself upon him ever more urgently. But the German environment, the Herder translation, and work on three lengthy essays so absorbed Quinet that material insecurity was less disturbing to him than it had been in the past.

Frequently during later life Quinet insisted upon the unity of his intellectual development, and maintained that all of the presentments of his adolescence had been confirmed in the age of maturity. The first important published presentation of his views is the 1827 *Introduction* to the Herder translation. The main tenets of the message which the translator directed to his French audience were familiar to all readers who knew the thought of Mme de Staël, Benjamin Constant, or Victor Cousin, and the undertaking appeared headed by a glowing tribute to the leader of the eclectic school. The two essays which introduced the first and third volumes of the Herder translation were, in their finished form, the product of Quinet's sojourn at Heidelberg. Although the political implications of the ideas discussed and defended were not obtrusive in these studies their tendency was undeniable, and it is worth noting that Quinet was never more genuinely a liberal than on the eve of the July Revolution.

The young man had sought in history for meaning and purpose, so that he might justify faith. Humanity, he wrote in the first essay, had been slow to develop the historic sense. Only after untold generations did the conviction develop that an invisible hand guided men and nations in the service of the law of Christ. This idea, in assigning to human actions a goal and an element of fixity, was the first which gave to history a philosophic character. With Bossuet this philosophy of history had reached its culmination. In his hands the history of humanity had become a sublime epic. Quinet professed no other historical belief. "Only that which was particular has become general . . . that which appeared in a particular place or time, has become the work of all places and all centuries. But we too, we believe in Revelation, that is to say in reason, justice, and liberty. . . ."[18] Humanity having established that God was the source, the eternal debate between the materialist and the idealist had been extended to the consideration of history. In what manner did God reveal himself? asked Quinet. It was the task of the "new science" to discover the answer. Two men then appeared, Vico, the idealist, and Herder, the materialist. Quinet found that "if . . . [Vico] gave as a point of support to the series of human actions thought in its sublime essence . . . [Herder] built upon the most gross manifestations of the material being. . . ."

Vico's, not Herder's, point of departure Quinet found "more solid." Particularly disturbing to him was the fatalism to which Herder seemed doomed. Herder's animal world, dominated by its physical environment until the moment when man began social progress, disquieted him. From whence did *this* impulsion come?

That first freedom from materialistic determinism which seemed so inexplicable to Herder, I see it reappear under a thousand different faces, in all of the succession of ages. Far from being a miraculous moment in the history of humanity, that act of emancipation has never ceased. It was repeated yesterday and is repeated today. Because of it we have . . . traditions and annals which possess unity and meaning. At this moment, by what miracle is it that we do not live under the law of the Middle Ages . . . ? Why is it? Because at different moments in history humanity has declared itself unwilling to accept the institutions which have been willed to it. Men have wished to modify or overthrow them, and at their own pleasure, and at their own risk and peril have made their own destiny.

How incompatible this really is with Herder we shall wait to examine. But this was Vico, as understood by Michelet, and by Ballanche as well. This was the explanation for progress: an ever recurring revelation served to guide man forward, toward a fuller understanding and realization of the Word. History, Quinet now wrote, in its commencement and in its end, is the spectacle of liberty, the protestation of humankind against the world which enchains it, the triumph of the infinite over the finite, the freeing of the spirit, the reign of the soul. The end of liberty would be the end of history.

Referring to Victor Cousin's identical statement, Croce noted that such words not only sounded differently in Germany, but had a quite different effect there than in France. The Italian liberal, in defining his own "modern" conception of liberty, rearranged the terminology of Quinet and Cousin scarcely at all, and concluded that liberty was a continual struggle in which the "final victory was impossible, because it would mean the death of all the combatants, that is, of all then living."[19] Not only may one wonder what the effect of such oratory really is; it cannot be startling that it should sound differently to separate audiences. In terms as general as these each private, class, or national interest may easily translate its ambition into the "protestation of humankind" against its unenlightened opponents. In this regard the difference between the French and German experience was not particularly great, a contention Quinet's development does something to support. The young man's liberalism, however, was made of more than this belief that history was a ceaseless struggle between good and evil.

Quinet preferred Vico to Herder. No matter how much he distorted Herder, the choice was a revealing one. Reacting above all against the deterministic materialism of the previous century, he could hardly help being attracted by Vico's idealism. The problem of Quinet's acceptance of the natural rights theory arises here, and although this acceptance was implicit rather than explicit in his early essays it was always present. A basic dogma of the French Enlightenment was the presupposition of an identical human nature at all times and at all places. Vico's theory of evolution would seem to indicate that man is not, as the natural rights theory contended, everywhere identical, but that he is shaped by the historical process. The difficulty of reconciling the eighteenth-century belief in progress with the conviction that human nature is always and everywhere the same thus arises, in a somewhat different form, for Quinet.

First it should be said that a presumed incompatibility of eighteenth-century universalism with a faith in progress gave Quinet no more conscious difficulty than it did Constant in his *De la Religion,* a work in which the two forms of optimism are very much in evidence. Whether the tone of disparagement is justified or not, Meinecke was correct enough when he wrote that Voltaire conceived of progress only as the "Annäherung an die Vernunft-und Zivilisationideal seiner Zeit."[20] Quinet would have been quite willing to admit his very similar guilt. Reason, he too believed, was everywhere and at all times the same; but progress was the process by which man's comprehension of Truth which was eternal was extended and purified, although understanding would never be complete or perfect. In any age the dispersion of the existing ideal to as large a portion of society as possible was of pressing concern. Natural rights were in part practical necessities which, when protected and guaranteed by society, insured that progress would continue. Of more fundamental importance, they were within the comprehension of all men; a modicum of "common sense" was all that was necessary for understanding them. They were based upon truths which were, as the phrase went, "self-evident."

Vico posed less of a problem for the adherent of the natural rights theory than did Herder, and for Quinet he posed no problem at all. Not only did Vico emphasize what is typical in history, rather than what is unique; he also gave natural law an important place in his synthesis. The difficulty might indeed be great if Vico had written no more on the subject that this:

It is equally beyond our power to enter in the vast imagination of those first men, whose minds were not in the least abstract, refined, or spiritualized, because they were entirely immersed in the senses, buffeted by the passions, buried in the body. That is why we said above that we can scarcely understand, still less imagine, how those first men thought who founded gentile humanity.[21]

Vico stated, however, that one of the fundamental purposes of his *New Science* was "to demonstrate that the natural law of nations originated *separately* among the various peoples. . . ."

Uniform ideas originating among entire peoples unknown to each other must have a common ground of truth.

This axiom is a great principle which establishes the common sense of the human race as the criterion taught to the nations by divine providence to define what is certain in the natural law of nations.[22]

Finally we find in his autobiography that "in our mind there are certain eternal truths that we cannot mistake or deny, and which are therefore not of our making."[23]

Vico believed that there were three kinds of reason. First was divine reason, which was understood only by God. Men knew it only in so far as it was revealed to them. "To the Hebrews first and then to the Christians, this had been by internal speech to their minds as the proper expression of a God all mind. . . ." This led Vico to conclude that "in good theology divine authority holds the same place as reason."[24] All of this Vico fitted to his more or less orthodox Catholicism. The natural rights theory, on the other hand, needs no more of a foundation than Vico's "common sense," and the minds of men which comprehend "divine reason," may provide.

Michelet, who wrote that he had no master but Vico, felt that his most important debt to the great Italian was to the latter's view of history as a struggle of liberty against fatality. In Mme de Staël Quinet had found the confirmation that the meaning of life itself was in this struggle. This feature of Vico's thought may well be taken as the decisive reason for Quinet's finding him "more solid" than Herder.

Herder's work, with its concept of individuality and the uniqueness of nations, may be said to be incompatible with the universalism of the French Enlightenment, but this escaped Quinet and was not the cause of his preference for Vico. In 1827 and 1828 he resisted what he thought were the fatalistic aspects of Herder's "disguised pantheism," although shortly thereafter he briefly succumbed to just that aspect of German thought. It is wrong to attribute a mechanistic doctrine of causation to Herder, but it is not so difficult to understand how Quinet did this as it is to explain his reading into Herder a kind of deterministic materialism.

Quinet found Herder's historicism both comforting and objectionable. Herder wrote:

What is the principal law which we observe in all great historical events? I think it is this: that every potentiality of this world is realized here. In part according to the situation and necessities of place; in part according to the conditions and opportunities of time; in part according to the innate or self-made character of peoples.[25]

This "astonishing serenity" calmed and refreshed the impatient youth. He never rose from Herder without feeling able to view events with greater equanimity. But how, asked Quinet, could man accept the law which Herder established? If humanity was not and could never be anything but in conformity with the accidents of time and place, could only be "ce qu'elle pouvait être et rien que ce qu'elle pouvait être," what of man's free will? What then of the rights of man?

Herder's progress, which Quinet understood to be produced by the action of natural circumstances, and the more or less spontaneous, irresistible, and collective human nature, tended to justify things as they were. Quinet always needed to believe in man's freedom of will, and his own pantheism never had this seemingly fatalistic complexion for long. He was, of course, unfair to Herder.

Meinecke made historicism a positive virtue, and, while he pointed out Herder's relative merit in this matter, recognized none the less that the philosopher was not free from the trait of universalism. Thus the ideal in Herder's own heart "remained the measure for treating the political side of world history." This moral judgment-stick was ever more in evidence as Herder grew older, and thus the *Ideen* is more contaminated than the earlier *Entwurfe*.[26] Herder believed that "pure reason and moral justice" were identical to Socrates, Confucius, Zoroaster, Plato, and Cicero, and that upon this fundamental basis *"unser ganzes Geschlecht ruhet."*[27] Quinet need not have found Herder incompatible with his own faith in inalienable rights.

Quinet's full development waited upon a diversity of frustrations; his concern with the application of truth to the event in the everyday political world was ever more dominant. Herder's secularized Christianity was a permanent influence upon his thought. The German philosopher's conception of the nation, the thought which Quinet later adapted most completely to his own purposes, he all but ignored before 1830. The 1828 *Essai sur les oeuvres de Herder* did mention that for Herder national forms were "sacred vessels, formed by the hand of God," and the "sole exterior cult worthy of the Author of things."[28] A passing reference here, in time this became the aspect of Herder most important for Quinet. In time the conclusion of this essay was sacrilege.

Farewell, hospitable land, peaceful land! What might I give in return for all that I have received from you? You have neither the sweet climate of France, nor the liberty yet more sweet of England.... The delirium of your inspiration is past, as the branch charged with fruit you incline to earth, and yet you remain the land of the soul, and of hope.[29]

The second work revealed more clearly Quinet's admiration for the variety of Christianity which he found in Herder, and an unwillingness to pay his respects to orthodoxy. Later he was more willing to compromise himself, until he arrived at the College of France. In 1828 he wrote that the more nearly each age of human development conformed to Revelation, the greater the progress which could be said to have been accomplished. But he asked that the terms "Revelation" and "Scriptures," "nature" and "reason," not be abused. One saw the letter opposed to nature, "but nature is itself a vast enough book." The first rule of Scriptures ought to be to give way to the common intelligence, which was the medium through which God truly revealed himself.[30]

De l'Origine des Dieux, written in 1828, is the last work by Quinet relevant to the present discussion which precedes July, 1830. This piece of writing is unsatisfactory from the standpoint of the usual Quinet admirer. Even Mme Quinet found it "obscure." Although little different in spirit from the two preceding essays, it gave one matter greater prominence, which may be thought to be at the heart of its objectionable character. Quinet announced that the task which truly awaited the modern genius was to create a universal authority.

The Christian symbol, in a sudden expansion, had, with the Church, dominated the Middle Ages, but had never freed itself from subjection to national traditions. Quinet proposed that local traditions, which had contradicted one another and fought among themselves for as long as they had been subordinated to the individual forms of the conscience of particular races, might, if freed from such bonds, take up their development and their natural order in the poetic conscience of humanity itself. Should the genius appear to break these molds, Dante's *Divine Comedy* would then appear to have been the first act in a kind of last judgment. The *Divine Comedy* of this improvised genius would have for its denouement not the taking of a city, the vengeance of a tribe, or the migration of a people, but the progressive law of the civil world. Preceding epics had been the contribution and the tableau of a race or of a nation; the epic of Dante opened a new cycle which Quinet hoped would seem the work and the image of humanity.

The above may serve to indicate how little Herder modified

either Quinet's eighteenth-century universalism or his cosmopolitanism. Herder is not to be "blamed" for Quinet's later development, nor to be held responsible for it. Herder was never a "patriot" in the sense in which Quinet became one. In 1828 the young Frenchman hoped that a future poet might use the annals of humanity as Homer had used those of the Greeks. For unity he should choose the unity of history and of nature. This poet should bring together individuals from across the centuries, no longer in the shadows of hell, or paradise, or the purgatory of the Middle Ages, but within an unlimited compass. This was the necessary and possible form of the epic of the modern world.[31]

Small wonder that this is slighted by those who admire the patriot. Cosmopolitanism was a basic characteristic of that woman Quinet yet so admired; the time was far off when the word would be a term of reproach on his lips. For the spell under which these words were written was not brief; Quinet's three most ambitious creative efforts of the ten years which follow had an important relationship to it—although, no doubt, the thought was seriously modified.[32] If the nation was here viewed as an outmoded form, which in a happier synthesis was to be submerged in a larger and all-inclusive perfection, this was not all that was at variance with the older Quinet.

At Lyon in 1838, and thenceforward, Quinet embraced religion as the substance of humanity, and preached that political and social revolution is accomplished only in the conception of an idea of God. Then he taught that religious revolution must always and without exception precede political or social change; and that history of the civil world was "eternally formed by its primary source," that is by its faith.[33] This represented a definite break with Mme de Staël, and, of course with Montesquieu, to whom Mme de Staël owed the view that political institutions were the source of all others, and a definite shift toward a more exclusive idealism. But, before 1830, Quinet sought firmer ground than idealism offered. On the other hand, his suspicion of any suggestion of materialistic determinism prevented his fully accepting Herder. This suspicion was a consistent trait. As protest against the existing order built up within him, Quinet assigned an ever larger role to the human will, and to immutable abstract verities.

After 1830 the part of Vico which remained a living part of Michelet's philosophy was neither the former's metaphysical theories nor his religious conceptions, but almost exclusively the law expressed by Vico of the power of humanity to make its own destiny. Quinet's course was similar in that he too placed greater stress upon this power, but divergent in that his original sympathy for Vico's metaphysical theories was increased.

Vico believed that his work fully demonstrated that the first governments of the world had "as their entire form religion." Aristocratic, then popular governments succeeded this first form, and religion "served the peoples as means for attaining them." Thus, if religion were lost among peoples "they have nothing left to enable them to live in society: no shield of defense, nor means of counsel, nor basis of support, nor even a form by which they may exist in the world at all."[34] Vico's thought that religion is the productive as well as the conserving principle of society was taken up by Quinet and developed. As Chassin would have it, Vico crippled the principle in restricting the flight and destroying the consequences, from the moment he immobilized the City of God in Catholicism, and in the name of a divine ideal "condemned humanity to turn eternally in a circle of despair." This may not be quite fair to Vico, but Quinet did take the principle and was not bound by the limitations of even Vico's somewhat doubtful orthodoxy.[35] Thus transformed, Vico's ideal city became a vantage point from which Quinet could view the past and present as "...a moralist, sure of himself...approving, disapproving, applauding or hooting, according to the impression of his conscience, in the name of all humanity."[36]

On the eve of the "glorious three days" of 1830 we have an ambitious and impecunious young romantic; a somewhat undisciplined enthusiast, impatient and nervously self-confident. In certain respects he had found himself. Mme de Staël had introduced him to German idealism, a modernized Christianity, which met his profoundly felt need for a faith which could stand against the skepticism so prevalent in the France of his youth, and yet not entail, as Catholicism or his mother's Calvinism seemed to do, the sacrifice of a belief in human progress due to rational and good human beings.

Bossuet offered an absolute unity and a philosophy of history which Vico and Herder taught him to fit to his own needs. Germany then became briefly a greater love than France—because in Germany there was faith, there was not the cynicism and indifference which seemed to him to characterize his own countrymen. That Chateaubriand vied briefly with Mme de Staël for his allegiance reveals how important he found it to discover a synthesis which did not view emotional behavior as ridiculous. He chose the Protestant way; his background made that almost necessary. Cousin assisted and encouraged him.

Heine wrote:

Cousin's eclecticism is a fine spun handbridge between a fleshy Scotch empiricism and the abstraction of German idealism, a bridge which may completely satisfy the needs of a few light-footed strollers, but which will come crashing down should the mass of mankind, with its heavy burdens of the heart, and its trampling chargers wish to cross.[37]

In the sequel Quinet found himself not light-footed enough, but in 1830 he showed fair promise of becoming an "official" spokesman of Cousin's doctrine.

A review of these years should not close without mentioning the fact that in Michelet Quinet had a generous and loyal friend.

4. Republican and Democrat, 1815-1830

AGREEMENT IS GENERAL that Quinet should be classed as a stalwart of the democratic-republican wing of the French Revolutionary tradition. Soltau was representative when he contrasted De Tocqueville with Quinet, commenting that the former nowhere came out "as the bold champion of positive democracy as the participation of all in the business of government as did Michelet, Quinet and their school."[1]

Under the Restoration the public expression of republican views met with arrest, imprisonment, or banishment. The republican movement was limited to activity within secret societies, which had a flourishing existence. Theorists headed the republican group, men who thought in terms of the distant future, and who in 1830 were not ready to assume responsibility for government, much less think of seizing that power. Even in 1848 the Republic was imposed upon these leaders by the people, and these men took control with faint hearts and trembling hands. During the Restoration the party followed the opportunistic policy of giving what support it could to the official opposition headed by the Liberals. The Liberals, once in power, took as their main objective the defense of the middle class against democracy, but before 1830 fought the good fight against Charles X.

Republicans were obscure on matters of doctrine. Mme de Staël was fiery in her opposition to Jacobinism; nevertheless she frequently spoke of republican institutions as the ideal. She typifies, as does Lafayette, around whom so much republican activity centered under the Restoration, the patient and conservative temper of many a theoretical republican. She felt that although democrats might say that what was needed was a king without a nobility, or the doing away with both, experience had shown the impossibility of doing away with either. During the last days of the Restoration the *National* and its controlling group came into prominence, a liberal monarchist group; in February, 1830, Thiers described the "republican" spirit for the readers of this paper:

France wishes to govern herself, because she has the capacity to do so. Will one say that this is a republican idea? So much the worse for those who enjoy taking fright at a word. This spirit, republican if one wishes, exists, manifests itself everywhere, and is becoming impossible to repress.[2]

Few republican leaders could have taken exception to his words. A representative and constitutional monarchy, in form not essentially different from that desired by the Liberals, was acceptable to the majority of an improperly labeled republican leadership. As Louis Blanc wrote, there was simply no truly republican party during this time. The aftermath of July, 1830, forced decision, and under the July Monarchy the gulf between Republicanism and Liberalism widened. By 1848 "the Republican is more often an undeveloped Socialist than an advanced Liberal." This describes the evolution of at least the extremist minority. Another aspect of the problem was suggested by Michel, when he wrote that the historian of the democratic school "would have some difficulty to isolate its action from that of the socialists in the years that separate 1830 and 1848."[3] Both are partly accurate statements, if one puts Marxist materialism from his mind in thinking of "socialism," but both apply after 1830.

Political science and doctrine played a subordinate role in the thinking of a party whose title leads one to another expectation, but the republican element was not without its passion, nor without a program for which it had unlimited enthusiasm. Between 1815 and 1848 one may say that the republican party, and the democratic party as well, favored military aggression with an enthusiasm and consistency which they rarely showed for either republican institutions or democratic practices. Under the Restoration an uneasy alliance between Liberal and Republican was accompanied by an easier, if no more sincere, alliance between Bonapartism and Republicanism, in which both paid lip-service to democracy, but with patriotism the adhesive agent.

The foreign policy of the republicans during the early July Monarchy was to liberate Germany and Italy, to appeal to the people of Europe against oppressive aristocracies, and to wash away the shame of Waterloo. Armand Carrel, who in 1830 felt that a Republic was neither desirable nor possible, in 1832 broke with the government, and then with monarchy itself, ostensibly because this foreign policy was not followed. But Carrel once told Quinet that he spent his life writing the very opposite of what he believed; he loved and admired England, every day he wrote a violent article against England; Cromwell seemed to him a hundred times greater than Napoleon, he wrote the reverse.[4] Waterloo and Napoleon were symbols not to be cast aside.

The Revolution of July was not made by those who benefited from it. "Like the victory of the republicans over the king, the victory of the liberals over the republicans was easy." Although some justice attaches to the charge of a "betrayal" of the Revolution, many a republican realized the justice of Cavaignac's later remark that "We were not in force." The real result was that the struggle which had begun in 1815, between the Bourbons and the Liberal party, had ended with the defeat of the Bourbons. The Liberals had wished to change the personnel of the previous regime; many of them thought of the Revolution as though it had been a ministerial crisis, and at first believed that the people had sacrificed themselves to uphold the Charter. This group did not understand "that a new idea had been born, and that the Revolution marked the first stirring of the democratic idea." Royer-Collard typifies the more perceptive element among the Liberals, and he is reported to have remarked at the event, "Moi aussi, je suis des victorieux, triste parmi les victorieux." But, as Schapiro notes, the Liberals of 1830 were not long in realizing "that in order to maintain their victory, they would have to pass to the other side of the barricade."

Thureau-Dangin explained the republicanism of Carrel by saying that when the monarchy at whose birth he had assisted offered him no more than a prefecture, vanity did the rest.[5] Quinet had a somewhat similar motivation, although in neither case should one be certain that it was decisive. These men do, however, exemplify a group, many of whom were theoretical republicans under the Restoration, which refused to pass to the other side of the barricade after July. Sincere in their liberalism, or disappointed and hungry for authority, they turned to the Left after July, 1830.

The July Revolution brought no solace to a bruised national spirit. Rather than fling defiance at the victors of Waterloo the new Monarchy spent all efforts to appease the irritated tempers of crowned heads. No opposition could fail to realize that an appeal to French patriotism was the best part of political wisdom. Thus Carrel wrote what he did not believe.

If "republican" under the Restoration was little more than a loose term, describing one moved by certain general and not strictly defined sentiments, "democrat" was little more precise in its meaning. It may be worth noting that even later authors of the more radical social doctrines were rather realistic about the preparedness of France for democracy. Proudhon's remark, "La propriété, c'est le vol," is famous; his "La démocratie, c'est l'envie" is equally characteristic. He wrote in 1851 that the masses were far from having reached a condition of being capable of benefiting themselves should they have the power of government. Democracy still remained a "fictitious word, which signified love of people, love of children, but not government of the people."[6] The Saint-Simonians made their main purpose the amelioration of the condition of the poorest classes of society, but were in agreement with Proudhon as to the incapacity of those classes to bring about such an accomplishment by their own efforts. The disciples of Saint-Simon posited the essential necessity for an absolute authority; De Maistre's writing was an important source for their argument. Louis Blanc was later in a minority among the more radical social reformers who believed that universal suffrage must, or even should, precede social reform.

Although the Ledru-Rollin school of republicans (of which Quinet became a member) made universal suffrage the key to their program in the late years of the July Monarchy, in 1830, as well as later, "democrat" better described the person who subscribed to several general premises than a person who insisted upon a necessary list of institutional arrangements. If republicans put their hope in the distant future, democrats were much farther from the prevailing sentiment, and it was only natural that their debate revolved about attitudes rather than a specific program. Lamartine, who after 1831 was an unsteady spokesman for democracy, stressed an important aspect of the French democratic sentiment when he declared that defiance of the country in the face of the state was "unintelligible nonsense" in a democracy. This expressed one of the principal differences between the French democratic and liberal viewpoints, if not the essential difference, although one may say that democrats shared the opinion with their worst enemies. The republican Debidour made a statement of principle at the outset of his *Histoire des rapports de l'Église et de l'État*, in which he declared that he had two basic and equally dear principles: freedom of worship and the sovereignty of the state; but if a conflict should arise between the two "the last word should always rest with the state."[7] This typifies the tradition, and the democrat thus resembled the seventeenth-century apologists of divine-right absolutism in refusing to limit the sphere of the state's activity, to the point of sacrificing the most sacred of individual liberties to the community interest. No logical difficulty was involved for Bossuet; for Quinet the case would be quite different.

Michelet clarified another aspect of the democratic viewpoint, one which in France separated him from most of the radical social reformers as well as from the Right. When Mickiewicz was preaching the need for "a man," Michelet wrote in his "Journal," "I say there is need for men."[8]

A further simplification takes one to the heart of the matter. Constant belonged with the most enlightened of the liberals, but we find him expressing the idea upon which democratic idealism is based, the hope which is a component part of the whole rationalistic optimistic structure, and which alone bears up a logical and meaningful democratic faith: "In order that these [future generations] may advance along the route which is open to them [as a result of immense discoveries in science] it will be necessary for them to have what we lack: conviction, enthusiasm, and *the power to sacrifice interest to opinion*."[9] If human nature permits man to sacrifice interest to opinion, and virtue is a distinguishing earmark of democratic society, only perversity could lead a man into any but the democratic camp. This optimism with respect to human nature we may say made the democrat, and the lack of it made his opponent. If the French republican was an impatient warrior, the democrat was an optimist. As Louis Blanc wrote, soon all theories would have been tested but the simplest and noblest, that of fraternity. "Jusqu'à ce que cette magnifique expérience ait été faite, veillons sur nos croyances. . . ."[10]

Aggressive nationalism was a part of the democratic program. Weill relates how even working-class political meetings, held secretly during the last years of the Restoration, culminated in attacks upon the treaties of 1815, and the demand that France have the Rhine. A working-class pamphlet of 1831 stated: "We have chased the government of the Bourbons, not because it rendered us miserable, for the people were never better off than between 1816 and 1829, but because it had been imposed upon us by the pretended victors; by foreign arms and domestic traitors."[11]

In all but the ruling element this was the constant cry. Among the groups who at first rallied to the July Monarchy were the Saint-Simonians. Through their press (Michel Chevalier was their great journalist in these years, and Sainte-Beuve one of the editors of the *Globe,* which became the daily of the cult in 1831)[12] they presented France as fitted for a missionary and conquering role, a people marked by God to initiate Europe into a universal but French-controlled communion. The annexation of Belgium was specifically demanded. For some glory, being a happier memory, was better remembered than the sacrifice it had cost. For others humiliation and frustration over the failure of the Revolution fired the sense of mission buried in their hearts.

Monod was surprised to find no evidence that the youthful Michelet, in the years between 1810 and 1815, had been moved either to pride upon the occasion of France's victory or to humiliation by her defeat. It was only later, at the time of his visit to England during the July Monarchy, that Michelet shared the feeling of hostility and rancor toward England "common to all Frenchmen who had grown up during the period of the Empire." In 1846 Michelet was "haunted" by the fear of anglomania, the admiration and imitation of English institutions—the heart of the doctrine represented by Guizot and the House of Orleans—which was killing France.

In 1846 Quinet expressed the view Michelet held in that year; before 1830 no trace of such a viewpoint is to be found. In England in 1825 Quinet breathed the freest air he had ever known. When Mme de Staël advocated the importation of the English constitution into France her pupil did not protest. He wrote with admiration and approval of an acquaintance who had spent five years in confinement for having spoken too openly of that constitution during the reign of Napoleon. The youth's letters from Paris down to 1830 show a singular lack of concern for those matters which were later to consume his life. At a time when the Paris student body was fired by an enthusiasm for the lost cause of the Revolution, when secret societies recruited great numbers of ardent members among those students, there is every indication that Quinet devoted his energies to breaking into precisely those literary circles whose opinions and outlook he was later to denounce as bringing death to France.

During the winter of 1829 and 1830 Quinet called upon Guizot weekly. He became a regular visitor at Mme Récamier's, where Chateaubriand was the center of attention. Cousin, the philosophical spokesman of Royer-Collard and Guizot, was still an intimate friend. This was the same Cousin for whom the Charter "spontaneously granted" by Louis XVIII was a "liberal and wise" constitution, and all that the moderate men of 1789 had dreamed of, and that Montesquieu had described; the same Cousin who saw in democracy the certain destruction of liberty, and who on the evening of July 27, 1830, in the office of the *Globe,* declared that the Bourbon flag was the only possible one for France. This man was still Quinet's idol.

5. July, 1830: *Emergence of the Patriot*

AFTER the Liberal victory in the 1827 French elections, in February, 1828, Vatimesnil was named *Grand-maître* of the University of France. Cousin and Guizot were then recalled to the Sorbonne in March, after an eight-year absence imposed by the clerical party. Quinet was overjoyed. The eleventh lesson of Cousin's 1828 course was devoted to Herder, and in August Quinet wrote from Heidelberg that it and the others had "explained Germany to me...and have aided to allow me to console myself to be so distant from you. I cannot doubt but that the philosophy of our century is contained in that vast school [German philosophy], the principal basis of which you have just pointed out in France."[1]

As soon as word reached Quinet that Cousin had been returned to the University, he wrote to his friend asking that if a *Commission d'antiquités* should be added to the expedition which the government was planning to send to Greece, he, Quinet, be recommended for appointment to it. Creutzer and Quinet forwarded similar requests to Degérando, Constant, Chateaubriand, and others, but when the government decided late that year to send such an expedition it was only with difficulty that Quinet's friends managed to have him named a member of the group.

Quinet at this time was impatient to marry Minna Moré, later his first wife, but could not hope to do so until he found some regular source of income. It was hoped that appointment to such an expedition, which in itself would briefly bolster his finances, might serve as a steppingstone to a permanent position. Cousin, Degérando, Constant, and particularly Michelet were anxious that something be turned up for him so that he might live in Paris. Cousin led Quinet to hope that he might be named to a chair of philosophy or history at Paris, and this was the solution all would have preferred. The state of Quinet's feelings was suggested by the letter he wrote to Michelet in August, 1828, asking his friend to bend all his efforts to seeing that he might be included as a member of the expedition to Greece: "You have a part of my destiny in your hands. Would that this might encourage you to serve me."[2] News of his appointment reached Quinet at Heidelberg in December.[3] Neither Cousin nor Creutzer approved of Quinet's design, but both had bowed before his determined pleading and supported his candidacy. Both believed that in view of the chaotic conditions then prevailing in Greece the young man could pursue his studies more profitably in Germany, and in January, 1829, Creutzer wrote to Cousin regarding Quinet's departure: "I have been of your opinion. . . . I have done all that depended upon me to make him give up his plan . . . in spite of everything he has persisted and I have been obliged to permit him to depart."[4]

The expedition sailed from Toulon on February 10, 1829; already Quinet was embroiled with his companions. Arriving in Greece, he went his independent way, and then returned to France alone in May. From Greece he wrote to Cousin justifying what he had done by stating that it would "return me to you the sooner." But playing the romantic poet brought upon him the disfavor of those who might have assisted his appointment to the University. Michelet sacrificed much time in his efforts to collect payment for a full year's services for his friend. When, in November, 1830, he succeeded, Quinet, not satisfied, requested salary for a second year which he said was needed in which to write a report of his "findings." When Royer-Collard, who had become Chief of the Division of Sciences and Letters, grudgingly promised three months' pay upon the delivery of the report, and swore that this was the limit of what he could do, Quinet dropped the matter and did nothing further.

Back in France Quinet divided his time between his family home at Charolles and Paris. The literary result of his travels in Greece, *La Grèce moderne,* was partly written and began to appear serially in December. During the fall of 1829, at Charolles, he met Lamartine. In Paris, where he resided after the first of the year, Mme Récamier requested his regular attendance at her Friday gatherings. Enthusiasm for Greece increased interest in a young writer who had only recently returned from the scene, and Quinet was lionized in a fashion quite unfamiliar to him. His travel account was also well received, but the displeasure which the administration still felt toward him was little modified. He saw Cousin and Guizot frequently in the first months of 1830.

In March Quinet returned to Minna at Heidelberg, with the promise of a professor's chair at Paris under a new ministry. He continued to work on *La Grèce moderne*. He was in Strasbourg, conferring with the Levraut firm which was preparing to publish this work, when word of the July Revolution reached him.

The Revolution of 1830 had a noticeable influence upon a number of French literary figures. Lamartine, Chateaubriand, Hugo, Lamennais, and De Vigny were all given pause by the event. Béranger observed that his confrères were all "like birds whose tree has fallen, and who are at a loss as to where to perch." The fate of the *Globe* is revealing. Its founders and most important editors, Guizot, Thiers, Villemain, and Vitet, each now took up some political or official role; the *Globe* ceased to be a literary organ and eventually passed into the hands of the Saint-Simonians. Poets, notably Hugo and Lamartine, could not resist the call to political action. Quinet is an interesting parallel.

On August 10 Michelet wrote that Quinet should come to Paris promptly; friends were in power, Guizot in the Interior, Cousin in the Instruction Ministry, but places were being claimed quickly. On the basis of this Quinet wrote to his mother that Cousin had seen to it that he be requested to come to Paris at once. But something larger than the ambition of the place-seeker had flamed up in Quinet at the news from Paris. Patriotism was born. His first thought was that the treaties of 1815 had been defied. In this August letter to his mother he reported that all along the Rhine people were drunk with joy, and waited only for the signal in order to *reunite* with France.

The break between Cousin and Quinet which now occurred has been most frequently assessed in terms more favorable to Cousin than to Quinet. Monod wrote that Cousin refused to name Quinet to the University post at Paris because he was neither *agrégé* nor *docteur,* and that this refusal resulted in the ferocious rancor which saw Quinet's love turn to hate. The ease with which the formality of the degree requirement was met when Quinet later received appointment to Lyon, not to speak of exceptions which

Cousin made in 1831, would make it appear that this detail need not have been decisive in 1830.

Letters of September, 1830 first revealed Quinet's disappointment. In these he related that Cousin had shown the most miserable character, his head having been turned by his sudden advancement. The master was profoundly fearful of being compromised by his former disciples. Quinet's bitterness that Cousin failed to grant him a University chair at Paris was immediate, deep, and lasting, but the younger man was impatient to find a place and held fire. Not philosophy but behavior caused his discontent. When Constant, who continued to support his appointment to the University, died that December Quinet was saddened. Villemain promised his help, Guizot made assurances, and in September, after the betrayal of Cousin, Quinet wrote to Minna Moré: "Either I will be sent as a professor to Strasbourg or I will obtain a sub-prefecture in Lorraine or in Alsace. The latter position would suit us better for it would give a greater chance of advancement."[5]

These remarks might be interpreted as an effort to put the best possible complexion on the most likely eventuality; but Quinet never evinced a high degree of enthusiasm to be a teacher. The solution had been one suggested by his friends. Probably this letter revealed the uncertainty of his desires, and an ambition to play a role in great events which became evident repeatedly in the future.

Coolness toward Guizot was first apparent in October, when Quinet reported that the Doctrinaire disapproved of the fact that the *Globe* and similar journals had showered praise on *La Grèce moderne*.[6] Guizot now seemed unlikely to support Quinet's candidature, in spite of his former promise to do so when the work was published. Royer-Collard made his unsatisfactory offer of settlement for Quinet's official report on Greece at this moment, and in November Quinet declared that the Doctrinaires "were in a state of ruin." By April of the following year hope was all but abandoned, although Quinet assured his mother that he had not given up completely. In May he made his decision. He was slow to act upon it, and first met strong resistance from all who felt that they had his interests at heart. To a friend at Lyon Quinet wrote: "Do not mention Cousin to me. He is a coward and utterly base, and we are going to launch *une guerre légitime* against him in our

journal." The journal referred to was *Revue des Deux Mondes;*
Quinet was one of the first persons called upon by François Buloz
when he took over and transformed the publication.[7] By carrying
out this intention Quinet put much of his past behind him.

The brevity of his enthusiasm for the new dispensation was
suggested by the pronouncement before one of his classes in the
1840's that "three days of truth in a lifetime" did not suffice.[8]
Peace and the status quo were at once the policy of the Liberal
Monarchy, and almost immediately Quinet was in the opposition.
Independence had been promised, definitive victory over the old
regime, the *émigrés,* the priests; but then the bitter fruit was tasted.
Quinet's voice, if unexpectedly, joined a protesting chorus.

During the Restoration republicans, democrats, Bonapartists,
and liberals had held in common two important attitudes: anticlericalism and a demand, in the name of national honor, for a
modification of the treaties of 1815. In July unity on these matters
had been the presupposition of the overthrow of Charles X. Then
the barricades were crossed. The Liberal forgot honor and embraced
the Church.

The expectation that the July Revolution would deal harshly
with the Church was natural; but the event was "nearly without
effect for the cult or for its ministers." The people did not attempt
to bring down the Church, and "the legislators of the new regime
showed themselves more moderate than did the people."[9] Within
a few years Quinet declared that in France "we are, by a notorious
miracle, at once at the *bourse* and at the confessional."[10] Proudhon
was concise:

> The bourgeoisie, what happy symptom! after a century of indiffer-
> ence, has suddenly been seized with a religious fervor. It has become
> advised that religion can be useful to its interests: at once it demands
> religion, a great deal of religion. A joint-stock company is organized by
> them for the restoration of religious ideas. Christ has been called to the
> assistance of the bourgeois gods Mammon, Plutus, Porus and Foenus.
> Christ did not answer: but the Church, orthodox and reformed, came
> running.[11]

Spokesmen of the Church were equal to comprehending what
had befallen and why. Dupanloup could not credit the early

leaders of the July Monarchy for having wished it. The result had been providential—but the July Revolution had served the Church in freeing it from many of the political prejudices, lies, and calumnies which had previously burdened it.[12] Cosmopolitan wealth had replaced cosmopolitan monarchy, and the Church was to become as much of an instrument of the one as it had been of the other. The most Voltairian among the bourgeois liberals of 1830 were, in many instances, of the conviction that a religion was necessary for the people; and as the people "seemed to have one ready-made which satisfied them, there was not a moment's dream of taking it away from them."

The Liberal had previously paid his respects to fundamental liberties; but with the advent of Casimir Périer there opened a long period during which the power of the state was used with consistent harshness against political opponents of the new regime. A fight to the knife was opened against the revolutionary party. At no time under the Restoration had press seizures and trials been so frequent as in 1831.

Whatever the pressures of personal disappointment, Quinet was consistent with his past in breaking with Cousin. Liberal rule, representing in Quinet's eyes a crassly egotistical materialism, turned him toward the democratic camp. His logic may be questioned; his course was not unique. The Revolution pretended to do away with classes. That was how Quinet, like Michelet, like all idealists in that tradition, interpreted its message. The July Monarchy, in his eyes, created and fomented class war; its policy, he wrote, was to crush the poor with the arrogance of the rich, to frighten the rich with the hatred of the poor, and to weaken national pride in order better to dominate the country. Only gold was worshiped. From exile he one day described the phenomenon:

When, after a long struggle against the outworn dogma in the name of a new idea, philosophers, supported by the sentiments and the hopes of all, obtain victory, and the power so long desired falls finally into their hands, something happens which no one could have foreseen. It is that the philosophers find domination so sweet that they forget the ideas in the name of which they took that power, and without further concerning themselves with truth, they dream of nothing more than enjoying in peace the authority acquired. Then they discover, first that the old dogma, attacked by them for so long, is the best harness with which to keep men under their yoke; and they put to use all of their artfulness to repair that harness which they have broken, and which appears divine to them now that it is in their power. For they thus obtain the double advantage of living in peace with their former enemies, and repressing their former partisans, now their principal embarrassment.[13]

At the end of August, 1831, discouraged and unwilling to wait longer for a position which seemed not to be forthcoming, Quinet retired to Germany and to Minna. Although he had planned an attack upon Cousin in May, he had yet held back. In July he published *De l'Avenir de la Religion,* an essay which did nothing to destroy whatever chance might have remained of official favor. In this essay his references to Catholicism were vague, and, more notably, nothing suggested his divorce from the official eclectic school. Quinet wrote that Catholicism could be expected to live for as long as did the present type of Western society. One day that type would alter, and with it, the cult made for it.[14] In suggesting that the French Revolution represented a striving to break away from the religious tradition of the past, and that it foreshadowed the future in this regard, he showed no impatience, and neither asked for nor predicted a sudden transformation. He was no less moderate than Cousin himself.

Quinet remained at Grunstadt during September and October, then returned to Charolles early in November after stopping off at Strasbourg. This brief period was one of the most decisive in his life. On November 2, 1831, from Strasbourg, Quinet sent Buloz an article, "De la Philosophie dans ses Rapports avec l'Histoire politique." He requested that Buloz also print in the *Revue des Deux Mondes* the article which he had sent Michelet from Grunstadt in October, and which Quinet assumed was in the editor's hands.

The article sent from Strasbourg was published by Buloz, in the first December issue of the *Revue.* Now publicly Quinet hurled his thunderbolt at Cousin, and at that system of philosophy to which he himself had been bound but recently. Although he avoided making a direct attack upon the government, Quinet the patriot was here first revealed. He had never been attached to the Jacobin or democratic tradition. One aspect of its revival seemed either to have stirred a responsive chord in Quinet, or at least to have fitted his mood of discouragement. The note quickly faded, but later returned to become his theme. Angry, he sought the applause of the crowd.

Quinet damned eclecticism for having been born under the sword of the Restoration. It was a degraded philosophy, and as such had suited a degraded France. Its popularity was indicative of a striking resignation in the face of the invading armies in whose train the philosophy had marched. Exhausted, unable to fill a role worthy of herself in the field of thought or action, France, in paying her respects to this alien doctrine, had practiced a pitiful diplomacy.

In this fashion Quinet appealed to patriotism, so that he might forego logic. Not daring to count himself among them (he let silence make the suggestion) he spoke of farsighted men who had suspected that when life again appeared in France the artificial combinations of eclecticism would fail the test. With a stirring of life the suspicion had been justified. Now, surely all could recognize that the system was but the distorted reflection of theories already in decline in Germany. All that some (Quinet could not state that he had been one of them) had believed to be the free emanation of French national genius was now found to be near ruin across the Rhine.

The demands of three days had sufficed to disperse the alien philosophy in such a manner that one searched in vain for its trace. By taking no part in the revolution philosophy had abdicated. After it had exchanged principles and lofty ambition for the first material advantage offered, no esteem could remain to it. An apostate idealism was worse than an avowed materialism. For those who had been present at the betrayal courage to name the crime was required. Whatever the cost, Quinet stated, he had faced the choice of laying aside his pen or accusing the criminal. With this essay he had chosen the latter course.[15]

At the close of his life Quinet wrote that in the days following the July Revolution a wise moderation had been the virtue most commended. Sagacity had consisted in the ability to forget, as soon as one had conquered, all the principles under whose banner victory had been won.[16] The inconsistency was on both sides, and Quinet would have been more just to have admitted that his own development took a change in course following July, 1830; and more, that a brief period of passionate protest on his part was followed by an unseemly calm, until he entered upon the rough waters of 1840 and found his true course. By dating the articles he wrote at this time incorrectly in later editions of his works he avoided admission also that his own sagacity lasted into the second year, when all hope of aid from Cousin had been abandoned.

The truth was that his own instability made the years between 1826 and 1834 a bitter and unhappy period of his life. The foundations of his philosophical outlook were as shifting as were his emotional attachments, and it was after a crisis in the latter that the real revolution in his attitudes became apparent. In a period marred by much personal disappointment he came to see differently, and more acutely; he came to wish for a more radical readjustment of a world less and less to his heart's desire. In 1830 Cousin failed to act in a manner consistent with his word; he sacrificed opinion to interest; he betrayed the ideal he had seemed to embody. The reaction in Germany to the events of July was an equally bitter disappointment to the young Frenchman who had believed that the German world was motivated by the idealism of her philosophers. Disillusion gave him profound insight.

When now Quinet's attack fell upon the government itself, the failure of the new monarchy to pursue an expansionist foreign policy was the ostensible cause for his anger. One may say that in foregoing an old enthusiasm Quinet did not cease to be enthusiastic. He joined his voice to a chorus which, if it was not to prevail, was most passionate and aggressive, that of militant nationalism. The cry masked Jacobin politics, but Quinet's political development trailed behind his emotional response; his adjustment to a different tradition than that which had formed him was gradual. He did not at once attack the bourgeoisie.

In 1831 Casimir Périer and his government prevailed over the forces which demanded a frankly revolutionary foreign policy. In debate against his critics he declaimed that "French blood belongs only to France." Later Louis Blanc wrote of this statement: "Rank impiety! Blasphemy of ignorance and incapacity! The genius of France has always been in its cosmopolitanism, and devotion to it has been imposed upon us by God as a condition of life." Disinterested behavior for France did not consist in renouncing force, but in employing it with devotion. France was commanded to watch over its power, "because it does not belong to us—it belongs to humanity."[17] This was the spirit to which Quinet addressed himself in 1832. To associate his nationalism with a supposed influence of Herder is impossible.

There was more than one hint in his past which might have made the shift predictable. The Rhine had always fascinated him. Late in 1827 he had written that upon his entering Coblentz "a strongly seditious" thought had passed through his mind (Quinet presumed that his mother understood him to mean the thought of a France extended to the Rhine), adding that he and all of his German friends believed that "it would be realized later." During the spring of 1830, being feted in Paris in a fashion new to him, although he continued to love Germany as much as previously, he was beginning to see things there with a great deal more independence. After July the Rhine became a main preoccupation; "our" Rhine frontier would now be taken, Grunstadt would then become French "again." Possibly never correct in the presumption that his Palatinate friends dreamed of returning to France, Quinet was soon forced to admit that they had felt a change of heart. A brief visit to Germany in February, 1831 disclosed that though Creutzer and other old friends at Heidelberg greeted him with all of their former hospitality, they were none the less full of prideful talk of drawing the sword at the moment of the first sign of French aggression on the left bank of the Rhine. This singular development Quinet attributed to the "weakness of our government."

Soon it was difficult to believe that there had been a time when Quinet could have written that the greatest thing taking place in France was the influence of new ideas which had originated in Germany, and that the greatest of all opportunities was open to the individual who could make himself the interpreter of this "supreme movement."

Depressed at his failure to find favor in the eyes of the new regime, impatient and unwilling to pursue favors any longer, Quinet left for Grunstadt in August, 1831. He was greeted there by an aroused anti-French atmosphere. The situation which he now

found in Germany was so shocking and, he felt, so menacing to
France, that he postponed the writing of his attack upon Cousin
momentarily and began the pamphlet, the beginning pages of
which he sent to Michelet in October. That month his engagement
with Minna Moré was broken. One may not weigh precisely the
influence of this event upon Quinet's development. Certainly no
other disappointment in his private life left so lasting an impression. More than thirty years later, during his years of exile in
Switzerland, Quinet had constantly recurring periods of depression
during which he was obsessed by the memory of the circumstances
surrounding the temporary breaking off of this engagement. Repeatedly he decried the fact that he and Minna had not married in
1828, and emotion overcame him as he recalled her "unpitying
hardness." German Lutheranism came to be embodied in the
terrible Dittmar, the brother-in-law who insistently pressed Minna
until she broke with a man who was French, a man who could not
possibly bring happiness to a profoundly devout and German
woman.[18]

Quinet returned to Charolles alone. Wretched and full of gall
he continued to work on his *De l'Allemagne et de la Révolution.*
Michelet had previously begged him to agree to a postponement,
or to forego publishing the pamphlet altogether, and had failed to
turn the first part of the manuscript over to Buloz while still hoping
that he might dissuade his friend. After an exchange of letters
between Charolles and Paris, Michelet wrote in November: "Finally,
to speak my mind fully, this pamphlet is of a nature which will end
your future in this country.... In the name of heaven wait a little
while."

What disturbed Michelet, and other friends at Paris, was not
Quinet's prophecy of what the German future held in store, but
the bitter manner in which the pamphlet attacked the July Monarchy. Neither Michelet nor Buloz proved able to halt its publication. When Michelet reduced his request to that of asking that at
least certain suppressions be made, Quinet answered: "My friend,
you who know so well the meaning of the dignity of thought, you
should understand what I suffer in seeing mine delayed, and
throttled, against declarations which I have repeated so many times."

Michelet, made "ill" by this letter, gave way and made arrangements for the publication of the pamphlet form. Buloz, feeling that the printing of the full text would inevitably result in government prosecution of the *Revue,* made important editorial modifications. On December 11 the editor had written the author that the article could not appear in the December 15 issue, since it was uncertain that he would have received Quinet's latest corrections by that time. He added:

I should inform you that there is another reason: a meeting of your friends was held to read your work. Lerminier, Janin and several other of our editors were present; all were frightened at the violence of your conclusion; all unanimously agreed to adjourn publication so as to give you more time for reflection; fearing that you would compromise your future, and that several passages, which I will point out, would destroy the effect of the whole.[19]

Opposition had but one effect upon Quinet: it fired his energy to move forward with the attack. Early in January *De l'Allemagne et de la Révolution* appeared in print, in its modified form in the *Revue des Deux Mondes,* and, unmodified, as a pamphlet.[20]

Quinet interpreted the French past and present; he prophesied the French and German future. The interpretation developed the patriotic position taken up in his recent article; the prophecy read the future with astonishing accuracy.

Belatedly a doctrine of Herder found its way to Quinet's heart. Now he repeated that each people had its peculiar characteristic, one aspect which fixed its personality; and this unique gift dominated and reappeared at each decisive epoch in the history of the nation. The problem then was to fix France's role. Pre-eminence in industry was given to England; in science to Germany; in liberty to the United States; in art to Italy. France had been given the instinct of civilization, and the need to initiate the progress of modern society. Should this need for exterior influence fail to find expression, France would descend below all the nations surrounding her; it was her best part, her genius, her happiness, her art. After 1831 Michelet believed that "the glorious fatherland is the pilot of the vessel of humanity." Michelet also knew Herder, but many a Frenchman ignorant of the German philosopher had reached this conclusion long before.

For two centuries destiny had made France the instrument of civilization; Quinet wrote that this was the idea for which she existed. This thought rallied the parties of France; held French territories united; and served as a natural attraction for conquered provinces. Quinet warned the July Monarchy of these facts. France could lead or die. The Revolution, in giving expression to the national genius, had moved toward the Rhine; but now that France seemed bent upon betraying her mission the force which had given her the power to convert others tended to abandon her. Provinces once taken grew astonished, and in spite of themselves they again felt the attraction of the German world.

Quinet insisted that internal reform could not be purchased at the price of world influence, and charged the government with just such a policy. France demanded a wider suffrage at home and wished to aid Italy to be born; the government traded suffrage for the defeat of Italian aspirations. French municipal government was reformed, and the Monarchy spent the favor thus gained by the desertion of Belgium. The nobility was sacrificed—but in exchange for that concession made to the spirit of the country and to necessity the Rhine was abandoned and Poland betrayed. Disaster was in store, he predicted, for a government which continued on such a course. Each step the Monarchy descended in appeasement of reactionary thrones abroad would cause more of the country to forsake it at home. Louis-Philippe was placed between two forces, reactionary Europe and national opinion; when he had ceded all to the one he would have ceded all to the other, and could then no longer survive.

Quinet replied to those who defended the policy as being one which would create a European equilibrium, that such a peace was war and death for France. The policy resolved itself into "pacifying the abyss in order to enter it without a raised voice and without emotion."

Quinet arrived at his *idée fixe:* France, synonymous with the Revolution, had a mission, which she could fulfil or betray, to lead humanity into the bright dawn. Should she fail in this, none could replace her.

The implications of this plea, and particularly of the manner in which he seemed to suggest his policy be carried out, may have partially escaped the disappointed office seeker, but the viewpoint it represented was not to prove a merely temporary aberration of Quinet's thought. The fact that many Frenchmen shared his understanding of the fatherland's proper role was important in the relatively prompt demise of the Monarchy. A large audience was receptive to these ideas. Quinet hoped for a more select following, but in the final analysis his talents rather than his ambition decided the part he played. Not that his talents were slight—nor was his change in attitude toward Cousin and Germany incomprehensible on grounds other than those of thwarted ambition.

The pamphlet had some success, particularly among the younger and militant element of the opposition, but attracted attention almost exclusively by its demand for an aggressive foreign policy and by its criticism of the government. The reputation which Quinet gained as a later Cassandra rested most firmly upon that section of the pamphlet which attracted little attention in 1832. He looked at Germany, but with a new vision. The fault had not been so much that Mme de Staël had been wrong, but that France was always something like a half-century behind reality in its opinion of her neighbor. The time had come, he wrote, to face the present and dangerous reality.

All at once Quinet seemed to realize that the enthusiasm which had characterized Germany at the beginning of the century had turned bitter. Germany had rediscovered the "sarcasm" of Luther in order to rail at its own dreams and past candor. Particularly did this apply to Prussia. No longer dreams or theories, but now "unity was the profound and continual thought at work across the Rhine." Religion, law, liberty, despotism, every live force, he contended, each in its fashion tended toward that culmination. Quinet conceded that at first view one might be astonished that the only popular government beyond the Rhine was almost the only one which was despotic in form. In Prussia, however, despotism was intelligent, alive, and enterprising. She drew sustenance from science as other despotisms based themselves on ignorance. Prussia lacked only a man who could see and recognize her destiny.

France must realize, cried Quinet, that the Holy Alliance was no longer on the thrones of Europe. It had descended to the peoples of Germany; and if France permitted them to do so, those peoples, divided since the Reformation, would rally about Prussia. France could, if she wished, continue to be lulled by the superficial dissensions and disorders which she had done her part to nourish. They would continue to be heard yet a little while. But soon it would be seen that the apparent struggle between liberty and despotism, that German chaos of peoples and kings which at present it seemed impossible to unscramble intelligently, was but a mirage.

One day there would be surging at the gates of France a community of interests, of ambition, of genius, of resentments; they would rise up this time, not from thrones, but from all the might of a race of men in the face of an obsessed and ruined France. Quinet's prophecy did not halt when he foresaw a man using the instrument of Prussia to accomplish the illiberal unification of Germany. The incorporation of Alsace and Lorraine would, he foretold, be one of the first objectives of a national Germany. All this passed unnoticed in 1832, but was the subject of a great deal of discussion in 1866.

6. *Poet to Publicist*

ANY IMMEDIATE HOPE of favor from the government had been put aside with the publication of his January, 1832 pamphlet, and Quinet remained at Certines bitter and heartbroken. Jerome Quinet died late in that same month. Edgar was working on *Ahasvérus*. He stayed on in the country with his mother until his father's estate had been settled, then in May left for Italy. The cholera epidemic which struck Paris at the end of March undoubtedly influenced his decision to stay in Charolles until his departure.

The Italian journey had been on Quinet's mind before his father's death, and a share in the inheritance enabled him to carry out the wish. He did not return to France until the autumn of 1833, bringing back the nearly completed manuscript of *Ahasvérus*, notes for a number of articles which later appeared in *Revue des Deux Mondes,* and a beginning of *Révolutions d'Italie.*

The death of his father changed Quinet's economic status but little. The only improvement, aside from the temporary one of a sum sufficient for him to live frugally in Italy during an extended visit, was that his mother now controlled the purse strings, and the young man hoped for more generosity than he had known from his father. At the very least, now Minna and he might be permitted to live at Certines. Reconciliation between the couple took place some time after Quinet's arrival in Italy, and in the fall of 1833 the son wrote home to his mother: "Today I ask of you, *comme un supplicié demande sa grâce,* to consent to my marriage to Minna." Not until late 1834 was this project realized, and then the couple resided in Germany, at the bride's request.

Quinet's mother did give her consent, and agreed that the couple might live with her at Certines, although it had certainly been their hope that she would assist them in setting up an establishment of their own at Paris. The traveler returned to Paris from Italy by way of Grunstadt, where these tentative plans were laid;

going on to Paris, he made arrangements for the publication of
Ahasvérus.

Nothing was more like Quinet than that his impatience for the
marriage to take place moderated when Minna had been rewon.
Remaining in Paris until March, long after the December publication of his new work, he entered into the literary and social
life of the capital with apparent relish. His mode of existence was
more consistent by far with the young man he had been in the
spring of 1830 than with the nascent radical of the late fall of
1831. Calmer and more confident he returned to his past. Sainte-
Beuve, De Tocqueville, Montalembert, Leon Faucher, Ary Scheffer,
and Corcelles formed a group with whom Quinet dined almost
daily during this stay in Paris. He became one of the inner circle
at Mme Récamier's salon which was favored with Chateaubriand's
reading of his *Mémoires d'outre-tombe.*

While Minna Moré waited at Grunstadt Quinet became a constant caller upon Miss Clarke, whom he had known before his trip
to Greece, and who was a close friend of Mme Récamier. The
wealthy Englishwoman now affected a violent passion for him;
on the occasion of his third visit she presented him with her
account books, so that he might take into consideration the state
of her fortune. Quinet's sister hoped that her brother might, for the
first time in his life, use common sense, but Edgar did not marry
Miss Clarke. Minna, however, suffered after her marriage from
attentions her husband continued to pay the Englishwoman, and
from the manner of her rival, suggested by Miss Clarke's remark
that "she did not recognize" the marriage.[1]

The prose poem *Ahasvérus* (The Wandering Jew), which an
admirer described as "the exact expression of the sickness which
then tormented humanity," the sickness of expectation and of waiting, was poorly received.[2] The moderate praise of Lamartine, Heine,
and Liszt did something to temper Quinet's disappointment at the
public reception.[3] Among those who were impressed was the
Princess Marie; she made two bas-reliefs of scenes from the poem.

In 1828 Quinet had hoped for a poet to appear who would
make use of the annals of humanity as Homer had used those of
the Greeks. For unity he should use the unity of history, and begin
where Dante had concluded. *Ahasvérus* was Quinet's own attempt

to realize that hope. Simultaneously with its publication Charles Magnin treated the work in a long essay, *"Ahasvérus* et de la nature du génie poétique," which appeared in the December 1, 1833 issue of *Revue des Deux Mondes.* Magnin pointed out that others, notably Goethe, had been attracted by the Ahasvérus legend, but had thought of making the hero the witness and spectator of humanity during the last eighteen centuries. In a larger and more poetic conception, Quinet conceived Ahasvérus as humanity itself, the personification of humankind during the Christian era.

Magnin had been advised of his friend's previous characterization of the *Divine Comedy.* The critic wrote that Dante's work had been the poetic expression of orthodox Christianity, of a young and confident Catholicism. But Christianity, at the present developing along pantheistic lines, was now opening up a new and vaster perspective. In the domain of religious poetry the epic had now become possible again. *Ahasvérus* was the expression of beliefs still in chrysalis and on the eve of spreading their wings.[4]

The reference to Goethe was in place. Brandes mentioned Quinet as one of the few French writers who were influenced by Goethe's *Faust.* Although there is no doubt but that the conception of *Ahasvérus* was influenced by Goethe, Quinet's reaction against Germany affected his attitude toward every representative of German culture. On his return from Italy he spent some weeks reading Goethe at Grunstadt before taking up the final revision of his own work, but he never spoke favorably of the great German after the 1831 crisis.[5]

Lanson dismissed the author's contribution to literature with the remark: "Quinet n'a pas réussi à faire une oeuvre: on peut lire ses *Lettres."* Quinet's prose poem was obscure and disorganized. But anyone desiring to contest Lanson's conclusion, on the basis of one of Quinet's creative works, would be forced to rest his case on *Ahasvérus.* It, at least, was not so marred by a prosy didactic quality as were other ventures into this field. Quinet was never quite a poet. He could not discipline his emotions, and was always noticeably self-conscious about the effect he wished to create by displaying them. Amiel, who was generous in his estimate of Quinet, finding him "rich in ideas" and "a serious, enthusiastic, courageous, noble writer" deserving a far greater reputation than he enjoyed in France, noted that his greatest fault was "subjective lyricism." The imprisonment of the author in his own personality was "a sort of infatuation."[6]

If by no extension of the word "great" may it be fitted to *Ahasvérus,* the work does have a valid literary note, and it did have literary influence. Quinet did receive recognition in France as a poet. One may, however, still conclude that no serious injustice was done his abilities when the indifferent reception given his imaginative works finally forced him back into other lines of endeavor.

In spite of the disorder and general confusion of *Ahasvérus* some things were not left in obscurity. The author concluded that orthodox Catholicism was an exhausted force, and that organized Protestantism was incapable of replacing it. He wrote of "the black depths of German science," of its Church without priest or God. Methodism was the "sect of death."[7] But later when Quinet was acting as a dogmatic spokesman of his own theology he insisted that *Ahasvérus* had not said what it seemed to say.

Thus his position was quite different when he came to write an introduction to the 1843 edition of the work. Then he protested that readers had failed to understand the conclusion the author wished them to draw. Critics declared that *Ahasvérus* ended in a cry of anguish, and on a note of despair. Not so, replied Quinet. The "Epilogue" was wrongly interpreted. It was meant to be a song of renovation. It is indeed difficult to read such a meaning into the passage in question. As Christ prepared to depart, the reign of His City having closed forever, he spoke to Eternity:

LE CHRIST.
Les mondes sont orphelins. Aimez-les à ma place, quand je ne serai plus.

L' ÉTERNITÉ.
Dans mon sein, je n'ai ni amour, ni haine.

LE CHRIST.
Est-ce une vierge qui vous a nourrie comme moi?

L' ÉTERNITÉ.
Personne ne m'a nourrie. Je n'ai ni père, ni mère.

LE CHRIST.

Qui donc vous ensevelira, quand, vous aussi, vous monterez votre Calvaire?

L' ÉTERNITE.

Je ne monte, ni ne descends; je n'ai ni sommet, ni vallée, ni joie, ni douleur.

At last Eternity was alone.

Ici finit le mystère d'Ahasvérus
Priez pour celui qui l'écrivit.

Doubt and despair were not to prevail for long. The spirit of the "alien philosophy" which seemed now to have failed Quinet, nevertheless prevailed throughout the work. But something new was added. A choir addressed France:

Men of Lodi ... of Marengo, where are you? Rise from the earth; you retired too soon. Come accomplish the task which your children lack the heart to achieve....

Only the battle chargers seemed to recall; when one laid hand upon them they yet cried: Lead me to graze upon a field of glory....

France ... it is late, rise that the world may fasten your sandals. You must attend the ball to lead the dance, not of the dead but of the living, not of the bourgeoisie but of empires. Dare tread underfoot the dust of men, of kings and of gods; in laughter stamp under a world's regrets, desires and terrors. The East ... awaits you, America too is ready; tomorrow and always have revolve about you a galaxy of nations in the harmony of your heavens....

Time presses. Remove from your assemblies and your governments those who speak in other terms than these....

If only the sea might render back that which remained of Napoleon as a force to aid in salvation; the Emperor who had defied the world with, "heads or tails, the universe or Saint Helena!"[8]

These pages had no context in *Ahasvérus;* Magnin's lengthy essay failed to note them or make the effort to explain their meaning. If it had not been buried in the middle section of a lengthy religious epic of obscure meaning, so thinly veiled an appeal for a change in rulers could not have escaped censorship or prosecution. The impassioned plea was too well hidden, and those who would have made a hero of its author failed to discover its existence. These pages, however, were the germ of a new faith—a faith in France and the Revolution.

Quinet returned from Italy willing, almost eager for a truce. The publication of *Ahasvérus* increased official hostility. A literary triumph would have been ample compensation had it materialized. The result was far less.

At the end of March, 1834, Quinet was called to Bourg by the illness of his sister. During this visit Certines was put in readiness for Minna, who was expected to move back with him following their marriage. Not until November did he leave for Germany. On January 13, 1835, a letter announced his marriage, but did not inform his mother that the event had taken place more than three weeks previously, on December 21. The couple decided to remain in Germany. Life was cheap there; *Ahasvérus* was selling fairly well; *Napoléon* was almost ready for publication; and Quinet believed that arrangements were being made for him to substitute for Fauriel at the Sorbonne and that he would eventually replace him there. Disappointments followed, however.

At Certines in May, 1834, Quinet had informed Michelet that he had begun "something unlike any of my previous efforts; I do not know what will become of it." This was a reference to his *Napoléon.* A fragment from the work appeared in the August 1, 1834 issue of the *Revue des Deux Mondes,* and in February the first printing of the completed work was ready to go on sale when the whole edition was destroyed by fire. An eleven-month postponement resulted. Quinet had written Sainte-Beuve in August, 1834, asking his advice and criticism and confessing his own doubts as to whether or not he possessed any talent at all. Before the January, 1836 publication Sainte-Beuve and others aided Quinet in cutting out some three thousand of the eight thousand verses of the original poem.

In the meantime constant efforts were made in Paris by Quinet's friends to enable him to return there, but the hope that he would substitute for Fauriel at the Sorbonne did not materialize. Fauriel, who held the chair of foreign literature, was willing to have Quinet replace him temporarily so that he might devote his own time more fully to his *Histoire de la Gaule Méridionale sous les con-*

quérants germains. But first it was necessary that Quinet "descend" from *Ahasvérus* "à un essai de critique, d'histoire littéraire qu'on pût présenter comme échantillon à la Sorbonne qui agrée les suppléans," and he refused to do this. Magnin, who had deferred to Quinet, finally filled Fauriel's place.[9]

Quinet, in his 1857 introduction to the poem *Napoléon,* ruefully admitted that the legendary hero had fallen upon him. He found himself crushed by the debris.[10] The 1836 introduction had informed the reader that the work was the second in a trilogy. *Ahasvérus* represented the poetry of the past, the general history of humanity. *Napoléon* belonged to the poetry of the present, and its subject was the individual, the hero. The author promised a third work "which would complete the sense of the first two"; this was a reference to *Prométhée,* which had now been in progress for some time.

The purpose Quinet announced was, however, more than simply to express the spirit of the present. He wished to commemorate the dead of Waterloo. Often, he wrote, he had shared the thought, which occurred so frequently to those of his generation, that it would have been best to have died in the battles of 1814 and 1815. Humanity's cause itself had been at stake. Recent events, he wrote, had confirmed his regret. Unfortunately he had been too young, but he could pay reverence to those who had died. By these words Quinet appropriated a legend which he did little to create. He was beginning to put the pieces together, to be consistent in all things with his patriotism. When the work appeared Sainte-Beuve wrote that the dominant idea of the poet, "that which perhaps best inspires him," was his sensitivity to the double wound of 1814 and 1815.[11] The author had been successful in communicating the essential part of his message.

Quinet explained and defended his choice of a hero. Napoleon was the personification of the latest phase in man's development, the democratic era. Napoleon fulfilled the first condition of taking his place beside the heroes of the past by absorbing within himself the spirit and aspirations of an entire generation. His role was to represent the development of the individual in modern times. Quinet believed that in the future the wars of the Revolution and of the Empire would form the heroic age of democracy and Napoleon, he firmly thought, would become the hero of popular poetry.

Most of this was commonplace. Quinet's generation, wrote Brandes, thought of the Emperor *als das personifizierte Volk*. Louis Blanc declared that the Emperor was the only political cult the people knew. During the early years of the July Monarchy "la foule ne se pouvait lasser de voir le petit chapeau, de revoir la redingote grise" on the Paris stage.[12] Quinet was not yet prepared to define or explain "democracy," but his use of the word may be clarified by comparing the viewpoint expressed above with that of Mickiewicz. The Polish poet served the legend with a more persistent loyalty.

At Vilna in 1812, fourteen-year-old Adam Mickiewicz was struck blind with admiration and love by the liberator who crossed the Nieman in June. Napoleon was a new messiah, leading a chosen people in a crusade to free all nationalities from their oppressors. In time Mickiewicz realized that the Poles (later all Slavs), not the French, were the people chosen to revive the laws of justice and liberty in the world. In France the Jacobin Republican made his peace with the Napoleonic tradition, so that he might put it to use in the struggle against the existing social order. Quinet in 1836 resembled Mickiewicz, in that he was still largely indifferent to the fight between aristocrats and democrats. Mickiewicz did not wish to battle for a Poland of the "left" or of the "right," but to free the "nation."[13] In 1836 Quinet had in mind the "freeing" of France.

Quinet is remembered particularly for the violence of his statements on the invasions of 1814 and 1815. They made their first appearance in *Napoléon*. All things might pass in time.

> But not tomorrow, not ever, will the footstep of
> the Stranger upon the rock efface or change.

There was another important innovation—his treatment of England. This reversal was as sudden as it was complete. He had now discarded his love for England. He could not bear the thought of Napoleon at Saint Helena:

> This is why I hate you, vile and vile England:
> Land of deceit, ship of misery....

> To efface the shame written on your name....
> Bathe day and night in the seas of Atlas,
> The entire ocean will never cleanse you.

> Your gold glitters in the sun, your purse is full.
> Your thought, your genius — a void.
> Your mask is Liberty. Your name is Slave....[14]

Quinet's subject and the concessions he made (as in the case of England) to popular prejudice failed to add up to success. The fault did not lie with circumstances, which were all favorable, but with the dullness of the work. The author tentatively, and on the wrong foot, again approached the democratic republican element. In 1832 he had quickly thought better of breaking off all association with the official and semiofficial world. After the January, 1832 pamphlet nothing of a like nature had followed. Again in 1836 he did not persist in the face of an indifferent reception at the hands of the party which attracted him ever more strongly.

Nagged by financial worries and unable to repay old personal debts involving small sums, Quinet remained in Germany during 1836, hoping that friends in Paris might finally have the influence to see him appointed to the University. Still he insisted on his own terms, and when Michelet prevailed upon Buloz to make an offer which would have enabled Quinet and his wife to move to Paris it was refused. Michelet wrote in October, 1836: "Why won't you accept, for several months at least, the offers Buloz has made: It would draw you out of that solitude in which it frightens me to see you remain. A man should not be alone."[15]

Quinet had done almost no writing for Buloz since early in 1834, and in October, 1836 his name appeared in the pages of the *Revue des Deux Mondes* after an unusually long interval. Depressed at the failure of his more ambitious works to batter down the walls of the indifference which seemed to surround him, he took up with a heavy heart the writing of a series of articles on Germany and Italy. Life seemed to be passing him by. So little had been accomplished, and to supply the type of thing Buloz wanted from him seemed a sacrifice of his better self. He could not bring himself to move to Paris, where he would be dependent upon turning out a regular stream of such work. Unhappy in Germany, he stayed on, completing his trilogy by continuing to work on *Prométhée*.

During the summer of 1837 his mother agreed to move to Paris, and to pool her resources with her son and daughter-in-law.

In October, or November, Quinet left Germany and moved to Paris, in order to be present during the printing of *Prométhée*. But Minna spent the winter at Nice with her mother-in-law and sister-in-law. The health of Quinet's sister necessitated this change in plans. A letter Edgar wrote to Minna during this unexpected separation chides her for weeping about money and their dependence upon others, and seems to indicate that the mother refused to support the couple alone in Paris and insisted that Minna accompany her to Nice.[16] Quinet was in Paris until March, when he left the city briefly to meet his family on their return from Italy. Back in Paris he was alone again, for Minna now visited Germany.

That winter in Paris was a time of decision for Quinet. The previous spring he had written to his mother that Lamennais's journal *(Le Monde)* was at his disposal; whether or not he would now substitute for Fauriel at the Sorbonne depended upon his own decision. With respect to the Sorbonne he either was misinformed or grossly exaggerated the truth. His admission that he did not know in what degree the two activities open to him could be reconciled is important. All bridges would be burned if he joined Lamennais. Although when he returned to Paris the ex-priest seemed to him one of two persons "who had remained at their post, and consistent with themselves," Quinet hesitated and did not leap. He turned along another path. Certainly the pressure to do so was great. Progressively unhappy in the German atmosphere, he was hounded by financial insecurity, and his wife was miserable. Much could be solved by compromise.

The schedule of his social activities that winter was strenuous: Tuesday, the Princess Belgiojoso; Wednesday, Mme Hoche; Thursday, Miss Clarke; Friday, Odillon Barrot; Saturday, Lamartine; Sunday, Mme Récamier. More important in winning the University chair he sought was the nature of the work he published. For the first time Quinet found favor in official circles. The cross of the Legion of Honor was a first result. Above all else the publication contributed to his nomination to a chair at Lyon. *Prométhée* appeared in March, 1838; in December he published an article critical of Strauss's *Life of Jesus*. The first of these two works preceded and seems to have been decisive in his appointment to a chair within the University of France.

Whatever the influence of external considerations, one would be hard pressed to decide that they entirely dominated the conception of *Prométhée*. For some time Quinet had been struggling for a greater degree of simplicity and clarity in expression than had yet characterized his work. *Napoléon* was largely free from his previous pantheism. And, although predicting the imminent disappearance of Catholicism in its present form, Quinet had not yet strongly attacked the Church. He had written in 1836, of his visit to Rome:

They are fortunate, I cried to myself leaving Rome that morning, still overwhelmed by the impression of the eve. Fortunate are those who believe, if mine be the feelings of those who doubt. Is it possible that such an institution has died? Is it made of the faith of our ancestors? Have I seen but a phantom, a ruin upon a ruin, or is it my heart which is dead?[17]

In 1838 he wrote to Mickiewicz, who was then an ardent Catholic: "Your faith, which I would wish to share, attracts me. It lifts me above this unhappy earth. You have in this a decided advantage over me. . . . Time passes and I yet know nothing of that which must be known. Dear friend, aid me to escape, or to bear that ignorance."[18]

These statements suggest a less positive position than in later life he wished to recall. In *Prométhée* a desire to appear tolerant and undogmatic, and a slightly veiled plea for sympathy for the author as he searched for a way out of darkness, were the dominant notes.

Quinet read parts of the manuscript at the Abbaye aux Bois in the fall of 1837. Chateaubriand and Ballanche were among those present. Ballanche, who also crossed Quinet's personal path through Michelet (Ballanche and Lamennais were fairly regular visitors at the Michelets' between 1830 and 1837), defined his own view of progressive Christianity at about this time. He did so in a fashion which might have permitted Quinet to believe himself a Catholic if Ballanche were. And Laprade, with a whole group of Catholic liberals at Lyon, soon received Quinet with warm enthusiasm—a group formerly directly influenced by Ballanche. Intrigued by the legend, Ballanche had written that "Prometheus is man forming himself by the energy of his thought." For Ballanche, and for

Quinet, he symbolized the struggle of the human will against fate, which was all of history.[19]

The *Revue des Deux Mondes* did not discuss *Prométhée* until August. The work convinced Magnin that Quinet should return to a prose medium. Sainte-Beuve agreed. He wrote that "Quinet is not a poet, in verse; or at least not to the same degree as in prose." More important in 1838, in so far as the author's advancement to the University was concerned, was Quinet's introduction to the work. His attitude more than his talent was under scrutiny. In this introduction Quinet replied to the orthodox-Christian critic.

If he had been fortunate enough to have retained the faith to which he had been born, "without any admixture of reflection," Quinet confessed he would not then have been entering into a treatment of the matters inherent in his subject. If it were impious to think that the Christianity of the nineteenth century was different from that of the twelfth, then the author confessed that he merited the accusation, "from which his obscurity had not always defended him." If, on the other hand,

to be religious was to recognize the presence of the infinite in all things; if a believer was one who kept the cult of the dead, and faith in the eternal resurrection; if it was to be a friend of God to search Him, to call Him; to recognize Him... in each moment of history and in all nature, without confounding Him with either the one or the other,

then, Quinet declared, he was the very opposite of impious.

No new creed was offered. Quinet presumed that his readers sensed the existing void, and could not escape realizing that the spirit of the century had shaken the confidence of his generation in the authority of the past. He did not wish to destroy but sought a path to healing and belief. Each age and each people formed its conception of God and the eternal. Prometheus was the personification of that constant striving for a more perfect understanding and expression of what was highest.[20]

Quinet's optimism had returned. He found that the history of successive religions was a record of man's ever greater mastery over matter. Hard-gained and partial victories led to an ever greater liberty and freedom of man's will. Each advance created the conditions for yet further progress. All of this was repetitious, and a return to the days of his enthusiasm for Cousin. Patriotism, in time, greatly modified Quinet's religion, and the hints of that future development were already clear. In *Prométhée,* however, the elements to which he more or less consistently adhered prevailed. The note of personal despair which ran through *Ahasvérus* was never in evidence again. Not that Quinet did not frequently experience periods of severe depression, but in the role he later played he believed it improper to confess this to the world.

The sweet reasonableness of *Prométhée* could only please. It contained no demand that the Rhine be seized, no violence, no bitterness, no veiled attack on an apostate eclecticism. When the work was successfully launched, Quinet began his *L'Examen de la Vie de Jésus.* He had reserved violent condemnation for "excessive pantheism." At no other time in Quinet's career is evidence of insincerity quite so overwhelming as on this occasion. For eight years unorthodoxy had been an important factor in his failure to receive the appointment which would have enabled him to settle in France with a comfortable, assured future. Frequently he had written in a fashion calculated to irritate the government, or to make difficult the task of friends who were anxious to help him, but now the most orthodox piece ever to come from his pen appeared opportunely. Quinet was not certain of an appointment until the end of September, 1838; the attack on Strauss did not appear until December. But the essay was written during the summer, and by December Quinet already was thinking of Paris.[21]

Michelet was elected to the College of France in February, 1838, in the face of strong opposition within the University, but with the support of Salvandy, the Minister of Public Instruction.[22] At this time Michelet was the tutor of Louis-Philippe's daughter, the Princess Clémentine. In June, 1838 Quinet, who was also in Paris, was informed by his friend that a faculty was being made up for Lyon, and that it could probably be arranged for him to have the chair of literature if he wished it. Michelet and the Princess Clémentine had spoken to Salvandy, who seemed well disposed to the idea.

First it would be necessary for Quinet to go through the formality of acquiring the necessary degrees. He decided to take them at Strasbourg, and in August received his *license.* Members of the faculty there requested that he give up the Lyon project in favor of remaining with them. A chair of foreign literature had been established at both places, and Sainte-Beuve was given the first choice to fill either. Had he chosen Lyon, Quinet would have received the position at Strasbourg. But Sainte-Beuve was interested in neither—the idea of life in the provinces was too repellent.

The thought was not appealing to Quinet. In December the *Revue des Deux Mondes* published his attack upon Strauss. *The Life of Jesus* had not then been translated into French; Littré began the French translation the following year. In attacking the work Quinet found, if he did not seek, orthodox approval for his defense of the real existence of the historical Jesus. Part hypocrisy, this essay nevertheless contained a modification of his past thought which may be said to have been permanent. The essay was consistent with Quinet's shift to a philosophy which gave the individual free will greater force and decisiveness.

He concentrated his attention on the German tendency of stripping the individual in order to enrich humanity. He was not cautious in his attack. Quinet professed to be persuaded that the personal Jesus was so much a part of the edifice of eighteen centuries of history that if He were removed every other part of that past would crumble to dust. To be logical one would inevitably be forced to admit a humanity without people, or peoples without individuals, generations of ideas without forms, who died, were reborn, and died again at the foot of an invisible cross where the impersonal Christ of pantheism hung eternally suspended. Though exaggerated, this was not hypocrisy. But as Renan wrote, nothing in the Strauss work could justify "the strange and absurd calumny by which one attempted to discredit it among superficial persons." Strauss did not deny the existence of Jesus, "but on each page of his book implied His existence."

The level of Quinet's criticism of Strauss is apparent from this: "Having disputed Moses the Decalogue, it is natural that one comes to dispute Jesus Christ the Sermon on the Mount." Discussing the German intellectual climate before the appearance of the work in question, Quinet was noncommittal and ironical; in a manner which suggested that he was a Catholic addressing a Catholic audience, he simply revealed the damning record. He then stated: "For fifteen pages, and in the same fashion as if it were a matter of an interpolation of Homer or Pindar, the author disputes Christ his cradle and his tomb."[23]

What was most objectionable, apart from the standard of historical scholarship it implied (and Quinet pretended to competence in such matters), was that this was inconsistent with anything he had ever written before, and with anything he ever wrote in the future. Coincidence can hardly explain the appropriate moment of its publication.

Quinet was at Heidelberg preparing for his doctorate when this article appeared. That same month, little enthusiastic at the prospect of spending one or two years anywhere in the provinces, Quinet followed Michelet's advice and chose Lyon over Strasbourg. He did so only in the hope that the time before he could move on to Paris would be short. He had known Lyon in his youth, and in 1836 wrote to a friend living there asking how he found it possible to pursue his studies "in the midst of that lamentable city."[24]

In January, 1839, Quinet received his doctorate from the University of Strasbourg.[25] His final appointment he owed mainly to Villemain and to Michelet, but Quinet was more dissatisfied than grateful as he traveled to Lyon. He opened his first course in April. Before it began he wrote to Buloz: "You realize that I must escape Lyon, and that I must neglect no opportunity to display the right I have not to remain buried here. Henceforth I will work to return to Paris, to you and to my friends. In this effort I frankly count upon the support of the *Revue....*"[26]

Michelet wrote, "Il faut plaire à Lyon pour n'y pas rester," and advised that a wise moderation would be the surest path by which to arrive at Paris. Quinet had immediate success; standing audiences of between 1,000 and 1,500 flocked to hear him speak. The following autumn crowds of 2,000 attended his lectures. But no enthusiasm he might inspire could compensate for that immense distance between Lyon and Paris, a distance he did not measure in miles or in hours.

Quinet the poet and philosopher and Quinet the publicist were not yet one. The patriot was an intruder in *Ahasvérus,* hardly present at all in *Prométhée.* In 1839 the serious life of a professor was in prospect. With a University position won, but with Paris still the goal, Quinet made a generous settlement with a past from which he had once seemed to separate in great bitterness and rage.

The publicist, writing in the fall of 1836, had assailed the principles of the Holy Alliance, and concluded that the self-respect of nations fluctuated in inverse proportion as the right of armed intervention in the affairs of another nation was established. The enforcement of such a principle might, indeed, repress tumult and stamp out sedition. A premature cosmopolitanism might be instituted. But it seemed to Quinet that loyalty to any supranational authority was a violation "of all that our ancestors honored." By abandoning the idea of the nation one degraded the fatherland, and Quinet wrote that love for France would never revive if the maxim of political cosmopolitanism were not opposed by an iron curtain. Unless patriotism were retained as a primary civic virtue, for at least another century, Western and Continental Europe would become nothing more than a bourgeois rabble, ready to become the prey of the first despot who wished to establish his authority over it.[27]

In 1839 it was the philosopher's turn. Quinet's immediate aim was to be promoted to Paris. Loud patriotism was associated with opposition to the government. At Lyon on April 10, Quinet gave the address which served as a point of departure for his first course. The expression "foreign literature," included in the title of his chair, was, he said, a poor one. He asked his audience how "foreign" could sensibly be applied to "the spectacle of the passions, or to the sorrows and beliefs of man as represented by the human word. As if all men were not citizens in the same city of beauty, art and immortality!"[28]

Quinet pleaded for a disappearance of national provincialism, like the past disappearance of local provincialism in France. Paris was indeed a magnet to bring these words to his lips, but he did not quite return to 1828. The patriot broke through. France, he told his listeners, was called by the nature of her geographic position to understand all other peoples. She could enrich herself by taking what was of value in each new foreign element, "without ever letting herself be absorbed by any." The thought of Quinet's early formative period did continue to be in evidence. Much was borrowed here from his 1828 statement, and the speaker did not seem to be the man seething under the treaties of 1815. But his emphasis had changed and the conclusion had been modified. Soon

he shored up the logical structure of his thought and brought nationalism within the fold of his all-embracing religion.

The Lyon lectures were published in 1842 as *Le Génie des Religions*. In so far as this work was a further step in Quinet's own
development, his announced purpose to reverse the popular view
that religious dogma was an outgrowth of, or was formed by,
political institutions was most significant. Quinet adopted Vico's
idealism. Thus he argued that modern institutions were an outgrowth of Christianity; the proof was that the religious faith existed
in Bethlehem before these institutions were known. And the Koran
preceded the caliphate.[29] The history of religions formed the gene-
alogy of the Eternal. From birth a unique and ineffaceable character
was apparent in the features, the heart, and the intellectual striving
of each race. This divine instinct alone made history comprehen-
sible; history was determined by it. It was in a people's god that
one found the truest expression of their spirit and genius, and
political and artistic forms were simply an outgrowth of this providential inspiration.[30] Later Quinet determined exactly the place of
France in the divine scheme.

The second edition of the work appeared in 1850, with an addi-
tional chapter on ancient Rome, an example which seemed to
Quinet to confirm his argument. In this chapter he wrote that the
Romans failed to destroy foreign religions because they were ignorant of the art of "moral extermination, the only one which kills."
This idea was foreign to the 1839 course, and to the first edition
of the book. Early in 1840 Ozanam, hoping that he would replace
Quinet at Lyon, did not expect to be as "brilliant" as Quinet. He
admitted modestly that his own teaching might "perhaps" be "more
solid."[31]

In view of what soon followed, the absence of a strongly expressed anti-Catholic sentiment was a noteworthy feature of Quinet's
lectures at Lyon. Victor Laprade was in his audience, and became
not only "an ardent disciple, but an enthusiastic friend." The
younger man was a member of a group inspired by a liberal and
humanitarian Catholicism which had centered at Lyon since 1835.
Possibly at the instigation of Quinet Laprade devoted himself to
the study of Ballanche.[32] In 1840 when Quinet abandoned Lyon he
offered the *suppléance* to this disciple; and in 1846, when he was

forced to renounce his course at the College of France, it was again
Laprade whom he proposed to replace him. No uncompromising
anti-Catholic could ever have attracted Laprade.

Saint-René Taillandier also attended the Lyon lectures, and was
turned in the direction of Germany by Quinet. That Quinet did
not emphasize his break with the German tradition while at Lyon
is made apparent by a letter sent to him by this young disciple in
July, 1840, from Heidelberg, in which Saint-René spoke of his
trip as a "pious pilgrimage to these places which are full of you. . . .
It is a Paradise on earth."[33]

Popularity at Lyon in no manner lessened the professor's passion to depart. With the beginning of the 1839 summer vacation
Quinet was at once off to Paris, to campaign for advancement. The
always friendly Villemain, Minister of Public Instruction since May,
promised his best. Michelet did all in his power to influence Fauriel
not to give his course, so that Quinet might substitute for him. In
autumn the younger teacher returned to Lyon, dispirited and angry.
The following March Fauriel wrote to him that he had only then
learned of Quinet's anger that the substitution had not materialized;
never for a moment had he considered not teaching that year. The
Sorbonne professor added, "I feel as deeply as yourself how tiresome
is your present position; my sympathy is heartfelt."[34]

In December, 1839, Quinet wrote to Villemain, not as *Grand-
Maître* of the University, but rather to Villemain the *grand écrivain*,
to explain that it was impossible that he remain in Lyon indefinitely.
Quinet had discovered that it was impossible for an individual to
struggle "against the instincts and habits of a population." He
enclosed a note from his doctor which stated that physical collapse
was certain if the professor did not receive a two-week holiday.[35]
The holiday was granted, but advancement did not come. On March
1, 1840, hope was further confounded by the replacement of Villemain by Cousin in the Ministry of Public Instruction. Leon Faucher,
whose efforts on Quinet's behalf in this matter were of long standing, approached Cousin for support. Effort was, in fact, futile until
such time as Cousin was replaced. But in April Quinet left Lyon,
sans congé. By midsummer he had made the decision to remain in
Paris, despite the unfortunate detail that he had not been called
there, and that the step meant the desertion of his post at Lyon.

Mother, son, and wife now finally shared a domicile. More swiftly than had been foreseen Villemain was back in office, deposing Cousin in October. Other events had been at work, however.

The Paris insurrection of May 12, 1839 was dispersed before nightfall. Yet it increased the power and prestige of the revolutionary parties, and in spite of its failure marked a rebirth of the republican Left. In the months that followed the government held rigidly firm before the growing demand for electoral reform, remained silent before energetic attacks upon the personal power of the king, and admitted its indifference to social questions which increasingly agitated the working class. In January, 1840, Lamartine voiced the fear of conservatives that serious difficulties might arise when Napoleon's ashes returned from Saint Helena. Heine noted in May that Napoleon was the unceasing topic of conversation: "Toujours lui! Napoleon und wieder Napoleon!" Later he wrote that the radical party in France, fearing the definite establishment of the Orleans dynasty, and the assurance to it of a long future, wished for a war so that the opportunity for a change in regime might be increased.

During the summer of 1840 Thiers, overestimating the power of Mehemet Ali, and seeking to strengthen his political position at home by victories in diplomacy, was duped and isolated by Palmerston. On July 15, 1840, the Treaty of London was signed. Thiers' bluff had been called; France could only throw in her hand, for in August Mehemet Ali met defeat. Thiers had defied Britain in the Middle East by lending encouragement and support to the Egyptian leader. The presumption of his military strength as an ally had given France this courage. Palmerston's disdain was justified by the Egyptian's defeat. In France the announcement of the treaty raised indignation to fever pitch. It seemed a new treaty of Chaumont. Thiers called up three years' classes, and war was in sight. But after the defeat of Mehemet Ali, only the Left and the legitimists continued to demand it, more in hope of defeat than of victory.

Lyon had been unbearable. In the exciting summer and fall of 1840 the College of France was less and less the goal Quinet pursued. As in 1831 his patience was finally exhausted. The announcement of the Treaty of London in July made it impossible to return to Lyon, and unimportant whether or not he were given a chair in Greek literature at Paris. On October 14 his pamphlet *1815 et 1840* was on the stalls. At that moment he was searching for collaborators for *"un journal de combat."* Enough capital to publish for four months would be sufficient, for decision would be soon. Already he was discouraged; war, he recognized, was but a feeble hope.[36] Thiers fell within two weeks. Quinet worked against time. He addressed patriots:

If the French Revolution was vanquished in 1815, public law, founded on the treaties of Vienna, is the legal, palpable, and permanent brand of that defeat. Under the yoke of treaties written with the blood of Waterloo, we remain legally for the world the vanquished of Waterloo. . . .

For France it is not so much a matter of conquering as of freeing herself, not of expanding, but of repairing; she should make no movement which does not lead toward deliverance from the public right of invasions. Anything in that direction is good, all that is contrary is bad. Monarchy, republic, *juste-milieu,* democracy, bourgeoisie, aristocracy, men of theory, practical men, men of politics, on this matter all have the same interest; it is the main point upon which their reconciliation is forced; for none of our parties will be anything but a shadow for as long as there is but a shadow France. Our internal debate will be sterile for the world and for ourselves, for exactly as long as, in any manner whatsoever, by diplomacy, or by war we have not risen from the sepulcher of Waterloo.[37]

The pamphleteer found it impossible to forgive the men who had ruled France since 1830 the blindness which had prevented their seeing the dangers which lay in the military feebleness of the State. Troubled by shouting in the street, they had ceased to see Europe. The Revolution had surrendered its sword in 1815. It had been the belief that she might retake it in 1830, but it had not happened that way at all.

The day following the appearance of this pamphlet an attempt upon the life of Louis-Philippe failed. Thiers had been kept in office so that he might assume the unpopularity of accepting peace. In the reaction following the assassination attempt, it was possible to drop him. Cousin left office with the Thiers government; Villemain came back as Minister of Public Instruction. Quinet seemed hardly to notice. On the last day of October he wrote: "We are not going to have war. The king does not wish it; he may well come to repent it."

The dismissal of the Thiers ministry, in late October, 1840, is a dividing point in the history of the July Monarchy. The policies and politics of the July Revolution had now met with total defeat. Peace and the personal power of the king were established as policy and fact; anticlericalism had long since died out. The resurgence of a warrior nationalism, attacks upon the irresponsible power of the monarch, and anticlericalism, all in the form of a bitter opposition to a regime thought to have been established upon these principles, now occurred. In that resurgence Quinet played a leading part; first by appeals for aggression. He wrote to his mother—on the day Villemain took office—that he was encouraged by the stir which his political pamphlet had caused. A new road seemed open to him. France had been humiliated and Edgar Quinet "translated that national sorrow."[38]

A second edition of *1815 et 1840* was prepared and appeared in the middle of November, with a new introduction. Quinet wrote of the recently formed ministry:

A coalition similar to that of 1815 forms against France in 1840. Who, do you think, is going to cover France against this new aggression. The man who was the agent, the defender and the friend of the coalition of 1815.

The ashes of Napoleon are returned to France; they approach, they are about to enter the port. Who, do you think, in the name of France, is going to be the first to receive and salute those remains: The man who was at Ghent while Napoleon was at Waterloo. Ah! if such is the hospitality which you prepare for those ashes they were better upon their rock; pray to heaven that should they touch a debased or enemy France that at that moment they be swallowed by the sea.[39]

Guizot remained in the government until February, 1848. Quinet never moderated this statement. The new edition of the pamphlet spelled out what had been left in partial obscurity before. The Rhine was an immediate objective of France, the first requirement of her recovery. Germany was invited to grant this peaceably, and to pursue her true destiny in the East. For Quinet did not mean to be unfriendly. Germany and France should join hands at the expense of Russia and England; but first Germany must disgorge the left bank of the Rhine. Thus peace depended upon Germany.

The ashes of Bonaparte were cold. The government survived their return, and in late December Quinet shifted his appeal. It was foolish to demand a war now hopelessly impossible, so another popular demand was championed; the democrat now emerged. The *Avertissement au pays* was Quinet's first piece of writing in which he discussed the French political problem in any detail. He came forward to state that democratic suffrage had become a prerequisite of a sound national spirit.

Quinet wrote that the spirit which divided France in two opposing camps was epitomized for him by Casimir Périer. Since his ministry it had been the consistent governmental policy to heighten the barrier between the people and the bourgeoisie. Defection had become the name for bourgeois-led efforts at rapprochement between these classes, sedition the term applied to the people's struggle to rise. The author believed that the strength of France under Napoleon had been in its unity, and in the fact that there had not been an "official" and a "real" France. Thus the failure of France to rise in 1840 was blamed on the debilitating internal division between the *pays légal* and the majority excluded from membership. Quinet concluded that only a France reconstructed by means of the binding force of democratic participation in national political life could deliver herself from the insults of the world.

In themselves political systems did not seem to matter to him. Gladly he would have accepted the leadership required from monarchy. An aristocracy would not have repelled him. For Quinet the democratic principle meant only the participation of all classes in the activities of government, not yet majority rule. Radicals who hoped to attain the goal, but rejected any means but majority rule, seemed to him the most dangerous adversaries of all movement or progress. Their immoderate pretensions condemned them to a stupefied quietism. The patriot also wished to state that if democracy desired no more than to augment and imitate the bourgeoisie he would willingly have held the suffrage where it then was. The bourgeoisie and their values were, he thought, already too prevalent, and Quinet disassociated himself from those who thought that all of the evil in France is of either bourgeois or democratic origin. I am much more tempted to believe that the greatest evil comes from their separation, and that things have reached a point at which it is not within the power of any party to save the country, and that salvation is not possible but in cementing and rallying the one to the other in the bosom of their common principle.[40]

National unity, recreated in the name of the fatherland, was the common principle which would allow France to smash the treaties of 1815, and restore herself to the fated role of European leadership. Quinet appropriated a democratic plank when it seemed suitable and necessary to his patriotism; he widened his audience and his appeal by seeming to move nearer to the most ardent of the patriots, the democratic party. It has been said that

according to Herder revelation is simply the providential guidance of the development of the human mind, through the influences operating on individuals and on peoples which combine to produce a certain result through their experience of nature and of the course of human events.... it is highly varied and progressive, and suits itself to place and time, to race and person. The progress of human civilization is not always and everywhere on the same road, or at the same rate; on the contrary, God makes use of special peoples and special times for special purposes; and hence comes "positive revelation" by chosen divine instruments.... for the realisation of that which is the end of the race as a whole, namely, of true *humanity*.[41]

For Quinet the divine instrument was France. His religion was being absorbed by his nationalism, and he began to foreshadow the prophets of *Machtpolitik*. Quinet's impatience for war in 1840 was based upon convictions which were quite compatible with Treitschke's belief that "most undoubtedly war is the one remedy of an ailing nation," or, "it is war which fosters the political idealism which the materialist rejects." French domination in Europe was not, however, desired for its own sake. Quinet never wrote or thought along the lines of Treitschke's statement: "We may depend upon the re-Germanizing of Alsace, but not of Livonia and Kurland. There is no other course open to us but to keep the subject race in as uncivilized a condition as possible, and thus prevent them from becoming a danger to the handful of their conquerors."[42]

In 1840 Quinet saw in war the possibility of a revived patriotism, but French aggression would have carried enlightenment with it. True, this concomitant of French victory was no longer thought of strictly in terms of benefits to be conferred upon the territory to be seized, and the good fortune which would befall the people on the left bank of the Rhine. But a re-energized France, restored to European leadership, would give the idea she represented new vitality everywhere. External influence was France's "vital principle." France had this providential mission, for *humanity*. Quinet did not heap insults on everything in Europe which was not French. He admired and respected all national groups, and his sincerity in this regard came to be believed in by republican nationalists from one end of the Continent to the other. The English and the Russians were low in his affections, but he blamed their history for their faults, not their blood. Nor was glorification of the French State Quinet's aim. Rather he wished to see the spread of the idea God had entrusted to France, an idea which was embodied in the not too carefully defined expression: the Revolution.

Democrats attacked the existing economic and political order behind the cover of aggressive nationalism. The ruling middle class reacted by becoming increasingly rigid in its opposition to an adventurous foreign policy. This group saw only its own economic interest, and so betrayed the national ideal. Democratic republicans were most receptive to Quinet's proposed foreign policy; he went to meet them by taking up their plea for democratic suffrage. He was not inconsistent in doing this (his tendencies had long been in this direction), and one may suspect that he had not done so earlier because it would have been dangerous to his chances for advancement to Paris. In a moment of enthusiasm he forgot ambition, or was attracted by another possibility, that of becoming a popular political figure.

A new road had seemed to open up and he entered upon it; but with a certain moderation after the moment of crisis had passed. The *Avertissement* was restrained, following upon the introduction to the second printing of *1815 et 1840*. As in 1832, a sudden violence was short lived. For more than ten years Paris had been his goal.

Friends stayed true, and in March Chateaubriand informed

Quinet that Villemain had him in mind for one of two chairs being created at the College of France. Hope in this matter was dulled by too frequent disappointment; but, to his surprise, the appointment was made in July. For once Quinet admitted a debt of gratitude: Villemain had been marvelous. Indeed, he would have preferred the chair of northern literature, but, "having shown color" on the Rhine, Quinet was granted the chair devoted to the study of the literature and institutions of southern Europe.

7. Church and University

THE STRUGGLE in France between the University and the Church dated from the creation of the University by Napoleon Bonaparte. Interludes of apparent peace were never more than a truce; periodically the fundamental antagonism became a matter of violent public debate. During the July Monarchy this battle reached its highest pitch from 1843 to 1846, and for those years was the most bitterly fought of all public issues. Edgar Quinet's term at the College of France was closely parallel—he opened his first course in February, 1842, and concluded his last in the spring of 1845.

These courses, and those of Michelet, are credited with having been one of the most direct causes of the "national and universal" revival of 1848; and with being the most important factor arousing public opinion, showing that in the University-Church fight "the problem of the Jesuits was really the vital issue."[1]

Before Napoleon's organization of the University, the 1802 law, establishing the system under which *lycées* were to operate, marked the commencement of the antagonism between Church and State in the educational field. Foucroy, charged by the First Consul to direct public instruction, fully realized that the clergy reconstituted by the Concordat would not postpone the effort to regain the monopoly it had enjoyed in the educational field before 1789. To forestall clerical success in this matter he decreed the exclusion of celibates from the direction of *lycées*. But in 1806 Fontanes replaced Foucroy as head of affairs relating to public instruction, and in 1808, when the University was organized, the act constituting the body stated that the base of its instruction was to be "the precepts of the Catholic religion."

The organic decree of March 17, 1808 placed a *Grand-Maître,* assisted by the *Conseil de l'Université* of thirty members, at the head of the University.[2] Under this body a group of Rectors headed the various academic fields. Controlled by these bodies, the universities dispensed higher education; secondary education was given over to the *lycées* of the larger cities, and the *collèges* of the less important ones. Both were placed under University control, the term University thus meaning "the State as educator." Primary education was left in the hands of the local schoolmaster, and practically nothing was done for primary education under this arrangement until 1833.

The charge that a University monoply existed must be examined, for this "monoply" became the target of Catholic attackers marching under the banner of "liberalism" in a battle in which vocabulary was all important. The monopoly existed only in this: after 1808, in order to be admitted to take the examination for the baccalaureate, necessary for entrance into the *faculté des lettres* of a state university, the student had to be sixteen years old and be prepared to be examined in all subjects taught in the highest grades of the *lycée*. The *baccalauréat ès lettres* was a prerequisite for those who wished to prepare themselves to teach, or to practice medicine or law. Only such persons ever took it. In September, 1818, when philosophy examinations had been consistently poor under this system, University influence was further increased by the decree that in the future a *certificat d'études* would be required of all baccalaureate candidates. The certificate would certify that the candidate had attended rhetoric and philosophy classes at a school where the University had approved the standards for those two subjects, *or,* the candidate might certify that a tutor, a parent, or a brother had instructed him in these subjects. Before 1815, and after 1828, these regulations put Catholic schools at a disadvantage in competing with the *lycée* for bourgeois youth, or forced Catholic schools to take cognizance in their classrooms of philosophical developments they preferred to ignore.

Private secondary educational institutions, other than ecclesiastical, could only exist upon authorization by the University. The University had the power to revoke such authorization at any time, and students at such institutions paid the *rétribution universitaire,* that is paid a tax to the University, and thus contributed to the support of the *lycée* with which the private institution competed.

This organization of the State was not, however, exclusive. In 1809 bishops were authorized to open ecclesiastical schools, to be devoted especially to the interests and needs of students who were

destined for the clergy (these schools were known officially as
écoles secondaires ecclésiastiques, popularly as the *petits séminaires).*
At the end of the Empire eighteen thousand students were attending
such schools, as against thirty-five thousand attending *lycées* and
collèges. Another eleven thousand secondary school students were
attending University-authorized private institutions. Primary schools
were frequently headed by members of the clergy; the priest taught
"morality" at all such schools. The situation prevailing at the end
of the Empire has been summed up as follows:

> One can understand that if *fonctionnaires* sent their children to the
> *lycée* or *collège,* religious families placed theirs in ecclesiastical schools.
> Thus was perpetuated in education that division of the country into two
> hostile Frances, the bequest of the Revolution and destined for a long
> future.[3]

Between 1809 and 1815 the University had some powers of
regulation over the *petits séminaires,* but when the Bourbons returned, and no institution was more criticized and attacked by their
partisans than was the University, certain of these controls were
erased.

The clergy, in 1814 and thereafter, had as its program either
the destruction of the University, or, if this were not possible, the
subjection of the University to the Church and the extension to
the Church of the liberty to open schools at all educational levels.
The State had no control over Church schools, but aided in their
support. Before examining the contending policies and programs of
defenders of the University and the clergy it should be stated that
the problem was much more than one of lay or clerical control of
education. As Quinet stated, the question was what morality would
be taught. In this struggle the Revolution and the Church were
each as tolerant of the morality of the other as the prevailing temper
of opinion demanded, never one whit more.

That the Church had the exclusive right to religious teaching,
and the right at least to supervise all other branches of learning, so
that any matter contrary to its faith or morality might be excluded,
was the all but unanimous conviction of the Restoration clergy. In
1815 the immediate issue before them became one of dealing with
the University. The Ultras decided upon its suppression, and bishops

called for this to be done; Lamennais and Chateaubriand led the attack.

Lamennais used such terms as "seminaries of atheism and vestibules of hell" in speaking of the University schools, but the policy of the Church was dominated by other considerations. Frayssinous is said to have remarked that Lamennais would have spoken with yet more violence had he known how truly deplorable the situation was. But, he asked, how replace the institution both wished to destroy? What do with 100,000 children? Neither the secular clergy nor the Jesuits felt equal to replacing the University overnight. Nor was Taine altogether wrong in believing that the Restoration government had no real desire to destroy the disciplined and centralized instrument the Empire had willed to it.

Restoration policy was to retain the University, while weakening its power and greatly assisting in the development of the Church schools outside its jurisdiction. The government doubled the budget of Church schools between 1815 and 1830, and more than 1,500 full scholarships and 2,700 half-scholarships were created beyond this budget increase in order to facilitate the attendance of poor children at these schools. Thus, so far as the Church was concerned, a policy which was second best was followed: the subjection of the University to the Church, and the extension to the Church of the liberty to open schools at all educational levels.

Subject to constant clerical aggression, the University gained steadily in popularity. When in the elections of 1827 the reaction against the religious politics of the Ultras resulted in a Chamber of Deputies with a moderate monarchist majority, the June ordinances of 1828 followed. The University was defended by the government for the first time since 1814. The Jesuits had borne the brunt of the anticlerical attack, an attack lately strengthened by the appearance of the Catholic Monarchist Montlosier's pamphlets. These Jesuits were the target of the first ordinance.

Frayssinous, *Grand-Maître* from 1822 to 1828, had shown the poor judgment to defend the Congregation, and to admit, by inference, the existence of some eight Jesuit colleges in France. The first June ordinance obliged all teachers to take an oath that they were not members of an unauthorized congregation. The second ordinance grew out of the alarm felt by the anticlerical party at the

competition to the University system developing in the form of
ecclesiastical secondary schools. These schools had been given their
original authorization largely to assist the Church in recruiting
priests, at a time when such recruitment posed a serious problem.
Under the Empire, and progressively during the Restoration, they
came to serve a very different purpose: that of forming the minds
of a large number of lay Catholics. The second June ordinance was
meant to arrest this development, by limiting the total number of
students who could be enrolled in such institutions in all of France
to twenty thousand, and by making compulsory the wearing of
ecclesiastical costume after two years of attendance. When seventy
French bishops signed a protest refusing to apply these ordinances
the government was forced to call upon Rome for assistance. The
Pope took advantage of this opportunity to exercise his authority
over the French clergy, and Jesuit colleges in France were closed.
The second ordinance was not rigorously enforced.

Charléty summed up the clerical program after 1830 in these
terms:

> Liberty of education...was the minimum for the present, the dis-
> appearance of all control by the state over private education was the
> hope; for the future, a complete victory over youth, *no private rival
> being presumed strong enough to measure itself against the organized
> power of the Church.*[4]

That separation of Church and State came to be an attractive idea
to a growing number of Catholics is understandable in view of this.
Catholic Liberal is an accurate label for the party originated by
Lamennais, and made into a permanent political force by Montalembert. Liberal, nowhere more than in France, is the label to
attach to that party which, seeing the handwriting of democracy on
the wall, created the gospel of the weak state. It seemed too that if
the State could be removed from the field of education the Church
would have a monopoly in that field.

During the July Monarchy the Church was mainly concerned
with improving its position with respect to secondary education.
Anticlericalism was one of the three principles victorious during
those "glorious three days," but a revolution which had the character of a sort of "revenge of irreligion against the clergy and

Catholicism" was promptly tamed. Before the end of seven months Casimir Périer, representing the "party of resistance," headed the government. The Catholic historian of the Monarchy judged that "compared to that which had preceded, and that which seemed the fatalistic consequence of July, that part [religious policy] of the ministry's policy testified, as did others, a real progress."[5]

By January, 1833, Montlosier charged that the "ecclesiastical party dominated the government." In May, 1835, De Tocqueville noted the virtual disappearance of liberal bourgeois anticlericalism. Talk hostile to the clergy or to Catholic doctrine seemed to have passed from the scene. De Tocqueville's explanation for this change deserves full citation, for it helps to emphasize that it was not an anti-Catholic one.

> Most of the liberals whose irreligious passions [for De Tocqueville, when he speaks of France, irreligious and anti-Catholic are synonymous terms] have formerly put them at the head of the opposition, now talk in quite different terms than they once did. All recognize the political utility of a religion and deplore the weakness of the religious spirit in the population.[6]

Guizot's 1833 education law partly explains why secondary education was almost solely at issue after 1840, when Catholic attacks on the University took the forefront of the political scene. It was not that the Church was little interested in primary education because the mass of the people did not vote; but rather that the 1833 law met all of its important demands on the matter. The law required that primary education include moral and religious instruction, and made the priest an ex-officio member of the committee established in each commune to oversee and control the public school.

So far as secondary education was concerned the July Revolution was another temporary setback for the Church, following upon the June ordinances of 1828. Many a Liberal who crossed the barricades was slow to enter the confessional, or to wish his son to do so. No matter how speedily he halted public expression of anti-Catholic sentiments, he continued to resist Catholic attacks upon the University.

The winning of the mind of bourgeois youth was the goal of

both Church and University; the battle lines were drawn between the spirit of the Revolution and the spirit of the Catholic religion. The University was determined not to give up the privileged position it enjoyed, which in time might serve to extirpate Catholicism from educated France. The Church fought for a more privileged position than that it already enjoyed. The fight was carried forward under the banner of liberty, until such time as it might become possible to demand the complete suppression of the University. No settlement was made before 1848. The February Revolution was followed by the unforeseen but logical victory of the clerical party in the passage of the Falloux laws.

Guizot worked constantly to meet the wishes of the Church, and in January, 1836, presented a bill which did away with all former University control over private schools: the bill provided that there would be no requirement of previous University authorization for establishing such schools, and in the future no requirement of certificates of study for presentation for the baccalaureate. Certain degree requirements were established for the heads of private institutions, none at all for professors. The government retained some right of inspection and some disciplinary authority, but only a civil tribunal, not the University as in the past, would henceforth have the authority to close a private educational establishment.

The bill presented by Guizot would have left ecclesiastical schools in their privileged position: the requirement of degrees for directors would not have applied to them. But when the Chamber of Deputies amended the bill in one respect the Church and Guizot ceased to support it. The Chamber added the provision that the head of a secondary school be required to take an oath that he did not belong to an unauthorized congregation. One prejudice had not died. Even in the Chamber of Deputies a majority could not be found which would willingly open the gates to Jesuit education. The clerical party, feeling that sentiment was running on their side, refused a victory tainted by compromise.

In 1836 the demand for liberty of education was particularly the property of the younger clergy, those who had followed Lamennais until the moment of his break with Rome, and who in the following years modified their former leader's doctrines. Lacordaire became their head within the Church. Montalembert remained their lay spokesman. They and their program had not wholly won the Catholic hierarchy in 1836. By 1840 further progress had been made along this line and a new effort was made to increase the power of the Church in the educational field. Montalembert negotiated a settlement with Cousin during the latter's term as *Grand-Maître* of the University. When Villemain replaced Cousin before action was taken to implement the settlement, Montalembert served as intermediary between Msgr. Affre and the new University head.

In 1841 a new project was submitted to the Chamber, only to fall before the opposition of the clerical party. Villemain insisted that ecclesiastical schools give up certain of their privileges. Most notably he would have imposed degree requirements upon professors which the clergy could not meet. Bishops judged that ecclesiastical schools were threatened by the measure. Rather than being a concession to their request for liberty the proposed step seemed to endanger important privileges already in their hands. Now the alarm was sounded. Attack upon the University seemed the best way of winning complete victory.

Dupanloup, later the real author of the Falloux laws, fixed the Catholic line, writing that the 1841 project was the first effort of the University to conserve, harden, and even extend its monopoly, in scorn of the Charter and of the public clamor. He declared that the project was a manifestly criminal attack against both liberty of education and religious liberty.

The non-Catholic view has rather been that at a moment when the government was being lax in enforcing a monopoly which it intended to end, just when the State was practicing *un laisser aller débonnaire,* a furious attack against the University was launched. The reason was not far to seek. Although the issue flamed into prominence in 1840, it had never been off the scene. Gustave Drouineau enjoyed a brilliant success in 1829 upon the publication of his five-volume neo-Christian novel; violent passages exposing University education explained a large part of its success in Catholic circles. The Catholic reaction was pronounced after 1830, particularly after 1833. The threat of democracy made new allies for the Church, and by 1840 enough ground had been recovered to bolster confidence for renewed all-out attack. By the end of the 1830's an intransigent Catholic youth was beginning to make itself felt within the University itself. In the year Quinet arrived at the College of France two courses were suspended following clerical attack. The Catholic *Univers* listed eighteen professors whom it charged with "irreligion." Among them were Cousin, Michelet, Jules Simon, Chevalier, Nisard, Jouffroy, Damiron, and Quinet.

Among the eventual beneficiaries of the liberty demanded by the Church the Jesuit order was most important. During the 1833-40 revival of Catholic power the Jesuits regained more ground than did any other of the interdicted orders. The anticlerical charge that the French clergy as a whole was increasingly inspired by ultramontane doctrine, and appropriated the interests and ambitions of the Jesuit order as its own, accurately describes what developed. By 1840 the Church was willing to fight the University on the Jesuit issue. It seemed that even on this ground victory could be won. The campaign against the University was "opened" by the appearance of the Jesuit Garot's pamphlet *Le Monopole universitaire dévoilé à la France catholique.* The floodgates of abuse swung open. This was in May, 1840. The intensity of the battle was still rising when Quinet reached his Paris pulpit in February, 1842.

Of the battle's importance Heine wrote, in June, 1843:

> The fight against the University, continually pressed by the clerical party ... still occupies the public. Perhaps this interest will soon be pushed aside by some new question of the day; but the quarrel itself will not be settled so quickly, for it is rooted in a division which is a century old, and may perhaps be regarded as the essential cause of all the revolutions in the life of the French State.[7]

8. The College Pulpit

THE REVOLUTIONARY and militaristic fevers which overcame Quinet in 1830 and 1840 were thought by many to have been only temporary aberrations. Though not a Catholic, he had not yet interjected aggressive passion into religious matters, and some saw in him a thinker searching for the God he had lost. The Catholic view is that at the College of France a transformation took place—a profound anti-Christian fanaticism became evident.[1]

Out of Quinet's courses at Paris came *la religion du Collège de France,* which Henry Michel summed up almost perfectly as a faith in "la magistrature du monde exercée par la France de la Révolution, héritière authentique et continuatrice légitime du Christ."[2] This "religion" has truly been the "inspiration of generation after generation of the rank and file . . . of French radicalism,"[3] and recently an adverse critic has stated that if Quinet's thought seems banal to Frenchmen today it is "precisely because it penetrated everywhere in the course of the Third Republic."[4]

Intense nationalism, rather than anti-Catholicism, was the note Quinet struck in his opening lecture in February, 1842. The spirit prevailing at the College of France, as well as Quinet's conception of his new role, is apparent from his description of his feelings, and the recital of his remarks, in the report he made to his mother of that first day.

The hall was packed. The speaker entered, pale and tense, and upon reaching the lectern put aside his one resource, a single page of notes. In silence he remained standing, looking out directly to his audience—"finally I began." The commencement was calm, the sympathy of the listeners apparent. One-third into the address Quinet was first halted by unanimous applause. He began to dare more. Far from the conclusion "deafening" applause answered when he asked: "Is it really true, as is repeated day in and day out, that here I have to do with a people who are finished...? No, no, if they are exhausted they will be refreshed; if they recline, they will rise up; if they are dead, they will be reborn." From this moment the hall was filled by a dialogue between the orator and the answering applause—applause which was "thundering" as he concluded:

In their crabbed imaginations I have often heard the peoples of the North say that France, bound to the Revolution, resembles Mazeppa being dragged far from the beaten track and torn by a steed no longer controlled by his hand. More than one vulture circles overhead, coveting the remains in advance.... This is perhaps true.... But it should be added that at the moment when all seemed lost, Mazeppa rose to the noise of the acclamation of those who had made him king.

As Quinet turned to depart Mickiewicz embraced him. Magnin and Ampère, "who knew the métier," were charmed.[5]

Quinet's courses of the spring and fall of 1842 were later brought together to form a part of his *Révolutions d'Italie.* This work was not published until after his three later courses had appeared in book form, and when completed (it appeared between 1848 and 1852 in three volumes) formed a conclusion rather than an introduction to this period of his development. After treating Italy in his first two courses he had begun to write the book, but found that "when I wished to unite those parts I saw no connection existed between them." He then asked himself, "what was the vital principle?" Quinet declared that next he searched the chronicles until he had found the thread for which he sought. For—and nothing was more characteristic—"I had no doubt that it existed."[6] The "thread," or the dogma, was that developed and expressed in the courses of 1843 and 1844; so these later courses, and the 1845 *Le Christianisme et la Révolution française,* preceded the published form of the *Révolutions d'Italie.*

Beginning early in 1843 religious pamphlets attacking the University multiplied, until they became "a mounting sea of calumnies and outrages which threatened to submerge it." There are two traditional descriptions of the next development. One is that, after untold provocation, in the spring of the year Quinet and Michelet, at the College of France, reduced their attackers to silence in a series of memorable lectures. The other description of the event would have it that, as a part of the University plot to maintain its monopoly and to evade the Charter, in the spring of 1843 the signal for a direct and violent attack on the clergy was given in the College of France itself, by two professors, Quinet and Michelet.

The decision made by Quinet and Michelet to turn their courses into an attack upon the Jesuits was in a sense, or in part, in order that they might answer the Catholic attack of the *Monopole universitaire,* a Catholic journal solely devoted to this battle, and the most scurrilous in the field. In 1843 Sainte-Beuve wrote that in France Jesuitism and Catholicism could hardly be distinguished. There had been a time when a French Catholic was completely astonished to discover the superstition and idolatry which prevailed at Rome, Toledo, or Antwerp, but he believed that henceforth "il n'y aura plus lieu a cet étonnement."[7] This too led Quinet and Michelet to their decision.

Heine wrote that the nature of the clerical attack upon Quinet and Michelet had the unfortunate effect of pushing these men, quite against their deepest natural inclination, to throw out the Christ child with the bath, and to force them into the element farthest to the left in the revolutionary Armada. The foreign policy of the Monarchy had done much the same thing, but in 1843 the spotlight was upon a different issue. Those forces which in 1840 had demanded the Rhine in 1843 were hunting Jesuits. The tide had long been running against the University, and as the Catholic reaction gained force the clerical party raised its sights. Cousin had been willing to compromise on many essentials with the Catholic attitude. Villemain, although he detested the Jesuits, was a devout Catholic. In 1843 destruction of the University, always the goal, was made the immediate program of the intransigent party.

Important in the Catholic revival was the tendency for the Church itself to define orthodoxy in ever narrower terms. Strictly speaking, Quinet had never been anything but a heretic; he began to attack the Church when it felt confident enough to draw the lines of faith in a fashion so as to exclude all who had hoped for some settlement between Rome and the modern spirit. Many who might hitherto have been hesitant to approve could now be expected to give a sympathetic ear to a more frank expression of his views than Quinet had previously ventured to make.

In 1843 Quinet was violently opposed to the foreign policy of

Guizot. He was soon to find Cousin's affirmation that the Catholic religion was the basis of the philosophy of the University humiliating—as a member of that body he felt implicated in his former friend's intellectual dishonesty. He did not yet profess republican ideas.

Now that his attack was mainly upon the Jesuits Quinet found more respectable company sharing his viewpoint than in 1840 when he had demanded the Rhine. Not that such company was wanting in either instance, but now the Voltairian liberal, who had not died out, came to Quinet's support. As a result the professor found new friends in high as well as low places. Shortly before the opening of his course on the Jesuits (the topic and the nature of which were foreseen), the Duchess of Orleans approached him to discover if he would be willing to take charge of the education of the Comte de Paris. At the height of the uproar over these lectures Quinet was invited to Vincennes by the Duc de Montpensier; he had at least one long and friendly conversation with the Duc d'Orleans upon another occasion within this period. Such contacts were not without meaning to a man who was never indifferent to recognition from his social superiors.[8]

The democrat, in fact, evidenced somewhat less ardor against the Jesuit than did the liberal who remained Voltairian in attitude. Thiers and Dupin, rather than members of the small republican group, spoke out in the Chamber of Deputies to demand strict application of the 1828 ordinances. Génin, in the republican *National,* was no more violent in his anticlerical attacks than was Libri in the *Journal des Débats,* a moderately liberal paper. The *Courier française,* the *Constitutional,* and the *Siècle* supported Quinet and Michelet, the last named publishing Quinet's 1843 and 1844 lectures the day following their delivery at the College of France. During the spring of 1843 Quinet found warm and avowed partisans in the literary world, among his colleagues at the University, even within the royal family, and in other circles as well, but particularly among these nonrepublican elements.

On May 3 Quinet began his course on the Jesuits. Many a stormy scene marked those lectures of May and June. Erckmann-Chatrian wrote that the Revolution, suspended since Louis-Philippe took the throne, "stirred itself back to life out of horror of Jesuitism." Quinet unchained the furies with his course. With Michelet and Mickiewicz he stirred a generation of ardent patriotic and anti-clerical students to a passion, while at the same time the people were aroused by episodes of a like tendency in the novels of Eugene Sue. "Hardly had those professors opened their mouths when applause broke forth like a tempest. At the end of a lecture one had not been able to make out four intelligible sentences."⁹ The first lessons were attended by large numbers of Catholic students, who came with the intention of silencing the professor, and who greeted the master with a storm of hissing and booing. Several lectures were heightened by physical combat between the clerical and revolutionary youth in attendance. More than once the administrator, pale and frightened, ran from his office to the auditorium where the lecture was being held to advise Quinet to dismiss the audience, protesting that if he did not the College of France might be leveled to the ground.¹⁰

Mme Quinet related that her husband spoke almost without notes, and that he wrote nothing beforehand. The truth is that Quinet sent an advance text of his lectures to the *Siècle*. The wife is unfairly charged with falsehood here, however, for Quinet, like Michelet, preferred to seem inspired. Michelet stated that duty forbade his making advance preparation—to do so would be to shackle the pure inspiration which otherwise never failed. Quinet in 1845 spoke in similar fashion; each night he retired unprepared to "deliver battle" the next day. Before the hour of the lecture everything came to him, from where he knew not.

Yet Monod wrote of Quinet's course on the Jesuits that it was, in contrast to that by Michelet on the same subject, "serious, solid, grave, rich in facts and documented. One sensed that they [the lectures] were based upon lengthy preparation."¹¹ When in July Michelet's and Quinet's lectures appeared in published form Sainte-Beuve referred scathingly to the fact that at the same time portraits of the two professors were put on sale *"comme des deux héros du jour."* But even he added, "La partie de Quinet est bien, très bien."¹² The adjective "grave" describes the orations poorly. On the other hand, keeping in mind the atmosphere which prevailed, there was merit in the degree to which the course was factual and serious. Quinet now entered into his true element. That part of his career which had a lasting influence began. He had failed to find himself

either as a poet or philosopher. At the College of France he began
to give effective expression to a democratic-republican program.
Throughout his life Quinet felt a deep need for adulation, a need
which was most nearly requited in the period of his life which now
opened.

A distinction between anticlericalism and anti-Catholicism cannot be made when speaking of Quinet from the time of these lectures. The Jesuits, not the Catholic Church, were his avowed target.
However, when accused of making a distinction which in fact he
did not recognize, he frankly replied that he separated only those
who wished to be separated. No debate seemed possible on the
proposition that the teachings of the Order were incompatible with
modern liberties. And Quinet wondered if Catholicism, by placing
itself under the banner of Jesuitism, really desired to reopen a war
already so destructive to the Church. If so, he forecast that a struggle
between ultramontanism and the Revolution could only result in
victory for the more Christian principle. The capital of the universal religious sentiment would henceforth be in France rather
than at Rome. While he did not exaggerate his own orthodoxy,
Quinet professed to believe in the future of Christianity: the preparation of the souls of men for that unity and solidarity promised by
the Gospel was the true spirit of the education of modern man.[13]

More than a half-century after Quinet's courses Troeltsch wrote:

> So long as the modern world is thought of purely in its political,
> social economic, and technical aspects, it can reconcile itself well
> enough ... with a somewhat softened form of Protestant orthodoxy,
> whereas Catholic orthodoxy constantly opposes it with a new Syllabus,
> and cancels again and again such accommodations as had already taken
> place.... [14]

Quinet, who thought of the modern world in religious terms, was
confronted by a resurgent and aggressive Catholic orthodoxy. The
Church seemed on the verge of overcoming the University. Jesuit
education for France was in the offing.

Quinet's liberalism was an outgrowth of his conviction that men
are free; that a man's actions spring from his own personality, and
that he is beholden for them to no authority other than that of his
own individual conscience. Prejudice and ignorance make it neces-

sary to restrict men's liberty, but the duty and purpose of organized society was to reduce prejudice and ignorance—to prepare all men for the enjoyment of full individual freedom. The Catholicism of the Church of Rome, wrote Croce, was "the most direct and logical negation of the liberal idea."[15] Jesuit doctrine was, however, a particular difficulty. On this score Boehmer, who was incomparably more dispassionate, and who searched for truth rather than evil, reached the conclusion which was most important to Quinet. The early question of "whether the Order would gain a deciding influence at the Vatican and in the religious life of the Catholic world" seemed to have been settled affirmatively "for all time," since 1607.[16]

A part of past failure to achieve the unity promised by the Gospel had resulted from the Protestant-Catholic division. Quinet hoped for a remedy to this. He reiterated that the character of a truly living religion communicated its force to, and was the foundation of, the political state. The ultramontane doctrine was philosophically and theoretically true. Submission should be given to the spiritual force. Here was a hint of the state political religion which Quinet later wished to establish by setting up a system of compulsory state education. In Jesuit hands, however, the ultramontane doctrine was death.[17]

One rule every Jesuit teacher was instructed to observe condemned the Order: the regulation that "no one, even in matters which have no danger for piety, is ever to pose a new question." This was indeed the word of the devil—the interdiction that the seed of progress be sown. The diametric opposite was the spirit of the Revolution, which was predicated upon a faith in progress. Quinet's emotional faith in the rationalistic spirit was at the core of his hatred of the Jesuits. What could be more evil than to make a virtue of blind obedience? When he attacked the practice followed by the Jesuits in India, of suppressing the Passion of Christ in the religion they spread, he was sincere in his anger. He detested the practice of deception as a deliberate policy with a perfect constancy all of his life. The practice was based upon a lack of faith in man's reason. Men who had the *Spiritual Exercises* and the *Constitutions* for codes were simply impossible educators for French youth.

It would be foolish to deny that retrograde Catholicism was the

real object of his attack. Also, popular prejudices with regard to
the Order must be made of first importance in any valid explanation of the special attention Quinet paid to the group. Was it not
damning evidence that the Society of Jesus had been brought back
to life in August, 1814? What better evidence of the opposition
between the Order and the Revolution! The lectures were replete
with similar logic. These were the statements which ended in
applause. The authoritarian and absolutistic aspects of the Jesuit
doctrine were, naturally, of serious importance to Quinet, but their
discussion in detail awaited his next course.

Quinet was constrained to justify his choice of topic. The professor's critics protested that the Jesuits had only a tenuous relationship to the field of study suggested by the title of his chair. He
made the retort that the relationship between the Order and the
fate of southern European literature was indissoluble. At the end
of the sixteenth century an atmosphere of death spread over Spain
and Italy. Quinet professed to see a small Society become great
upon the substance of the national genius of two magnificent
peoples. The orator denied that he could or would study the effect
without considering the cause. He might, indeed, have found other
causes, but preferred this very timely one. He might also have
defined "death."

In certain important respects Quinet must be distinguished from
the typical mid-century liberal historian in these matters—for
example, from Macaulay, who wrote: "Our firm belief is that the
North owes its great civilization and prosperity chiefly to the moral
effect of the Protestant Reformation, and that the decay of the
Southern countries is to be mainly ascribed to the great Catholic
revival."[18] Quinet never wrote of or believed in Macaulay's "great
civilization of the North." Nor did he ever think of passing judgment on a culture on the basis of its "prosperity." When he visited
Spain in 1843 he believed that the country's greatest fortune lay
in the very fact that bourgeois materialism had not infected its
people. Not that Quinet's doctrine of causation was not equally
crude.

Quinet's most serious difficulty was with causation in the field
in which he was most fundamentally concerned. To associate
artistic and cultural achievement with liberal or democratic political

institutions, or with "liberty," is a common error, not at all peculiar to those who, like Quinet in this instance, carry it to a ridiculous extreme. This is in no sense an apology. Quinet made his untenable position the justification for making the Company of Jesus the subject of his course. Believing that religion was the source of all social phenomena, and detesting Catholicism, he simply drew his conclusions. Quinet was important in preventing a definitive Church victory over the University during the 1840's. At this level his performance can be taken seriously, his more ambitious pretensions notwithstanding.

Mme Quinet related that the storm over his course was so great that it was suspended in October, 1843, when Quinet should soon have taken up his teaching post for the fall term. Only after a ministerial change was he able to reopen his course in February, 1844.[19] Although this account has become part of the legend, there is evidence to disprove it. Quinet left Paris shortly before his course was to have opened, and visited Lyon during the last days of October. Among friends he wished to see was Victor Laprade. The continued affection between these two men is an interesting fact, although it ought not be forgotten that Polish followers of Mickiewicz cheered Quinet at the College of France, and, Mickiewicz at their head, attended Catholic services *en masse* each Sunday. From Lyon Quinet departed for Spain.

In view of the title of his chair at the College of France, Quinet's desire to know Spain at first hand was justifiable. His taking French leave of the University was in character. That all was not well within the bosom of his family is not to be entirely overlooked. For different and sometimes certainly unwelcome reasons, he and Minna were apart more than together during their marriage. Earlier separations have been noted; then when Quinet moved to Paris almost a year elapsed before Minna joined him. Her visits to Germany thereafter were frequent and extended. One of the few traces of some difficulty, one which the second Mme Quinet could not destroy, is a notation in Michelet's "Journal" in September, 1842: "I wish to appeal to Quinet for his wife. In order for her to be beautiful again it would suffice that he love her a little."[20]

Whatever the cause for Quinet's sudden visit to Spain, it was not the suspension of his course. In Madrid, on January 10, 1844, he received the following notice from Paris. The letter had been sent on October 24, 1843, by Fauriel:

As for your trip to Spain, I scarcely dreamed of it further at a time so advanced in the year, and at the moment of the opening of your courses at your college. But since there you are, on your way, I have nothing to do but make the best of it. I saw Villemain as you asked; he is being amiable about the matter but wishes that you write as soon as possible to M. Letronne, President of the College, to inform him of the step you have taken and of an inevitable postponement in your course.[21]

The course referred to was the one which should have opened in November. It was particularly unfair that Mme Quinet should have placed the onus of the imaginary suspension on Villemain. On November 23, the Minister of Public Instruction wrote to Quinet granting a request that the originally unauthorized absence be further extended. The plea of research would, he wrote, be the formal justification. He added: "Since you have indicated no limit to the time you desire, I am sending you the regular forms for requesting such a leave."[22] This letter reached Quinet at Cadiz in January, before he received the previously dispatched note from Fauriel. Immediately he informed Minna that Villemain had written in an extremely friendly manner, and stretched the truth to add that the Minister "approves completely of my trip." On February 26 he was back on French soil. *Mes Vacances en Espagne,* Quinet's account of this interlude, was written and published in 1846.

On March 20 the returning warrior gave the first of his nine lectures that spring at the College of France. No ministerial change had taken place, and Quinet took up a more radical position than in his previous course. Villemain's leniency is suggested by the fact that University regulations stipulated that Quinet give forty lectures a year. He gave seven in 1843, nine in 1844, and fifteen in 1845. Michelet was little different in this regard, appearing thirteen and twelve times respectively during the last two of these years.

With the course of 1844 Quinet was frankly done with Catholicism. His announced purpose was to make apparent that a distinction between Jesuitism and Catholicism could no longer be made. The previous year he had been content to "refute" the past, to lay bare an insidious evil; now he insisted that Jesuitism had compromised Catholicism, that one had become the other. Would Catholicism in turn compromise Christianity? This was the danger to be faced.[23]

From this moment Michelet and Quinet have been said to have begun moving along different paths, Quinet remaining at heart a Christian, continuing to believe that the Revolution was a natural transformation of the Christian faith, whereas Michelet was now to interpret the Revolution as a revolt against the Christian dogma of Grace. Michelet, at Cologne on July 14, 1847, recorded in his "Journal" that France was drifting intellectually, allowing its thought to become obscure. He regretted that "Even we, Quinet and I . . . we have seemed to drift, especially in so far as one has been able to believe that we think Christianity can be reconciled with the Revolution."[24] Regarding the doctrine of grace Quinet was no more of a Christian than Michelet. An outright antagonism to historical Christianity, and to liberal Protestantism as well as modern Catholicism, was increasingly apparent in Michelet's thought after 1843. On the first two points he parted company with his friend.[25]

The 1844 course, *L'Ultramontanisme,* treated of Catholicism or liberty, which Proudhon too termed that "fatal dilemma." Quinet made a notable return to the eighteenth century, and paid moving tribute to the positive side of the Enlightenment. Nearly a century before Carl Becker reminded another audience,[26] Quinet recognized that the Enlightenment "had not overturned, but had replaced the Church." Voltaire, Rousseau, and Montesquieu were the "triple crown of that new papacy which France had presented to the world."

Quinet went further, and declared that although there were many things in which the eighteenth century had ceased to believe, ". . . it is equally certain that the essential aspect of that century was a universal faith in that which was most important in the Christian heritage, I mean in the power of the invisible, in the mind. In this all men of that time are as one."[27]

Quinet portrayed Voltaire as the true representative of the Christian tradition; everywhere violence or injustice showed its face he saw his hero answer with anathema—jeering and overcoming the infidel Church with the arms of the Christian spirit.

Voltaire was an instructive choice. It aids us to define Quinet's
"Christianity." To present Voltaire in this light was to go far
beyond Mme de Staël in secularizing Christianity. Vestigial orthodox
scruples Quinet might have felt almost twenty years earlier when
translating Herder certainly could have existed no longer. But
Quinet's long-lasting admiration for Voltaire was due to the great
philosophe's implacable opposition to the Catholic Church, not to
any great philosophic affinity. With the Jesuits his adversaries, he
did the obvious in calling upon Voltaire. And he declared that the
worst of the capitulation following upon Waterloo had been the
fall from grace of the greatest representative of the French eighteenth century. He believed the time had come to erase at least
that shame.

Quinet put rhetorical questions to those who saw an age of
faith and a true Christian society in the past. The reign of force,
the Inquisition, authority vested in the caprice of one man: was
this "the very Christian kingdom?" To the contrary, fraternity and
equality had more and more descended to the plane of reality; the
liberty of the individual had been consecrated in law; the Christian
ideal had penetrated little by little into institutions, and had become
the substance and the sustenance of modern law. The mere epithet
"pantheism" was deemed by the Church sufficient rebuttal to all
this. What then was the Church's understanding of religion? "Who
indeed is your Christ?"

You search Christ in the sepulcher of the past; but Christ has left
his sepulcher; He has moved on, has changed place; He lives. . . . He
descends into the modern world. Ah! you who think that with a word
you may put France under interdict, your great misfortune [is that] . . .
you search your God there where He no longer is; there where He is,
you do not know or you do not any longer wish to see.[28]

Vico and Bossuet were mentioned but Herder was not. As once
before, Quinet reduced the originality of Vico to a single thought:
the realization that civilizations depart from an idea of God as rivers
from their source. Like Bossuet, Vico had observed that the world
is submitted to the government of Providence. Quinet defined his
own position by saying that "from ruin to ruin, from Church to
Church, man had not ceased for a day to gravitate toward God."

To be complete, he declared, the philosophy of history must note the manifestation of divine action in all human things. Humanity is the true, the real Church.[29]

Catholicism no longer represented "religion"; the evidence was 1789. Quinet declared that then, for the first time since the existence of that Church, the temporal world had changed without the change having been provoked by a corresponding movement of the Church. As it was axiomatic that religion was the sole dynamic factor in history, the only possible conclusion was that "religion" had left the religious institution. For three centuries not a page had been added to the Catholic conception; the Council of Trent had been its last breath. Could one imagine, he asked, that the spirit of God had spoken only to the ancient prophets?[30]

Quinet took the position that science was the true religion; Galileo, Kepler, and Newton were the prophets of the modern world; Galileo was the martyr of the modern church. This science, he declared, must encompass and grow with the continuing revelation of natural law (or Providence), which lived in nature and in history. To mutilate and paralyze religion or science in order to render the alliance between them more commodious was to flee the question, not to solve it. Science promised to reconcile all men and peoples, for it knew neither sects nor heresies.[31] Quinet did not claim finality for the eighteenth century. One could honor its heroes by not imitating them.

What was most important he had found in Herder. For if orthodoxy were made compatible with science this would not be enough. The contempt of Rome for nationalities was nothing other than contempt for life in its most profound manifestation. The original form which a people received at birth was the seal of God, whereas the social ideal offered to southern Europe by the Roman Church was a vast cosmopolitanism in which all national personality would be dissolved. Italy had fallen into the trap; in imitating that example France would inescapably suffer the same fate.[32]

Quinet's name is closely associated with a development in France foreign to his conception of society as rightfully organized: the separation of Church and State. The necessities of the French situation finally led him to advocate such a step; his ideal was a

different one. In the spring of 1844, more logically, he attacked the
Catholic Church for seeming to desire that separation. He could not,
even at that date, decry the prospect of separation of the State from
Catholicism, but he scorned the apparent willingness of a highly
vocal element within the Church to see that institution "desert
the nation."[33]

The memorable lectures of 1843 and 1844 did less than
"silence" the adversaries of the University, but were a factor in
another shift of Catholic policy. The demand of the clergy, when
not for outright destruction of University education, had been for its
modification or amelioration along Catholic lines. When attack
seemed only to increase resistance Montalembert was in time able
to convince many of the Catholic party that the hope of improving
the University was illusory, and to spread his belief that the University could not be "representative of anything but indifference in
religious matters." This did not seem criminal to him; it was "a
result of the state of society." He attacked the views of Michelet
and Quinet, but defended their right to freedom of expression; in
return he demanded that a like liberty be granted to the Jesuits.

By 1844 Montalembert's program had resulted in a Catholic
understanding to serve religious liberty under the banner of civil
liberty. His program brought the clergy under this strange flag.
A true liberty, he argued, could not condone that the University
education should be imposed upon those parents who were concerned with the preservation of the Catholic faith among their children. The only solution was to grant complete liberty at all levels
of education. Montalembert always disclaimed that his motive was
an eventual Church monopoly. That he was sincere in this is sometimes granted; that the clergy was sincere when it followed his
leadership is less frequently admitted. In any case his argument was
such that the defenders of the University sought a somewhat different ground on which to fight. The demand for liberty stole their
thunder; they shifted their emphasis to a different aspect of the
problem, though not an aspect they had ever ignored.

After 1840 the government had continued to seek a transaction,
and in February, 1844, at the moment Quinet was beginning his
lectures on ultramontanism, a bill favorable to the clergy was submitted to the legislature on behalf of the Crown. The important

concession stipulated that the certificate of university studies would no longer be necessary for presentation for the baccalaureate. Cousin was prominent in the debate. He defended the University with the latest weapon, protesting that the bill, the certain result of which would be the creation of large numbers of new confessional colleges, would shake the unity of the country: "From childhood we would learn to flee one another, to enclose ourselves in different camps, priests at our head; a marvelous apprenticeship for that civil charity we call patriotism." Should the bill become law and two competing systems be established, "this country, which in its misfortunes has at least conserved one immense resource, the force of its unity, would lose it."

Thiers wished to preserve the status quo because "above all else we must conserve the unity of our national spirit." The French Catholic need not have been silenced by this. Dupanloup could in all sincerity reply that the "sacred duty of teachers, everywhere and always" was to bring up youth in love of their fatherland, and "to inspire it with zeal for its glory and devotion to its interests." This was the first sense in which "education ought to be national."[34]

No amount of debate could obscure that the difficulty was not here. When Dupanloup continued that he was just as firmly convinced that education should not be "political," and that the only political lesson suitable for children was that they be taught to "love, respect and obey," he was nearer to the problem. How contend that Catholic education was not "political"? Only by assuming the Church to be in possession of immutable truth. As in 1840, however, the bill was rejected. Favorable to the clergy, the measure would have withdrawn certain clerical privileges, by establishing regulations as to the competence for *all* teachers. Worse, it was amended so as to exclude Jesuits from teaching, by requiring an oath from teachers that they belonged to no unauthorized congregation.

That Cousin came to the defense of his former protégé in this debate was to his credit, but there was nothing perverse in Quinet's continued and bitter attacks on the official eclectic position, embodied in Cousin's frequently quoted statement that his school of philosophy was patient. It was quite happy "to see the masses, the people, that is to say nearly all of humanity, enter into the arms of Christianity; it contents itself to offer them a friendly hand, and to aid them to raise themselves to a yet higher plane."[35] This supercilious note was as infuriating to Quinet as it was to the Catholic, and when Saisset, a disciple of Cousin, attacked Michelet for deviation from this sweet reasonableness Quinet promptly answered for his friend in one of his February, 1845 lectures.[36] Saisset repeated the familiar argument that religion was the philosophy of the people, philosophy the religion of the educated. Philosophy should gradually extend its empire, but any effort to hurry progress by the preaching of a natural religion would create moral anarchy, just as the sudden institution of universal suffrage would create political anarchy. This position had the merit of infuriating the enthusiastic among both clerical and anticlerical, but was not a banner under which men would march.

Jacques Maritain in his *Man and the State* labors with "the problem of means." His discussion may clarify the politics of both Church and University in France in 1844. Man in an evil environment is confronted with a hard choice. He may refuse to commit himself to "political" activity because the only means at his disposal are incompatible with moral law; on the other hand he can leave aside moral law and accept evil means in order to eradicate evil.

The second position assumes that the end justifies the means and that no God exists. For, as ... David Rousset put it ... "you cannot have moral principles playing the part of an umpire dividing bad and good means from each other unless you keep those moral principles out of historical, social relativity, and therefore find foundations for them outside the human species, that is to say, be it pleasant or not, in God." Let it be added that the one who takes the stand under discussion cannot help being himself corrupted in the long run by his *total* adaptation to a corrupted environment.

The word to note is "total." Inserting it does more than make the meaning elusive; meaning has been divorced from all that precedes, and variable and contrary application to specific events is now permitted. Maritain continues: "Reason must never abdicate. The task of ethics is humble but it is also magnanimous in carrying the mutable application of immutable moral principles even in the midst of the agonies of an unhappy world, as far as there ... is a gleam of humanity."[37] This suggests that "mutable application" is but the use of means adapted to a corrupt modern society, one in which error so prevails that means, to be successful, must be adapted to error and be corrupted by it. For example: the hope of re-establishing the universal authority of Catholic truth by means of force is irrational in a world in which skepticism prevails; although the Inquisition was justifiable and proper, because in an environment much near to truth than our own it could enforce conformity to truth, to demand its immediate re-establishment today would be to "abdicate reason." The principle of using force in such matters, however, is immutable.

Soltau believed that Maritain's thought fulfilled Quinet's prophecy that a new scholasticism was almost certain to appear. As a derogatory epithet (which it was for Quinet, and one may presume, for Soltau as well) "scholasticism" means the practice of perverting the meaning of words, as Quinet charged the Church did in demanding "liberty" in order that it might one day be destroyed.

The University more frequently applied another adjective to the program of its adversary, one which Heine thought apt for describing both disputants: "jesuitical."[38] Neither Church nor University was honest about its objectives. Both professed indignation at methods of the other, methods which neither had qualms about practicing in the pursuance of its own cause. The Church denied that the goal was a completely Catholic France; the University denied that it wished to extirpate Catholicism. Both, but the University particularly, expressed horror that belief should ever be enforced by inquisitors and arms.

In 1844 at the College of France Quinet decided finally that religious sentiment had left the Church, and declared lay society in its pursuit of scientific truth to be the modern expression of humanity's search for God. The next year, his last in the college pulpit, he embraced the democratic state, which in the pursuance of the "general interest" had powers limited only by certain immutable principles, prime among these being the dignity of the human personality. Quinet easily concluded that the development of the human personality to its fullest limits—the justification and purpose of social organization—was impossible where Catholicism formed attitudes and controlled minds. Thus later he came to believe that the general interest demanded that Catholicism be rooted out, by whatever means.

Then Quinet, like Dupanloup, could not escape the unhappy circumstance that the application of his program was impossible given the French environment. He, too, was faced with the problem of a mutable application of immutable principles. As events disclosed the tragedy of truth, he followed logic to its inexorable conclusion and discarded toleration as a principle. This, however, is to anticipate.

When a brief mental illness incapacitated Villemain in December, 1844, Guizot took prompt advantage of his colleague's misfortune and replaced him with Salvandy (on February 1, 1845); Salvandy quickly indicated that the confidence placed in him by the Catholic party was not mistaken. One of the new Minister's first acts was to address "severe but powerless remonstrances" to the administrator of the College of France regarding the courses Quinet and Michelet were giving. He wrote in part, "the disorders astonish and wound public feeling."[39] Then Mickiewicz was suspended. If there is the slightest justice in the charge that Quinet deserved the suspension which came in late 1845, there is much more in the case of the Polish prophet, whose one preoccupation after the spring of 1844 was to spread the word of the new messiah, Towianski. On March 19 Mickiewicz had announced to his audience at the College of France:

The joy which I have experienced, and which will not be taken from me, the joy which has moved me to be charged with the mission to come before you, will be the joy of all my life, and all my lives. I proclaim myself in the face of heaven to be the living witness of the new revelation.[40]

Quinet's courses were a continual source of embarrassment to the government, but the only means of silencing him was through the faculty of the College of France. At the semiannual meeting of that body in July, 1845, Salvandy requested the assembly of professors to insist that Quinet and Michelet restrict their lectures to the limits suggested by the titles of their respective chairs. Twenty-four professors were present, and the debate lasted six hours. Letronne read Salvandy's letter asking that the faculty invite

Michelet and Quinet to cease their extravagances. Michelet defended himself briefly, Quinet at great length. Michel Chevalier suggested that the faculty put the matter to a vote. The first count revealed a division of twelve to twelve. On the second ballot Michelet and Quinet were upheld by a vote of thirteen to eleven. Both Quinet and Michelet voted.[41]

When his plea was rejected Salvandy did not desist. Quinet occupied the chair of "Southern Languages and Literature." The faculty, which had several times approved Quinet's program, that is the actual title of his course, "Comparative literature and institutions of southern Europe," requested him to remove the word "institutions" from the title. He refused, but in November, 1845 the course was officially listed with the deletion made. On December 2, Quinet wrote to the Minister that he could not in good faith accept the change, and that he would not take up his chair until such time as the word was restored.[42]

Guizot's characteristic solution to end the uproar had prevailed. He hoped the criticism of sensible men might be ended by silencing the extremists at the University, and by prevailing upon Rome to request that the French Jesuits retire. The Minister had pursued this policy although Montalembert and his followers had wished to gain "liberty" for the Company in return for permitting University figures like Quinet the free expression of their convictions. De Tocqueville expressed the uneasiness of the moderate party in a January, 1844 address. He reproached the government for remaining silent while, on one hand, bishops attacked the University in an injurious and calumnious manner with impunity, and, on the other, important men, "irritated by those unjust attacks, speaking in the name of the State, in chairs created and maintained by the State, attacked not only the portion of the clergy which menaced lay instruction, not even just all the clergy, but Catholicism itself, Christianity itself."[43] The policy Guizot pursued largely met the wishes of men who shared De Tocqueville's viewpoint.

The fifteen lectures Quinet delivered in the spring and summer of 1845, and the lectures he would have delivered beginning in November, had he not made the decision to retire, were published as *Le Christianisme et la Révolution française*. In his dedication to Michelet the author insisted that if this work had been written far

from the madding crowd there would have been no essential difference in the conclusions reached; but he acknowledged that the
public clamor which had surrounded the statement of his message
had necessarily affected the form it had taken. The first part of the
argument was weak.

The 1845 course presented the first clear design of Quinet's
doctrine which associated the idea of religious renovation with a
democratic and social revolution—a conception which found its
most complete expression in his 1849 *Enseignement du Peuple.*
Quinet now presented a program little different from that of the
politically advanced group who wrote for *Revue indépendante,*
among whom Leroux, George Sand, Schloecher, Duprat, and
Renouvier were most important. Hostile to the Voltairian spirit
and to Catholicism, this sect hoped for a religious revolution which
would replace the existing Christian churches with a new Christianity, which would be an offshoot of democracy and of modern
social aspirations. In 1843 and 1844 the *Revue* applauded Quinet's
announcement of a future religious unity. In 1845 we find Quinet
nearer to their democratic and social attitudes.

The more important impetus to move in the democratic direction may, however, be thought to have been the attacks of the
spokesmen of the eclectic school. We have mentioned that one of
Quinet's 1845 lectures specifically answered Saisset's criticism of
Michelet. What, Quinet asked, had been the tactics? In order to
obtain the triumph of a week one had pretended to come to an
understanding. How different was the example of Christ in the
desert! Quinet believed that if one admitted for a moment that a
God was necessary for the people, that was to say continual progress
of the spirit among some and eternal immobility of belief among
the rest, the union of society was broken. France would then be
divided into two irreconcilable camps, everlastingly separated by
an abyss which would never cease to deepen, and the work of
Christianity would be destroyed.[44]

Quinet announced that a truce had to be established between
the City of God and the city of men—the one and the other
reunited in the same principle. He believed the conscious desire
for this culmination to be so great that should the sacred phrase
"follow me" be pronounced, whatever the source, should it be from

the Vatican, from a throne, from the heart of a people, "I do not say all Christianity, but all humanity, prepared at that cry to recognize the voice of the future, will march at once."[45] Even this last was two parts rhetoric, for he proved the Vatican and thrones incapable. But there was a chosen people. Quinet sounded the call to arms, in hushed tones, but in a fashion little likely to be misunderstood. France must speak. Humanity would follow. The new order he proposed could not take place without suffering; that was not possible. His generation could not escape the laws of history; but its suffering would make the peace of those who followed.[46]

After his last lecture in August, 1845, Quinet wrote to his mother, "the campaign is finished." Although he and Michelet never identified themselves with Mickiewicz without reservation, the three had a single place in the heart of many a student, and when "the campaign was finished" Quinet and Mickiewicz were presented with a medal at a large student demonstration. Michelet, absent from Paris, could not attend. The token of admiration and affection was adorned on one side by the profiles of the three warriors. In the presentation ceremonies the student representative declared that these men "alone have not deserted the great teaching of the greatest days of our history, and, thanks to these professors, our greatest tradition has been renewed among us."[47]

Students and workers were the two Parisian groups devoted to the Republic; Weill supported this characterization of student opinion by noting that in February, 1848, "all of the schools were rivals in patriotic ardor and furnished the Hôtel de Ville with gratuitous and devoted auxiliaries.... All the youth of the Latin Quarter acclaimed Edgar Quinet when his course ... was reopened at the College of France."[48] On December 3, 1845, the day following the publication of Quinet's refusal to submit to a change in the title of his course, some three thousand students formed at the Place de l'École de Médicine and at the Place du Panthéon. Converging into one group, they marched in a body to Quinet's residence. Their "republicanism," at least on that day, was limited to the attitudes expressed in these parts of the address delivered by a student who spoke in the name of all those who had assembled:

Our applause has reverberated beyond the walls of the College of

France. There has been fear to see us fired by a true patriotism, by the
enthusiasm of the great days of [the Revolution]....

...it is our cause you have lent support, it is for us that you have
fought the ultramontane reaction against the spirit of the Revolution,
with as much firmness as eloquence.

Quinet's response fitted the spirit of the occasion: "How little the
fate of one person affects the cause! The seed is sown, the cry of
awakening has gone forth. The new generation has heard. It will
not sleep. You will honor your fatherland, and that will be the
recompense of my efforts, if, in fact, they have so merited." The
gathering then retired. As the group passed under the windows
of the Minister of Public Instruction the chant *"À bas les jésuites
...Vive Quinet"* was heard. General disorder, culminating in numer-
ous arrests in the Latin Quarter, ended the morning.[49]

Publication of the undelivered lectures went on through December and January. At the opening of the second semester, in February,
1846, the College of France again received from the Minister the
order to delete the word "institutions" from the description of
Quinet's course. Not until April, 1846 did Quinet formally resign,
in a letter which fully presented his case. He appealed to the royal
ordinance of March, 1831, which stipulated the purposes and
privileges of the College of France. The line drawn between academic freedom and academic license will determine to which side
the observer will grant his sympathy, and those who arrive at
differing conclusions find reason a poor means of dissipating the
area of disagreement between them.[50] Quinet's decision not to compromise led to his separation from his remaining Liberal friends.
It was now that he moved into the Ledru-Rollin camp. This was a
rather significant step to the left politically, particularly in so far
as it affected the company he kept. A temporarily increased preoccupation with matters of political organization was another result
of the move.

Unfriendly critics, and even the more or less friendly Monod,
have cast doubt upon Quinet's true motive for resigning his teaching post. They suggest that he was becoming bored, and so pushed
the quarrel to the breaking point; or that he sought popularity with
the mob, and expected he might win a greater share as a martyr

seemingly sacrificed to clerical opinion. Convincing material evidence is lacking.

Years later Quinet wrote that all of the pleasure of teaching at Paris had been poisoned for him as he came to realize that living in the midst of a crowd of friends and addressing cheering audiences was deceiving him as to the reality of things. He came to understand that the number he reached with his message was so small that, whatever his success in influencing it, he was not affecting the depth of the general ignorance. Among the mass of Frenchmen his voice had no echo.[51] If Quinet was impatient for a different role, the fact that a new demand had forged to the forefront of public debate might have influenced his actions. By 1846 electoral reform had superseded the Church-University battle in the center of the political arena. Reaching the masses was a growing preoccupation for Quinet; events would now rapidly underscore the essential importance of doing so.

9. February, 1848 to December, 1851

PARLIAMENTARY REFORM, by means of an extension of the suffrage, was proposed in the Chamber of Deputies seventeen times between 1831 and 1847. In each instance the government in power opposed and defeated these proposals. During the summer of 1846 electoral reform was the most debated issue at the time of the elections. Quinet made an unsuccessful bid for a seat in the Chamber, running on a platform of universal suffrage under the auspices of Ledru-Rollin, the leader of the left wing of the republican party. Following this defeat Quinet turned his attentions to his unfinished work on Italy, the subject of his first lectures at the College of France. His purpose, as always, was didactic: Italy should serve as an example to France.

In 1848 Ernest Renan found the spectacle of the physical suffering of the poor lamentable; but he wrote that this touched him infinitely less than to see the immense majority of humanity condemned to intellectual helotism, and men, perhaps his intellectual superiors, reduced to a beastlike existence. To raise these men up to the level of humanity was, he thought, the "true religion, the only serious and saintly matter facing society." For this reason the conquest of material well-being, which seemed to him to be the work of the nineteenth century, was not profane. It was saintly, when one considered that it was the condition of the freeing of the spirit.[1] Quinet was slow to concern himself with these matters. Although he believed it to be one of the more noble traits of his time that each day seemed to bring forth new proposals for the amelioration of the infirmities and physical misery of the people, the hunger of the soul and of the spirit seemed more redoubtable to him. The intimate connection apparent to Renan escaped Quinet. This may be explained in two ways. Quinet's romanticism retained something of a German character, and German idealism was little concerned with economic and social problems. His own essentially middle-class viewpoint, which he never wholly overcame, was probably a more important cause, however. But because the moral regeneration of France was of primary concern to him, Quinet was never attracted by currents in German thought which were out of keeping with this purpose. Schleiermacher's statement that "it is an insult to religion to try and make it the handmaid of morality" he could not really have understood.

The tragedy which followed upon February, 1848 brought about a different orientation in Quinet's thought. He learned that an ignorant people could not fulfil the mission of France. The Second Republic established that fact for him. Elevating the people forced itself upon him as the great problem. Quinet never did devote his efforts to the working out of a system of economic and social reform, but the factor of a necessary and proper material standard for the masses was one he ceased to ignore. And the superstition and ignorance of the people, proved to him by the ease with which they were won to reaction after February, 1848, turned him to the problem of their intellectual elevation. Of at least equal importance here was his conviction, which developed slowly but which had grown to sturdy stature before 1848, that the bourgeoisie was unhealthy, was amoral, that is to say was not "national."

The 1846 *Mes Vacances en Espagne* first revealed the trend. *Les Révolutions d'Italie* marked the height of his concern with the masses. In the former work he pointed out that everywhere in France there were examples of two men,

who for fifty years have met in the street, every day at the same place; a nod has never been exchanged between them. They are in proximity during their entire lives, and yet eternity would pass and their lips would not part. For one is rich and the other is poor. One has found his place on earth, he occupies it; the other still wanders without knowing where to rest, he lives and dies standing.[2]

In *Les Révolutions d'Italie* Quinet turned to Italy and found the parallel, and the explanation for the sharpness of this division.

France was on the eve of changing governments again. Quinet increased the violence of his attack upon the existing system. The enemies who were ruining France were seen at the same work in Italy. Not only was the French bourgeoisie corrupt, so was the

Italian, and by implication that of all Europe. The people of Paris acted before Quinet's encouragement to revolution reached the press.

Quinet now made Catholicism responsible for the class struggle. The essential fact in the social history of Italy was that the plebeians, having hardly emerged from the people, turned with fury upon their origins. Whereas in ancient Rome patrician and plebeian had been contained by their national sentiment, in Italy intolerance, being at the base of religious belief, broke out into political life. The bourgeoisie made no concession to the people, and the people no concession to the bourgeoisie.

With his ability to discipline history Quinet found ready examples in fourteenth-century Italy. When Guelph and Ghibelline reciprocally changed banners in a bourgeois or proletarian interest the root of this action was that an intolerant and cosmopolitan religion increased class strife and prevented the existence of that fraternity which can develop only if national feeling is strong and deep. Lest the lesson go unheeded Quinet reminded the reader that the French Revolution had been resolved in the reign of a new *popolani grassi,* whose resemblance to the Italian was striking: the same parvenu spirit, the same blind abandonment of all national instinct. Indeed the *popolani grassi* of the July Monarchy were attempting something new under the sun in foregoing the virtues of the Italian. In abandoning God, country, humanity, heroism, beauty, science, and art to their adversaries they were in truth abandoning too large a share to the impatient fortune of the *peuple maigre.*[3]

The February Revolution returned Quinet to the College of France, and he was charged with making the ceremonial address at the beginning of the first term to open under the new dispensation. With Michelet at his side he spoke to the assembled faculty and students on March 8. Mme Quinet declared that not "since the dawn of Liberty in '89, had a patriot tasted more radiant happiness." Quinet described the recent events:

If ever a miracle has been consummated on this earth, it is that which you have seen with your eyes and made with your hands....

Each [class] performed its duty at the place marked for it by Providence; and the sentiment of that duty accomplished seals eternally that alliance which the monarchy strove to destroy. It believed that it had formed two peoples, enemies the one of the other, but they found one another on the barricades. . . .

The masses have entrained and conducted their chiefs [the learned and educated]. Such is the spirit of this last revolution, accomplished by faith, by the weak, by the poor, by the small, that is in greater conformity than ever to the Christian spirit of the Gospels. . . .

If, by a misunderstanding which would seem impossible, the spirit of concord which animates us were misjudged by the princes, if the frontiers of the sacred soil were menaced, or if our friends should be in peril of death . . . with what joy, with what intoxication, with what felicity all of us would take up the arms of yesterday . . . But I stop . . . I have more need to tame than to stir your warrior enthusiasm.[4]

Quinet had been returned in triumph, but was not to devote his energies to the College of France. Instead he dedicated himself to political activity, and was elected to the Constituent Assembly in the April elections.

"One of the strangest paradoxes of a strange period" now occurred, for the Revolution provided the Church with "two of the most signal victories she won in the whole of modern history."[5] The overthrow of the Roman Republic and the passage of the Falloux laws were the work of a French Republic. One might also say that a Republic in name granted victories which were signal if not paradoxical. More nearly paradoxical had been the action of the conservative bourgeoisie during the last days of the July Monarchy, when they worked "with an unpitying ardor to dissolve a regime which they had so great a fear to see disappear."[6]

A Republic was forced upon republicans by the Paris mob. Democratic concessions made during the five days following the Revolution threatened to pass the limits of a simple political revolution, and were made only in order to calm the people of Paris. The partisans of the new government looked on with increasing fright as innovations were imposed by the populace. Thus the conflict which would end in the June Days began with the Revolution itself.

Universal suffrage was declared, and an electorate of less than one-quarter of a million overnight became one of nine millions, a majority of whom could not read. Democrats were now on the verge of having to face reality, and a struggle immediately broke

out between the *Réforme,* or left-republican element, and the
National, or center-republican group of the Provisional Government. The date on which to hold the elections for the Constituent
Assembly was at issue. Originally it had been fixed at April 9, but
the members of the democratic faction demanded postponement,
correctly judging that the country would return a large majority
against them. On March 17 a mass demonstration in Paris protested
the government's decision to adhere to the original date. The government held firm momentarily, but on March 26 postponed the
date to April 23, now realizing that a delay would strengthen the
Right.

Republican clubs in Paris debated the responsibilities of the
citizen should a nonprogressive majority be returned to the Assembly, frequently concluding that insurrection would be the most
sacred of duties. Another issue divided the government itself along
similar lines: Ledru-Rollin headed the minority faction which
wished France to intervene directly in Europe to aid peoples against
their monarchs.

On one hand it may be said that the "democrat of 1848 was
an ardent patriot and often a frank Jingo"; on the other that whereas
the entire nation was passionately concerned about questions of foreign policy, "in 1848 it no longer dreamed of warlike propaganda."
The controlling element of the Provisional Government, the men
of the *National,* very quickly put aside the thought of fostering
such propaganda. These men saw that pursuance of such a policy
would have put them at the mercy of the democratic minority,
whose social radicalism frightened them, and which was made up
of individuals who were all that is suggested by the expression
"frank jingoes." On March 1, Lamartine informed the Duke of
Wellington: "The Provisional Government . . . will make an energetic declaration to the nations of Europe, but the Duke of Wellington will understand its true meaning."[7]

After much soul-searching Ledru-Rollin proved the sincerity of
his liberal optimism, sacrificing himself and his party to it. By
mid-April he seemed to be convinced that conciliation of the bourgeoisie, now dedicated to reaction, was impossible, and to be inclined
toward taking up arms against the government of which he was
still a part. But at the last moment he stood with the Government,

called out the National Guard on April 16 to crush a popular demonstration for Poland, and so helped to bring about "the definitive defeat of the party of social reform"—that is to say, his own. He received paltry thanks for his action. Quinet found little to choose between the foreign policy after July, 1830 and that after February, 1848, but the worst of the second nightmare was not this.

Debidour wrote of the days immediately following the February Revolution, "the clergy had never been so popular in our country." The enthusiastic reception which the Church accorded the event was his suggested explanation, for the clergy wasted no tears on Louis-Philippe. The Church understood at once that its own interest was not to try uselessly to bar irresistible events, but rather to put itself at their head.

During the Restoration the middle class had professed horror of the clerical party; under the July Monarchy this attitude had been significantly modified, even reversed among the most conservative. However, the tradition that the danger was from the Right, and the fact that until late in the 1840's, when Montalembert began to influence greater numbers within the Catholic hierarchy, the Church was closely associated with the legitimate branch of the royal family, had limited government favor. The group at the *National,* wishing to replace Guizot, had been prominent in the anticlerical attack. All changed "as if by enchantment" after the February Revolution. The peril was now democracy, and the Church offered its aid. Thus it was that Victor Cousin, meeting Rémusat on the streets of Paris on February 25, had raised his arms to heaven and cried: "Courons nous jeter aux pieds des évêques; eux seuls peuvent nous sauver aujourd'hui."[8]

The Provisional Government was hardly installed when, "from one end of France to the other, the Church deafened it with its acclamations and weighed it down with its promises."[9] It should be remembered that Pius IX was still the "liberal Pope," and that the liberal lay Catholic world was enthusiastic and expectant. The April elections fell on Easter. Church services were arranged so that in many localities electors were led in a body to the polling places by their priests. Fifteen ecclesiastics were elected to the Assembly, among them three bishops, and in an election in which almost all candidates ran as republicans, practically none were elected who were openly opposed by the clergy. Quinet was an exception. Still waiting for the result on April 25, he wrote to Minna from Point d'Ain that he was told the people had resisted "the furious campaign of the clergy against him." On April 28, from Bourg, he announced his victory.[10] The men of May 24, 1873, presented themselves as *républicains rouges* in 1848 and were elected. When the results were known Barbès wrote in the *Réforme,* on April 29: "We counted on bad enough elections; it must be admitted that the event has surpassed our worst expectations."

Carnot, the former Saint-Simonian, served as Minister of Public Instruction in the Provisional Government. How little he resembled Quinet is apparent from his statement of February 25, the day after he assumed office: "The reunion of the two administrations [religious and university] under a single direction is the guarantee of the just conciliation between the equally respectable interests which will be established."[11]

Thus on the very morning of the Revolution Quinet might have felt alarm. Not until March 19 did the Provisional Government order the dissolution of nonauthorized congregations and corporations, with specific reference to Jesuits, and then not at the demand of friends of the University. Only after the working class had taken matters into its own hands, devastating several Jesuit buildings, and when this movement threatened to spread, did the government act. Worse, worker antagonism was not religious. The Jesuit communities attacked competed with certain classes of labor, and in a time of depressed employment the feeling against such competition flamed up.

In the moderation of his views on Catholicism, Carnot resembled Cousin. The new minister had a great deal more of a "socialist" concern about the general level of education than Cousin, but he thought of education as a means of imparting skills rather than as a method for instilling doctrines. His cardinal effort was to establish free and compulsory primary education, without any notion of reducing the dominant influence of the clergy in this field. In the field of secondary education he wished to grant "liberty" to the Catholics, if they would accept some regulation of ecclesiastical schools. By reducing the cost of State secondary education, through the creation of a much larger scholarship fund to aid needy students to attend the State *collèges,* he felt that "liberty" would not hand secondary education over to the Church. Meeting Montalembert's demands would have meant just that. Carnot's solution was one moderate men might have accepted; in fact it represented helpless innocence. Carnot, however, was a more typical republican than was Quinet. Many republicans were genuinely surprised when Montalembert and his party accepted the servitude of the Second Empire as the price of "liberty" of education.[12]

Definitive action had, perforce, to wait for a permanent government. The Constituent Assembly first met on May 4. A conservative majority, consisting of diverse elements and extending from Catholic legitimists to former Republicans of the *National,* took charge. When on May 15 the National Guard proved loyal, in the face of the popular demand that aid be sent to Poland, the government felt strong enough for a final trial of strength, and began to carry out a policy which culminated in the June Days.

The insurrection began at 6:00 A.M. on June 23, and lasted three days. "It was a battle between the classes, the battle of the bourgeoisie and the army against the workers."[13] In that hour of decision Quinet did not hesitate. Commander of the eleventh legion of the Paris National Guard, on May 15 his task had been to cover the Luxembourg. During the June Days his troops upheld law and order in the area of the Panthéon. Eventually he resigned his commission, in protest to the violence of the governmental repression which followed the uprising of June, 1849. But, although never fully forgiven in "left" circles for the lateness of that resignation, Quinet remained certain that his 1848 action had been justified.[14]

The Revolution of 1848 was terminated on June 26, 1848. An era of political and social reaction followed. Ozanam remarked in 1849 that there was not a Voltairian to be found who, if he had several thousand francs a year in dividends, did not wish to send the rest of the world to mass, on the condition that he not attend himself. Cousin and Thiers were two representatives of the non-Catholic world who turned at once to the Church as a force able to maintain now not only the masses in obedience, but all society in health. As early as March, 1848, Thiers wrote: "As for liberty of education, I have changed; I have done so, not because of a revolution in my convictions, but because of a revolution in the state of society."[15] Short months before he and Cousin had defended the University; with many others they now surrendered.

Marx ridiculed those optimists, whom he classified as "social democrats," whose essential character was in their demand for republican institutions as a means, not to suppress the two extremes of the social order (the capitalist and the wage earner) but to attenuate their antagonism and to transform it into harmony. He had in mind his adversary Proudhon, who characteristically wrote, "Resolve the bourgeoisie and the proletariat into the middle class . . . such is . . . the true question of February." Marx could scoff because the event had been so little promising to the optimist and democrat. His sarcasm reached far beyond Proudhon, to all of those for whom February had been a moment of generous hope.

Quinet could not take the path of Thiers or Marx. Their policies were antagonistic, but it was the materialism of both which he could not accept. In this period of general disillusion even the mild Pecqueur, upon observing the unwillingness of the privileged classes to accept the diminution of their privileges, began in 1849 to speak of the "inevitable and uniform solution of social problems by violence."[16] Quinet reacted differently, at first. After June 26 he was saddened like the bourgeois democrat in Lyon who wrote:

For me, who have had a lifetime dream of the fraternal republic according to the Gospel, that is to say the triumph of reason, of morality, of justice; who have aspired only for the form of government which would be able to assure the happiness of all, the liberty of all, the well-being of all, I have shame for my country, I have shame for modern civilization.[17]

June 26 may have ended the Revolution. Quinet did not admit it; his resilience, his unwillingness to admit defeat, became more apparent as adversity mounted. Although the horizons of hope had quickly narrowed, Quinet's readjustment was equally swift. The ignorance of the people had lost the Revolution. More revealing in this regard even than the elections of April was that of December, when Louis Napoleon received 75 per cent of the popular vote. Early in the summer of 1849 Quinet published his *L'Enseignement du Peuple*. A fifth edition went to press before the close of the year.

The inculcation of respect for the authority of a tradition and for the institutions representing that tradition, and the planting in the minds of youth of the premises and prejudices, doctrines and dogmas suitable to an easy acceptance of the authority in question is part of education. The problem of educational control—that is, which of two opposing traditions will have the privilege of teaching French youth—has been and remains one of the problems which has most divided France since the Revolution. Napoleon voiced the opinion of both camps when he stated:

There will never be a fixed political state of things in this country until we have a body of teachers instructed on established principles. So long as people are not taught from their earliest years whether they ought to be republicans or royalists, Christians or infidels, the state cannot properly be called a nation.

Here the term "two Frances" is perfectly descriptive: Catholic France and the France of the Revolution. Not that the issue or the attitude was born in 1789. A characteristic of seventeenth-century French political theory was the absence of individual rights of a nature to check the public power. In Bossuet, whom Quinet so frequently resembles, such rights are all but absent. For the seventeenth century the political danger of "two peoples" was in itself justification for enforcing uniformity of cult and faith. In its nineteenth-century context the problem appeared somewhat differently. First Quinet posed the question:

Catholicism being the national religion, how establish modern liberties on a religious principle which damns them. This problem has been the most fundamental in the history of France for sixty years; one finds it everywhere....

For it seems, at least for the time being, that the French nation wishes neither to renounce the Catholic religion nor modern liberty; we pretend to maintain one with the tenacity of habit, the other with the enthusiasm of novelty. This is the practical reality.[18]

Recent experience had forced Quinet into a new attitude. The reality, not the ideal, was now his concern. He stated that the question was not at all to decide whether or not in an ideal democracy

education should be organized and administered by the State; that
had become "an abstraction without any application to France."
Whether, given a country in which the clergy formed a caste, it
was not necessary for the lay principle to be organized in a manner
so as to balance the action of that caste, had to be answered. A
quarter of a century later Gambetta declared of Quinet:

> He uttered the true cry, that which will remain the rallying cry of
> democracy. He said: "In order to save the country from the dangers
> which menace it at home and abroad, instruct the people in conformity
> to its genius; grant it lay education."
> It is Quinet, my fellow citizens, who first pronounced those words.[19]

In so far as this was true Quinet had done so in the face of an
unfortunate circumstance, for he bowed to no one in the conviction
that education must have more than a strictly lay character. He
too demanded that it have a religious base. The tragedy which he
faced in 1849 was that for his compatriots religion was synonymous
with organized churches. To constitute education without the Catholic Church seemed impious to a majority of them.

The months just past had solved the enigma. In all of the debate
on matters of social organization Quinet noted an astonishing absence of any mention of the moral and religious factor. Quinet was
far from alone in the view that this was a mistake. The early Saint-
Simonians had stressed that "l'institution sociale, politique, considérée dans son ensemble, sera une institution religieuse," and were
convinced that "l'humanité a un avenir religieux." Even Louis Blanc
had been distressed during the July Monarchy to see his friends
confound liberty of conscience with complete suppression of any
state religion, for by declaring itself indifferent in religious matters
the State was bound to abdicate an essential part of its authority and
function. But as regarded the main tenor of non-Catholic thought
Quinet was not wrong. He wrote that France must awake to the
fact that the religious problem enveloped the political and economic
one, and that no solution of the latter could be more than hypotheti-
cal for as long as the first had not been resolved. Quinet was coming
to realize that the people of France did not share his modernized
Christianity; they were, as he came to see, and in his own terms,
without faith. He began in 1849 to grope his way to the remedy.

In *L'Enseignement du Peuple* Quinet indicated what he thought was the difference between the Revolution of 1789 and that of 1848. The first had believed that it could save the world by its own spiritual energy, and it had given birth to great events and great men. The second had believed that it could not save the world without the support of the priest, and the expedition to Rome had been a logically necessary result. Had France, or had it not, the spirit of life; did the Revolution feel within itself the power to make men without assistance from the Church? Quinet was certain that the first condition of achieving freedom was in such a faith, and the hope that lay society might emancipate itself was a fatuous one for as long as it doubted its own self-sufficiency. If France possessed such self-sufficiency, upon what principle was it based?[20]

With *Le Peuple* Michelet preceded his friend in making a full statement of their common conviction regarding what should be taught. He dedicated the work to Quinet:

This book is more than a book, it is myself. For this reason it belongs to you....

With justice you have remarked that our thoughts, spoken or not, agree always. We live from a single heart....A wonderful harmony which could surprise, but is it not natural? All the variety of our works has been rooted in the same source: the sentiment of France and the idea of the Fatherland.[21]

This dedication, and the like warmth of Quinet's dedication to Michelet of his *Le Christianisme et la Révolution française,* have frequently served to justify quoting one of the two men to suggest what the other thought regarding an issue on which he did not express an opinion. The practice is questionable enough. It is none the less true that Michelet and Quinet were never so close as during the last days of the July Monarchy, and that both were steadfast in their adherence to the first principle they held in common: France's mission was to lead humanity.

In the section "La Patrie," of *Le Peuple,* we find Michelet, like Quinet, grasping at patriotism as the common ground on which all classes of French society could unite. This was, of course, not new on the French scene. In 1795 Daunou had written that "in the midst of diverse cults, freely exercised, but submitted to the laws of the Republic, patriotism will soon become the common cult of all Frenchmen." He asked what agency could be a better instrument of this "general conciliation" than public instruction. Michelet, indeed, asked for much more than this. The fatherland should be taught as a religion, indoctrinated from the first day of the primary school program. Monolithic loyalty to the ideas of '89, and a profound sense of the holy mission of France to give the world spiritual and intellectual leadership, was the cult Michelet believed the school must serve.

The first problem in politics was education. The second problem in politics was education. And the third? Education! The first question in education was: "Do you have faith? do you instil faith?" For the child must believe. The child must believe that "La patrie, ma patrie peut seule sauver le monde."[22]

For Quinet the ideal would have been to unite indissolubly the religion of the fatherland and lay science in the same system of education. Before his audience at the College of France he had claimed his purpose to be the creation of an all-inclusive system, "more Catholic than Rome." After 1848 he felt a new and permanent urgency that this faith be implanted in youth at the earliest age. More than the fate of France was at stake. *L'Enseignement du Peuple* concluded: "If ever the destruction of the French fatherland should be consummated, all the world would be swallowed up in that death. Then truly the death of Achilles, all and entire the ancient world would be sacrificed on that tomb."[23]

But what of the practical reality, the religious conditions of French society? Quinet restated a now familiar idea, here as an explanation of the limitations of what could be accomplished immediately in France. What had occurred on the political scene had been but the reflection of what existed in the religious world. Religion, he repeated, was the ideal toward which the nation tended, and which it progressively realized in its civil institutions. A people who had lost the idea of God, by the same token, lost all ideal. Quinet could not imagine how it could continue to orient its collective life. Unable to orient her collective life, what was reasonable to demand of France?

Quinet believed he had proven two laws to be axiomatic: Catholic states perish; political liberty cannot be realized in a Catholic state. Thus the only answer for France was complete separation of Church and State. Two means existed by which a nation might escape the ruin which accompanied the decline of its religion (in Quinet's sense of the term). By far the more desirable was a religious revolution, a substitution of a new faith for the old. The inferior choice, but one forced upon a nation without positive faith, was to separate absolutely lay and ecclesiastical society. Quinet believed that it was not only an inferior method, but one which could only be effective upon the condition that the separation be total. Nor was he sanguine about the promptitude with which France might follow even the second course. In spite of the debate since February, 1848 about "liberty," he noted that salaries had been voted for the clergy almost without discussion. By that action "liberty" had been rendered impossible.[24]

Three proposals were made by Quinet: first, suppress salaries of the clergy; second, make education free and compulsory; third, separate lay education and ecclesiastical education of particular sects. Everything depended upon meeting the last condition. Only by adherence to this third rule could the national unity of France and true liberty of conscience be obtained. Otherwise each religion and each dogma would have its own schools, or all would have representation in every school. In the first instance as many nations as communions would result; in the second all beliefs would necessarily be taught by one person who could do justice only to his own.[25]

There was not a little irony in the fact that this work, in which Quinet presented a program far removed from that he would have wished were possible for France, is the one for which he has been primarily remembered. If ideas influence events no other suggestion of Quinet had nearly so important an effect on later French history. Nor should it escape one that the real objective is hidden. Separation of Church and State accompanied by free and compulsory education at State schools, in which no positive religion would be allowed an influence or a voice, was a daring and aggressive demand. If it were met, monopoly would be truly gained. Quinet was finding himself. Events continued to light the way.

Napoleon was swept into the presidency in December, 1848. The following May the Constituent Assembly gave way to the Legislative Assembly, after elections in which the deceit of April,

1848 was scorned. Monarchists of every stripe, legitimists, Orlean-
ists, Bonapartists, and Catholics united behind the program of Order,
Family, and Property. Falloux, who took the position at the behest
of Dupanloup, was Minister of Public Instruction in Napoleon's
first cabinet. In this capacity he held up discussion of an education
bill during the last months of the Constituent Assembly. In June
he submitted to the Legislative Assembly a bill drawn up by an
extra-parliamentary commission which had been headed by himself,
and which had included Montalembert, Dupanloup, Thiers, De
Riancey, and six (out of the total twenty-four on the commission)
representatives of the University. On June 13 the demonstration led
by Ledru-Rollin against the expedition to Rome was crushed; after
the clerical victory at Rome came Montalembert's "domestic Roman
campaign."

The Church recognized the right of the State, or University, to
have a voice in the regulation of primary and secondary education,
and the State accepted the participation of the Church in the direction of the University. The Falloux law, "in the thought of the
Minister and of his friends" ought to have been the "great charter
of clerical education in France." When more than "liberty" was
offered, liberty was compromised. Montalembert had done what he
had criticized the Church for doing under the Restoration. The
Church made a pact with the State, and tied itself to the social policies of the bourgeoisie, as in the past it had wedded itself to the
program of Charles X. Seignobos aptly termed the law "a political
measure for the defense of society against the revolution."[26]

The result did not meet either the dire or hopeful expectations
of the contesting parties. Liberty of education, invoked to justify
the bill, was no more accomplished than the supremacy which had
been hoped for. The Church did become a more powerful rival of
the State; but the conclusion that by the measure French youth was
cut into two masses "oriented in opposite directions," and that one
is thus forced to see in the law "one of the decisive events of the
nineteenth century,"[27] is difficult to defend. Such had been the
prophecy of Thiers and Cousin with respect to similar proposals
before 1848. Quinet continued to make the same forecast. But was
the law at fault, or did it only serve to intensify a struggle between
two adversaries of too nearly similar strength and staying power to

hope that one of them might, in anything less than generations, reduce the other to unimportance?

The events following February, 1848 forced many besides Quinet to reconsider certain past and easy premises. The most difficult paradox was the attitude of the middle class. A particularly popular liberal shibboleth had always held that freedom from economic want made independence of judgment in political matters possible. The aftermath of the February Revolution brought home with particular force quite another suggestion, and Quinet concluded that the servitude of man's intelligence seemed rather to augment in proportion to his wealth. He remarked that it was a singular material independence which had for condition the absolute servitude of the mind and soul.[28] The actions of the educated suggested disturbing things about the nature of man, but this was not what gave him pause. His suspicion that the bourgeoisie was unsound was in a sense only justified. But the *people,* the people who had seemed inspired when Quinet addressed the College of France in March, 1848, what of them?

Flaubert described Paris on February 23, 1848:

—Plus de missions!
—Plus de baccalauréat!
— À bas les grades universitaires!
—Conservons-les, dit Sénécal, mais qu'ils soient conférés par le suffrage universel, par le Peuple, seul vrai juge![29]

Edgar Quinet was never Sénécal, but in the hour of victory declared:

See and weigh that lesson! All seemed lost according to calculation or human wisdom, at the moment when all was won and saved by the inspiration, by the instinct, by the divine genius of the masses. The people, naked, pressed on by wisdom from on high, by the folly of the cross, consummated the impossible.[30]

Came April, June, and December, the expedition to Rome, the Falloux law, all leading to December 2, 1851, each and all approved by a majority of Frenchmen. Helpless in the path of an inexorable tide Quinet sat in the Legislative Assembly, voting with the minority, turning out brochures of hopeless protest,[31] and, in the fall of 1851, publishing the second volume of *Révolutions d'Italie*. Minna Quinet died in March, 1851.

For as long as reaction seemed to have a tint of legality Quinet remained within the bounds of loyal opposition. On the morning of December 2 he escaped arrest, and remained underground in Paris until further resistance had become hopeless. He then fled to Brussels, where he arrived on December 11. An eighteen-year exile had begun. He was assisted in his flight by a Mme Asky, whom he married in July, 1852.[32]

Late in 1852 the last volume of *Révolutions d'Italie* was published; it was a resumé of Quinet's *"histoire morale de décembre 1851 à juillet 1852."* He wrote of recent events in Italy; the French parallel was his real concern. At the College of France the unequivocal incompatibility of the two authorities struggling for control had been Quinet's theme, but conclusions with respect to policy had not been clearly formulated. Now the age of innocence was past. The very nature of things decreed that either Catholicism or the French Revolution would destroy the other. The day when the Revolution became imbued with a willingness to make a settlement with its eternal enemy it delivered itself bound and gagged.

The defeat of the Revolution in Italy and France, Quinet wrote, had come about largely because of the attitude of the masses. The hatred of the majority of the Italian people for the Revolution was the work of Jesuit education, well done and achieved in silence. By means of that education men had been riveted to servitude, spiritual slavery had become the very flesh of the people, and they had lost all desire to be freed. As always religion had determined politics. In France the July Monarchy had fallen for having too greatly despised the people, the Republic for having esteemed them too highly. Each Catholic people was like a child; eternally in tutelage it sought a master, and if not given one it imposed one upon you.[33] This thought was on the morning of disaster; time brought it to maturity.

One may believe that had the Second Republic prevailed, had reaction stopped short of Napoleon III, Quinet, remaining in France, in all probability devoting his efforts to political activity, would have spent his energies in holding the line here, in winning a concession there, and that in time he would have become, much more typically than was ever to be the case, a spokesman of the "left." But the opinion of an electorate need never concern him in exile—bitter and isolated, a more serious and less sanguine vision came to him. He set his course in the closing lines of his work on Italy:

I commenced this work, and I conclude it, in dedicating it to the Italian exile, precursor of all the exiles of the earth....

But you who live with right, wherever you may be, if you remain true to yourself you are in the land of your father. They cannot take from you the city of the conscience. You nourish the flame of justice; would you then believe yourself absent from your foyer?

If the fatherland dies become yourself the ideal of the new fatherland. In order to remake a world what is required? A grain of sand, a fixed point, pure and luminous. Strive to become that incorruptible point.

Be a conscience. To form a new world but awaits to encounter an atom of truth in the emptiness of deserted heavens.[34]

Croce wrote of those in France who refused to submit in 1851: "We are still moved today by the pages written at this time by De Tocqueville, Quinet, Prévost-Paradol, and other men of their type."[35] Such a statement highlights the difficulties inherent in such generalizations. No "type" can be represented by so divergent a trio. But Croce's lines on "the poet militant," who exemplified the "liberal ideal," aid one to understand Quinet's personal evaluation of his own exile. And there is little room for argument with the Italian liberal's belief that Quinet responded nobly to this cruel culmination of all his hopes.

10. *Exile and Maturity*

DURING the greater part of the first seven years following his December, 1851 flight from France, Quinet resided in Brussels. Here he and the second Mme Quinet were members of a small French colony of political refugees. Earning a livelihood was not a problem for the self-exiled prophet after his marriage in 1852. Mme Quinet enjoyed a modest private income and the couple, if not affluent, did not suffer want. Many others in their banished company did.

The feverish intensity of Quinet's literary activity during these years in Belgium culminated in a near physical and mental breakdown in 1857. First he completed the third volume of his *Les Révolutions d'Italie.* Next he published *Les Esclaves,* a tragedy in verse which was never produced and was practically never read. *Marnix de Sainte-Aldegonde, Les Roumains, Lettre à Sue, La Révolution religieuse au XIXe Siècle, L'Histoire de la Campagne de 1815* (which was not published until 1861), *Histoire de mes Idées,* and the preparation of his ten-volume *Oeuvres complètes* for publication followed. The purpose of every line Quinet wrote was the same: reawaken the French conscience. His determination to remain outside France until his country repudiated the despot who had overthrown legitimate government was unwavering.

Orsini's unsuccessful attempt to assassinate Napoleon III led, indirectly, to Quinet's decision, made six months later in June, 1858, to move to Switzerland. After the Orsini incident the Belgian authorities were constrained to maintain more rigid surveillance over the activities of political exiles within their borders, and Quinet and his wife found the resulting situation unbearable. In September, 1858 the couple moved to the hamlet of Veytaux, at the eastern extremity of Lake Geneva, where they remained until September 6, 1870. *Merlin l'Enchanteur, La Révolution,* and *La Création* were the products of this period. Except for the summer months, the Quinets lived in seclusion until the last years of their stay in Switz-

erland. But during the season of clement weather friends and admirers made the pilgrimage to the exile's retreat. After 1865 Quinet
found increasing pleasure in the society of Geneva's *beau monde,*
and the harshest weeks of winter came to be spent in that city.
During the final year of the Second Empire he did a considerable
amount of writing for the opposition press.[1]

Sedan was the signal for Quinet's immediate return to France.
News that a provisional government had been established reached
him on September 5; within forty-eight hours he arrived in Paris.
Not only France, but Quinet as well, had changed during the long
interval.

Modern liberties are several. In practical politics their enjoyment depends upon the existence of certain institutional arrangements. Their bedrock foundation is the recognition of rights believed
to be "natural," or accepted as being so. What rights are "natural"
is as much a subject for debate as are questions relating to the institutions necessary to liberty in a given environmental setting. And
representatives of Revolutionary France were as noisy and as narrow
in their defense of their private political theology as the human
record would lead us to expect. In 1849 Quinet had asked that
secondary questions be put aside in the face of a fundamental embarrassment. First and above all freedom of thought must be guaranteed—once this had been granted he would be generous regarding
all the rest. On this "right" liberty was based; there could be no
denial of one without the destruction of the other. Truth proved
itself by prevailing; its right to expression was the guarantee of
progress. Error fled before it.

The coup d'état of Louis Napoleon brought about the comple-
tion of Quinet's thought. According to his past definition, one valid
enough, he began to preach the destruction of liberty. The exclusive
possession of absolute truth logically justifies intolerance: is it not
stupid to permit the growth of error when one is armed with the
sole means of universal salvation? Out of the unshakable conviction
that Providence stood revealed in the Revolution and in his own
secularized Christianity, Quinet embraced the logic of faith.

Faltering steps were taken in the disillusion of the summer of
1848. Quinet, confronted by the problems facing a democracy
brought into being in a corrupt age, concluded that any democracy

which emerged with the long habit of servitude, without taking any precautions against its enemies, necessarily became their dupe. In order that the philanthropic laws of democracy be applied and survive it was necessary that men already be changed and improved by the laws of democracy. The Gordian knot—now draw the sword: Quinet did.

It is a favorite idea of the liberalism of our day that brute force can do absolutely nothing against ideas. As for me, I confess not to have the same conviction of that helplessness.... When I consider that men of theory themselves reject the force which God sometimes places in their hands, and which they tremble to use, I ask myself if this is not an indication of scepticism rather than assurance. A certain degree of faith is always necessary in order to dare touch the ax.[2]

This was somewhat disingenuous. Liberalism did not hold that force could do nothing against ideas, but that the use of force in such matters was an evil thing.

Quinet found after 1852 that his former liberal idealism failed to explain the tragic course of recent history; he adjusted his philosophy to the event. The transformation included three important judgments. First in importance was his discovery of what he insisted was a law of history: Catholicism can only be destroyed by force. Second, he faced the logic of his own past attitudes and publicly re-evaluated the Revolution itself, and, in judging it a failure, placed that failure at the door of the unfortunate fact that the Reformation had been stamped out in France. Last, he turned in a bitter attack upon historicism, and upon the optimism of *tout est bien*. The three conclusions were consistent with his basic concept that a people's religious belief determined its history. All that he jettisoned was liberalism.

THE LAST VOLUME of *Révolutions d'Italie* saw the author face up to the accusation that he was foreign to the philosophy of his time. He confessed he did not believe that a nation could win freedom from slavery without putting iron to the service of right. Quinet could find no historical precedent for the belief that ideas prevailed without the necessity that one take up arms for them. The lesson of his own time in particular led him to persist in the conviction that

the sword, in certain instances, could accomplish more in a day
than all of the wisdom of the earth in several centuries.[3] Recent
personal experience in Paris, on the days between December 2 and
6, 1851, may be suspected to have been large in his mind as he
wrote these words. The first two years of exile were devoted to a
work which completed their meaning.

Marnix de Sainte-Aldegonde, which appeared in 1854, was
frankly didactic. In his introduction to the work Quinet announced
that each forgotten historical figure who reappeared, as his subject
was doing, brought with him some forgotten and needed message.
The three lessons taught by a study of the life of Marnix were: the
perfect accord of his life and his word; the fact that he had understood all things in the light of his religion; and the fact that he
had realized the *necessity* for intolerance. Quinet examined a revolution which had succeeded. He found that these were the reasons
for its success and that failure marked any contrary course.

The Reformation, Quinet wrote, had been the face which liberty
had shown to the world at the close of the Middle Ages. It was
too often ignored that those peoples who had been unable to con-
quer that liberty had to the present remained powerless to establish
any other. The obvious question then became, where and how had
the Reformation succeeded? Only by violence, by stern and ruthless
intolerance, had the germs of Protestantism been destroyed in the
southern provinces of the Low Countries. Quinet believed that it
would be easier still to show that everywhere Protestantism had left
liberty to the Catholic Church the Reformation had promptly disappeared without trace.[4]

How exactly history seemed to repeat itself! Writing of the
conference at which the Dutch had refused the Catholic offer that
universal suffrage be instituted in all of the provinces, Quinet asked
the secret of the Protestant minority's wisdom. The simple answer
was that the Dutch had possessed the firm resolve to be victorious,
the unshakable resolution not to cede their victory to a demand of
logic. The author knew that the moment any revolution was victorious the invitation that it perish for the honor of its principles
came from all sides, and that it was rare that such an invitation did
not win a majority. History, however, hated the dupe and put him
almost at the level of the guilty. This, Quinet concluded, was but

half an injustice; to be abused was almost always to be in a false
situation.[5]

Before man in the majority could recognize the higher truth all
means of communicating with him must be seized and held. This
was the logic of the position Quinet now took. It differed from that
of De Maistre in the authority it would make of the Pope. Not that
what Quinet described as having been the Dutch example could, in
any sense, have been duplicated in the France of 1848. The intima-
tion that, on the morning of the February Revolution, suffrage
might have been arranged to give complete power to the minority
who shared his opinions, or that these men might themselves have
prevented any elections whatsoever, was pure fantasy. Quinet himself had dreamed of no such possibility.

The forces of "disorder" were vanquished in June, and Quinet
had chosen against them. Where, indeed, might he have found
allies? Croce wrote that the Catholic Church posed problems for
liberalism which, "in certain particular cases," permitted that a
"rigorous and radical procedure" be used against it. Favorable conditions for such a procedure must first be prepared by the Church,
by its "indiscretion and disregard for moral sentiments." The certain
"particular case," seemingly, would then be at hand.[6] This was to
say that a willing public opinion was a necessary condition of success.
In France the Dreyfus case provided it. In 1848 the Church, to state
the matter cautiously, was less unpopular than was usual during the
nineteenth century. Quinet, however, less willing than Croce to
weigh the politically feasible against the program he wished to implement, made no concession to reality. The Italian Liberal also
described the necessity governments sometimes feel, in periods of
society's mental and moral depression, "for an alliance with the not
always distinguished forces the Church has at her disposal." The
practice need not be put in such censorious language, but one
instance of the phenomenon was displayed by the Provisional Government. The group from the *National,* which was in control, shared
much of Quinet's anti-Catholicism. These men, however, did not act
blindly, but with deliberate purpose. It was quite another thing to
share Quinet's religious convictions, and this was the difference.

The Dutch revolution, the exile wrote, had succeeded because
it had been based upon a religious revolution; because it had dared

to take itself seriously, and to give itself time to take root before granting amnesty to the adversary. It had dared to use the ax. The provinces in which the revolution had failed had evidenced a different logic and had paid the price.

The lesson for the present was spelled out in detail in Quinet's later writing. He denied that religious unity or another universal church was possible, and criticized those who seemingly strove for such a goal. To propose a universal acceptance of a particular sect or formula was to wish for the rebirth of the past at the moment of rejecting it. A universal church or universal philosophy was impossible in the face of modern individualism; those who dreamed of either had not truly thrown off the Catholic heritage.[7] So Quinet wrote, but with less than complete sincerity, and more to disparage the Saint-Simonians than to express his true position. He too asked for unity after all, demanding a universal attack upon Catholicism. Proposing neither a system nor a dogma, though suggesting that the faith of the *Vicaire savoyard,* and its almost exact counterpart, Unitarianism, could most easily be conciliated with the modern age, Quinet demanded an alliance "of all free minds" in order to break in common the "spirit which possessed and sterilized the earth."[8]

The world of enlightened men should, he advised, concentrate every energy upon the point which was the center of all attacks directed against reason: the Roman Church. The defender of the Church was invited to speak his mind, but to speak of conciliation between Catholicism and Democracy was now unforgivable; the incompatibility was complete. Self-deception on this matter was criminal.[9]

The thought embodied in the above paragraphs is the basis for the frequent statement that Quinet desired a Protestant Reformation for France. Ruggiero noted that Liberalism, although less utopian than the democratic or socialist school, demanded a religious reformation "necessitated by the hostility of the Roman Church towards its social and political programme." The Italian Liberal added: "In Quinet and his successors the idea often appears that the Catholic countries must have a Protestant Reformation of their own, if they wished to raise themselves to the level of other nations."[10] Putting the matter in this light distorts not only Quinet's thought, but his motivation as well. First, it need hardly be said that few

panaceas were more utopian than that which Quinet offered to
France. Also, Quinet's politics and his religion were one. The
increased intensity of his attack upon the Roman Church after 1848
is to be attributed, not to a greater antagonism to the philosophy and
politics of Catholicism (for some time previously his hatred had
been total), but to his sudden awareness of the extent of the power
which the Church wielded in France. Quinet's fury became ruthless
when he saw that the majority of Frenchmen believed more in their
priests than in prophets of the philosophy of the Revolution. The
Church gained steadily in France after 1830. During the Restoration the alliance between throne and altar had been in defiance of
French opinion. Under the Second Empire political opportunism
seemed to advise close ties between Church and State. These developments are important to an understanding of Quinet's progressive
intolerance. He wished to raise France to the "level" of no other
country, but to the height of her own destiny.

Near the end of his stay in Belgium Quinet wrote that those in
authority who would undertake to uproot superstition should remove
that superstition from the people and render its exercise *absolutely
and materially impossible,* at the same time removing all hope that
it might ever be reborn. There were indeed several ways of van-
quishing an outworn religion, but first among them was the use of
force by the established authority. Whatever one might say of
this means, Quinet believed it was the only one which ever succeeded in destroying an ancient belief. There had never been a
religion so senseless or so absurd that it had been possible to erase
it from earth solely by freedom of speech. Although the whole
world repeated that force could accomplish nothing against ideas,
the whole world was witness to the contrary.[11]

The first volume of the first edition of Quinet's *Révolution* was
published in 1865, and aroused a storm of protest from many who
had never been critical of Quinet before. Although his message of
intolerance was not the primary cause of this protest, Quinet was,
for the first time, widely charged with this sin. The *Critique de la
Révolution,* which was first published in January, 1867, and which
was printed as an introduction to *La Révolution* in all subsequent
editions of the longer work, was the author's answer to these critics.
In defending himself against the charge of having preached intoler-

ance Quinet retracted nothing; his defense resolved itself in the statement that tolerance was a virtue, but that intolerance was permissible against the intolerant, that is to say against the Catholic. His one concession was that separation of Church and State was all one could possibly hope for in France.[12]

Quinet defeated his own purpose when he wrote that Catholics of the De Maistre school, who vaunted the necessity for the Inquisition in the past, would never convince him that they were now friends of liberty until they renounced in the past what they pretended to renounce in the present. This covered his own case, in so far as it touched upon the past. His own renunciation of intolerance for the present was not sincere.

An attack upon the revolutionary Terror, much more than Quinet's views on intolerance, explains the unfriendly response his former friends gave *La Révolution*. In this work he repeated that indifference could never destroy a religion; a religion never died unless "the formal order was given" it to do so. But what Quinet attacked in the Terror was not its intolerance. He attacked its uselessness. Comparing Danton and Robespierre with Moses, the Terror of the Revolution with Hebrew terrorism, he concluded that if Moses had been content to entrain the Jews in the desert, while allowing them to carry with them their ancient idols, his people would not have failed to return to the spirit of Egypt. In vain Moses would have redoubled his menaces and exterminations; he would have killed without profit for the future, and the blood uselessly spilt would have cried out against him. Danton and Robespierre were remembered just as Moses would have been. The less they had dared as regarded Catholicism, the more they dared in the nonreligious field. Such audacity was sterile. The Jacobins had used the right weapon, but not against the right enemy. When Quinet defended himself against the charge of intolerance, by pointing out his opposition to the Terror, he indulged in a form of deceit he professed to detest in others.[13]

Quinet's new history did have real significance. He re-evaluated the Revolution. As late as 1849 he still wrote of the Revolution as a religious transformation which had endowed men moved by its spirit with unnatural powers, as a movement confident of its self-sufficiency, and thus capable of mighty accomplishments. Decem-

ber 2, 1851, following as it did upon a long series of like deceptions
for men of his faith, seemed to demand that one re-examine a
received interpretation of the Revolution itself. How speak of success after the experience of the years between 1830 and 1851? For
Quinet the courage to do so finally failed, and the question became
something else.

No other historical work by Quinet ever received much praise
from a representative of the "scientific" dispensation in the field of
historical writing. But when Aulard opened his course on the French
Revolution at the Sorbonne he said of Quinet:

It is proper that his name be mentioned with respect at the opening of
a course in the history of the French Revolution.... For, if this course
is possible, if it exists, it is because Edgar Quinet wrote. Yes, his work,
worthy of Montesquieu, truly inaugurated the critical study of the
Revolution.[14]

La Révolution was undertaken, the author declared, in order to
discover the laws which might explain why such prodigious efforts
had failed. For events had pressed upon Quinet the inescapable conclusion that the result had not been commensurate with the cost it
had entailed. But he need not have searched far for causes. The
Revolution could be explained by squaring it with the view that
political history takes its shape from the religious faith of a people.
Although he had frequently criticized his nation for making the
same assumption, in this work Quinet assumed that a positive
religion was meant by "religion." This done, the failure of the
Revolution was apparent. Where could one find the religion of liberty professed by a Kléber? Where were its rites, its altars? It had
disappeared from the souls of men more completely than from the
material world.[15]

His colleagues greeted the work with pained astonishment. It
seemed to Quinet that their attitude was a quite Catholic one. They
asked that all adherents of the Revolution "believe all or renounce
the whole." The Revolution, Quinet wrote, was not a supernatural
fact. He insisted that one might examine it without being against it.
Theologians judged men according to their theology, rather than
after their actions and character, but he refused to write as a
theologian of the Revolution. Professing his willingness to sacrifice

his life for democracy, Quinet declared that he would not sacrifice justice and reason upon any altar. The moment was overdue to break out of the iron circle of attributing results to fate. The necessity of things had not made the Terror; false ideas were to blame.[16]

In *Le Christianisme et la Révolution* Quinet had confronted the paradox that France, alone among modern nations, had carried out a political revolution before having consummated a religious one. Logically he should have found this impossible, and he had escaped the dilemma by stressing the positive faith of the eighteenth century and by making this a type of "religious" revolution. Now that his optimism had fled he concluded that really there had been no revolution at all, failing a truly religious one. In the 1845 lectures he had pointed out the Catholic characteristics of the post-1789 upheaval, and this far his later *Révolution* had been foreshadowed. In the former work Quinet pointed out that the English and American revolutions had known nothing which compared with the Terror, and explained that both had been born of Protestantism; whereas France, obliged to break out of the confines of Catholicism, had found it impossible to escape the tradition of intolerance and infallibility. This was of course before Quinet himself had begun to insist upon the virtues of intolerance. Not only were the evils of the Revolution to be attributed to the Catholic heritage, but almost nothing of value had been won without borrowing from the traditions of the Church. The virtue of proselytism and the tendencies toward universality and toward greater political unity and centralization were Catholic in inspiration. The face of Catholicism had changed; its spirit remained. The discrepancies between this and his still traditional view regarding the greatness of the Revolutionary accomplishment were not apparent to Quinet until later.[17]

In *La Révolution* Quinet remarked that to judge if a revolution had succeeded only one question need be answered: had men been changed? Upon this basis the failure of the French Revolution was apparent, for in reality an ideal, a flag, several slogans about justice were all Quinet believed remained of the great political upheaval. Three words left to the world as heritage, and millions vainly dead for them. There was something sublime in this, but sublime failure. The only permanent act of the Revolution, the establishment of civil equality, had been accomplished without struggle and by common consent, had taken place "by itself." After August 5, 1789 there had remained "the problem of liberty," that is to say the whole difficulty. Political and religious questions had unchained the furies.[18]

By definition a revolution was the transformation of a religious ideal. Quinet repeated that no great revolution had failed to have the pre-existing religion for its most bitter antagonist; no victory had ever been won unless the old faith had been repressed until such time as new moral habits had been imprinted upon the nation. He granted that the position of France had been difficult. In no epoch in its past had the nation known liberty. Accustomed to passive obedience after having passed ten centuries upon its knees, it had found three years too short greatly to modify its posture.[19]

Quinet attributed a large part of the failure of the Revolution to the fact that the Reformation had not won France from Catholicism. Seemingly the other peoples of Europe who had known or found liberty had seen it supported upon a tripod of the Reformation, the Renaissance, and philosophy. The revocation of the Edict of Nantes was thus one of the most decisive acts in the history of France; the support of the Reformation had been taken from French liberty. The tripod *chancela comme dans le vide.*[20]

Although the difficulty had been great, the error of the Revolution was no less. Leaders had found themselves before an obstacle, the people being separated from their chiefs by the long habit of superstition. But when the leadership convinced itself that it was impossible for the people to cross the gulf, and, from fear of being brought into dispute with the masses, chiefs imposed upon themselves respect for superstition Quinet believed they had voluntarily placed themselves in a hopeless position. They put to death anyone who wished to attack Catholicism, thus engaging themselves, out of respect for the people, to respect what enslaved the people. Leaders who believed themselves powerless to change anything in the domain of the spirit became so in fact.

A religion for the people was necessary! The harshness of his past attacks upon this aspect of official eclectic doctrine did not prevent Quinet from now taking a similar position. He now argued that the course of the Revolution proved how little attraction vague philosophical concepts held for a people long bound to a positive faith. The enlightened author warned those who believed that science would one day replace religion that they poorly understood the nature of man. For although science and religion drew ever nearer, there would always be questions which science could not answer, and these mysteries would form the inexhaustible source of future religions. The failure of leaders of the Revolution to realize the need for a positive religion for the people, so that Catholicism might have been destroyed with the consent of the masses, had meant the failure of the Revolution. As always Quinet used history to teach by example, forming the past into well-ordered battalions. He had some conception of what was impossible in the present, but was impatient with the past for having failed to accomplish miracles.[21]

Robespierre was blamed. He had undertaken to elevate a small edifice of Greek or Roman style upon a Gothic base, and this impossible architecture had crumbled of itself as he built. He rendered a revolution impossible, thinking he had saved it. The hope to preserve Catholicism for the masses and create a cult of a Supreme Being for official adepts had been doomed to failure.[22] But the modification Quinet made was one of degree, not of kind. As he would have given a monopoly to truth and exterminated error, so truth itself must exercise caution, and must satisfy the common taste for a positive religion with external trappings. Philosophy was for the elite. He did not cite Cousin.

Another matter Quinet particularly stressed in his post-1852 writings was the responsibility of the historian "to fill in the midst of the drama of events the office of the antique choir. . . ." Thus the historian should maintain and proclaim justice, "in spite of good or bad fortune." The adherents of the doctrine of progress, however, did not seem indifferent to historical crimes, but determined to justify them. The lessons of history could never be learned, thought Quinet, until all actions, independent of time and place, were measured against an absolute and immutable standard. Thierry and Buchez and Roux became celebrated for their rehabilitation of the great crimes of history. They justified all that occurred in the annals of France upon the plea of necessity; all failures of the past had been "premature."[23] Quinet had first paid special attention to the evil these men practiced in his *Philosophie de l'Histoire de France* of 1855:

Le tout est bien may be understood and maintained to a certain point if one applies it as did Leibnitz, to the whole, to the universe and to humanity, which survives and heals the wounds it has made. But if you apply the same maxim blindly, as did Candide, to the particular history of each nation, of each man, if the faults of people and of individuals produce nothing but the greatest good, if their servility makes their liberty, if their vices engender their virtues, the moral order is abolished. History is no longer the great judgment of the Eternal. You remove justice with conscience; much more, you remove reality.[24]

Quinet was a patriot. He wrote history. But he was no relation of the nationalist historian. Whatever his shortcomings, he was vastly superior to the ordinary twentieth-century historian who in describing the facts tends always to justify them. He damned French historians who, confident that past suffering was the necessary road to the political rights by which the nation's history was crowned, dealt only in praise. He might have found the result amusing if the effect of such thinking had not been so tragic. Quinet outlined a few of the examples which he found most ridiculous. One excused arbitrary authority under the *ancien régime* because it had been needed to organize equality; in the new France arbitrary authority seemed necessary in order to organize liberty; next one arrived at the providential necessity for the despotism of the Terror, which engendered the necessity, more providential than before, of a despotism which overthrew and succeeded it. The procedure could be continued up to the moment at which he wrote; the only virtue was force, and what was supported and justified up to 1789 was deserted and condemned the moment force was detached from it.[25] Mid-twentieth-century national history demonstrates how pertinent this remains.

The exile cried that the doctrine of progress must cease to be perverted and made to cloak the infamies of the past. Proud to have made his contribution to the modern faith that man might advance, Quinet had never dreamed of the day when the doctrine would be formed into an instrument against all progress. The time had nevertheless arrived. Men concluded that man, whatever his activity, "doing good or evil, drinking, eating, and creeping served progress." Progress meant but one thing, the higher development of man's spirit, and Quinet felt that much of the difficulty which had arisen could be erased the moment this basic definition was re-established.²⁶ In praising the human race for what time added in the way of material results, one made it an infinite glory to man that the earth continued to turn.²⁷

Some years ago Ortega y Gasset described how our world of intensive specialization fashions doctors and scientists who are as much "mass men" as any day laborers. He made this circumstance the prominent feature of what he thought was a general return to barbarism. Long before, Quinet had warned that material progress, with its increased demands for specialization, held more danger than promise for the only type of progress which deserved the name. Quinet predicted that philosophy would come to be disdained because no one understood it any longer; only vanity would survive. The lowest would set himself up as a model for others, and the most intolerable of all possible situations would come to prevail: the necessity to endure and pay respect to the fatuousness of the slave. For although the development of mechanical contrivances demanded a more than equal development of the energies of the spirit, increasingly the spirit was buried beneath what one complacently termed a victory over nature. How ridiculous it was to imagine that railroads would bestow dignity, security, and liberty, without man's lifting his finger:

> I wish finally to take from you that last bit of self-deception. Servitude will outdistance you along those iron rails; it will be in advance of you if you have no other means of escaping it. Railroads will entrain none but the ideas you supply, and if it is to be a slave conception rails, steam, electricity, will be able to transport nothing but your slavery to the ends of the earth.²⁸

Materialism was that slavery.

Such were Quinet's conclusions. During the last years of the Second Empire the political climate of France grew more promising, and Quinet again began to devote effort to influencing opinion along specific lines of policy by taking part in the polemic of day-to-day political discussion. Sedan permitted him to return to the fatherland and to give the last five years of his life to the fight for republican institutions in France. The mutable application of immutable principles became a duty, but by neither word nor act did he retract the conclusions of exile.

11. *Conclusion*

IN THE EARLY MORNING of September 7, 1870, Quinet arrived in Paris. Hugo, too, came home. On the ninth, appeals to the people from both men were printed by the mayor of Paris and posted throughout the city. Quinet's concluded: "Nous combattrons en pleine lumière; nous défendrons la cause du genre humain. Cette cause ne peut périr."[1] Soon the Prussians surrounded Paris. During the siege Quinet's constant and passionate appeals to the people for continued resistance always bespoke the absolute certainty of eventual victory.[2]

In the elections of February, 1871, "the only collective influence was that of the clergy"; the most unexpected result (the resurrection of the Legitimist party) "was chiefly explicable" by their intervention. The enemy had not changed. But in Paris, at least, opinion differed. Running as a representative of the party demanding a continuation of the war with Prussia, Quinet was paid a stirring tribute by the electors of the Seine. The department sent forty-three members to the National Assembly, and Quinet was fifth on this list. Only Louis Blanc, Victor Hugo, Gambetta, and Garibaldi received more votes.

The new Assembly met at Bordeaux. In a state of illness which seemed almost certain to be fatal, Quinet left Paris and arrived at the seat of the government in time for the first full meeting of the new body. Garibaldi, realizing that further resistance to the Germans was impossible, left for Caprera on the evening of the first day the Assembly met. He had been refused the privilege of addressing the body by the antirepublican majority which controlled it. Before departing he turned his spacious quarters over to Quinet.

Quinet promptly associated himself with the extreme left, signing the manifesto of this small group which declared that neither "the National Assembly nor the entire French nation has the smallest right to make a single Alsatian or Lorrainer a subject of

162

Prussia." Thus, mustering what energies remained to him, Quinet resisted to the end any peace settlement which signed away Alsace-Lorraine. Debate on this issue was held on March 1. Henri Martin, Brisson, Delescluze, Floquet, and Clemenceau had put down their names to speak for a continuation of the war. When the hour came all waived their right to do so. Jules Simon wrote: "What could they have said after such speakers as Victor Hugo, Edgar Quinet, Louis Blanc?"[3]

In spite of his broken health Quinet moved to Versailles with the National Assembly, and was present at every sitting of that body until his death in the spring of 1875. The most vehement adversaries of the Quinet who wrote *La Révolution* were Louis Blanc and Peyrat. At Versailles these two men became Quinet's political allies and his most intimate friends. This was natural. Gabriel Hanotaux noted that the work of Michelet and Quinet penetrated into the schools of the Empire and "had prepared fresh and ardent recruits for the Republican ideal."[4] But there had also developed a new school of republicans, a group who proclaimed the bankruptcy of the men of 1848, and who made expediency, not principle, the guiding factor in their policy. Their man was Gambetta, a republican who even as a youth had admired Cavour much more than either Garibaldi or Mazzini.

Writing of the years between 1865 and 1870 Juliette Adam noted the sharp separation between "un républicain humanitaire et scientifique et une républicaine idéaliste et nationale." She wondered if any event, even the proclamation of the Republic, could create unity between them. At the same time she was conscious that the new generation was increasingly attracted by positivist doctrines, and that an ever smaller group stayed true "to our great leaders, Ledru-Rollin, Victor Hugo, Edgar Quinet, Louis Blanc, Schloecher."[5] By 1870 Comte was master—the positivist had replaced the idealist of 1848. But the old leaders were still necessary to the party, particularly at election time.

Indeed Quinet was selected to be first president of the *Union républicaine,* formed at Versailles in the spring of 1871. But, as Mme Adam wrote, he was one of those ancestors "qu'on honore mais qui n'entrainent plus."[6] When, late in 1873, Gambetta frankly went over to a policy of "opportunism" Quinet was one of the five "intransigents" in the republican group who refused to follow him.

The establishment of the Republic hurried Quinet's death. His will was broken, "for the first time." In the weeks before the passage of the Wallon Amendment Quinet stood firm before the entreaties of Gambetta and his followers. On January 29, 1875, the Laboulaye Amendment was before the Assembly. It provided that the magic words "The Government of the Republic" introduce the clauses of the government bill establishing a two-chamber legislature. To be sure, the republican group had for months after February, 1871 denied the Assembly constituent powers, and had long campaigned for dissolution. And Gambetta, as late as 1873, had condemned a second chamber as the "outcome of an unnatural combination... an everlasting cause of strife." But the old formula, "Périsse la République plutôt qu'un principe," was now out of style.

On January 29 Quinet entered the Assembly determined to abstain from voting, and until the ballot was almost completed he, Louis Blanc, Madier de Montjau, Peyrat, and Marcou stood firm. Then the rumor spread that five more votes would carry the amendment. The rumor was false, but suited to "opportunism." Louis Blanc describes the incident: "We let ourselves be dragged to the tribune, and one after the other we threw our ballots into the box, amidst general excitement and the noise of plaudits which pierced our hearts...."[7] In spite of this sacrifice the amendment failed by twenty-three votes, but on the following day the Wallon Amendment succeeded. On this day a change of one vote would have sufficed to have placed the form of government in question. Quinet's spirit had been broken. On the thirtieth, with his four colleagues, he voted for the Wallon Amendment.

On February 25 the constitutional laws of the Senate were voted. The composition of the Senate was settled; the Republic was an accomplished fact. The extreme left did not vote. Louis Blanc described Quinet on this day. "He, too, stood his ground, but at what a cost! I can still see the grand old man collapsing into his seat, so overwrought that the tears were trickling down his cheeks."[8]

After his return from exile Quinet continued to write. *L'Esprit Nouveau,* which appeared in November, 1874 and was the last of his works published during his lifetime, went through three editions within one month. His health had improved in 1873, but the end was near. In February, 1874, he opened his newspaper to discover that Michelet was dead. Quinet had not been informed of his illness, but the misunderstandings of recent years did not assuage the survivor's grief. He told Edmond Adam, "C'est un appel, je ne lui survivrai pas longtemps...."⁹ Then a year later, suddenly and without warning, on March 27, 1875, Quinet died. On his desk over one hundred letters awaited reply. Republicans and democrats of Spain, Argentina, Italy, Portugal, England, Germany, Greece, and Switzerland were represented in that correspondence.¹⁰ His burial at Montparnasse was a great republican occasion. More than 100,000 heard Gambetta speak over his grave; this orator was unembarrassed by the audience which would have found Clemenceau a much more appropriate speaker. Victor Hugo also spoke.

When the news of the death reached Garibaldi he wrote that Edgar Quinet would have an immortal cult in the hearts of Italians, and of free men of all nations. Portuguese republicans sent word from Lisbon: "We cannot forget that Edgar Quinet is an apostle and emancipator of all persecuted and crushed nationalities.... He was one of our most revered friends, in all things he has the right to our gratitude."¹¹

In the year of the one-hundredth anniversary of his birth one of the principal streets of Bucharest was renamed in Quinet's honor. At that time a Roumanian statesman was profoundly certain "that the name of the hero would live eternally in the grateful hearts of the Roumanian people."¹²

Quinet was above all else a patriot and a religious thinker. That the essence of his nationalism was emphatically nearer to that embodied in Wilson's Fourteen Points than to that of Hitler and Mussolini, or even that of Barrès, is at least suggested by this European reputation. It is, in fact, said of Michelet that he held the political principles which were adopted at Versailles in 1919. But if Quinet's (and Michelet's) thought is maligned when it is said to be a direct line precursor of twentieth-century totalitarian philosophies, it must be remembered that Delcassé and Clemenceau belonged to the party which was most influenced by Quinet's form of patriotism. True, they too represented it but poorly—adequately enough only to suggest that the Fourteen Points is not exactly an example of it.

Hanotaux, himself a representative of Opportunism, was frank to admit that at the bottom of this idea "lies Nationalism." "Opportunism," he stated, "is eminently patriotic. The Collectivity 'France' is enough for it; there it limits its ideal."[13] This represents a perversion of all that Quinet stood for. Gambetta was just as far from Quinet on this score. In 1870 Garibaldi offered to command one of the armies of the *Défense nationale*. Gambetta's reply was peremptory: "La loi ne veut pas qu'un étranger commande à des soldats français...."[14] Quinet's quite different ideal is suggested by his reference to "the joyful sound of the cannon of Sedan."[15]

In spite of his consecrating his life to the history of his fatherland, Michelet belonged to the cosmopolitan tradition. As Oscar Haac notes, he believed only that no other nation served humanity so well as did France. This last brings us near to the reality of Quinet's belief. His disciple, Chassin, summed up his master's place by saying that he had given birth to a new genius, one which was neither German nor Italian, but French, "that is to say universal."[16] Quinet could have put it no better. In this sense Garibaldi was ever so much more "French" than officers of the Empire upon whom Gambetta placed his hopes in 1870. Quinet's cult of the nation was never independent of eternal values, but France was the chosen vehicle; hers was a mission "for the glory of the world." Spain and Italy were necessary to European society; they would be reborn only if France showed the way. If France receded a single step, if she denied her providential role, "the world would be thrown into confusion." *"Only* France had the religion of justice, the passion for justice."[17] But France was not always true to herself.

In the years between 1851 and 1870 Quinet was disheartened and angry that so many of his Republican friends cheered French diplomatic and military successes. When, in July, 1870, only ten members of the opposition in the French Chamber voted against war credits, he cried out, "Where is hope?"[18] Should France betray her mission to fulfil and complete for all of humanity the promise of 1789, her role could not be filled by another; but Quinet never followed the fatherland in error. "My country, right or wrong" was completely foreign to his outlook. He demanded from his people selflessness and dedication to a universal ideal. France failed again and again to fulfil the destiny he thought was hers. Quinet continued to believe that the world's best hope was in his fatherland, but between 1830 and 1875 France had few harsher critics.[19]

Three-quarters of a century later victory has gone to new barbarians. Quinet would almost certainly agree with those of his mid-twentieth century countrymen who accept this evaluation. Has the Roman Church been to blame? If not, Quinet was in error. His only logical position would have to be that French leadership has failed to establish itself because the nation could not free itself from the Catholic tradition. Would a Protestant France have changed all of modern history? This is hardly a serious question. It brings us to a problem of Quinet's religious thought. Was he a Protestant?

On frequent occasions during Quinet's lifetime it was suggested to him that his conversion to Protestantism was desirable. But Calvinism, Lutheranism, and Methodism were almost as distasteful to him as Catholicism. Mme Quinet assured Protestant missionaries that God was quite content with her husband's religious faith. She is our witness that Quinet privately reiterated that he did not wish to make France Protestant, that he believed the date too advanced.[20] On the other hand J. J. Kaspar, one of Quinet's early twentieth-century French Protestant admirers, wrote: "That religious revolution so ardently desired by Quinet, and which I wish as well, I hope that it might evolve out of a synthesis of the living forces of Protestantism, of free thought (one of whose leaders is E. Lavisse) and socialism (one of whose chiefs is Liebknecht)."[21]

Kaspar believed that Quinet never declared himself a Protestant because there was no real European equivalent of American Unitarianism. Quinet did know the work of Emerson, Channing, and Parker, and felt that their views were very near to his own. During the American Civil War he hoped for Lincoln to speak out more clearly on the slavery issue, "as would be worthy of the country" of those religious thinkers.[22] Not that one need cross either the Rhine or the Atlantic to discover the essence of his religious faith.

Of Émile he wrote, "C'est le plus bel ouvrage de Rousseau."[23] In Émile one finds Quinet's Protestantism. In France, however, the broad foundation for such a faith did not exist. The revocation of the Edict of Nantes was the most tragic event in the French past because it had destroyed the necessary base. Separation of Church and State, and a State monopoly of education was thus the most satisfactory solution possible—or the only one. The school was to inculcate the secular faith of the Revolution, and a religious transformation was to be accomplished in this fashion.

The practice of intolerance had to wait until such time as a State monopoly of education had done its work, until the proper climate of opinion had been created. When Cavour's program, "l'Église libre dans l'État libre," seemed to be having some appeal for French anticlericals, Quinet made the retort: "Autant vaudrait dire: Émancipez le Czarisme. Le Czar libre dans la Russie libre!"[24] For on the subject of Catholicism Quinet was a fanatic, which is to say that he was a fanatic pure and simple. In his own faith reposed truth; all which was antagonistic to it was evil and false. If Quinet's nationalism was neither intolerant nor exclusive, his religion was both and took precedence. He could not bear dissent, or compromise.

A faith in the authority of natural reason, man's free will, and a conscience through which God spoke in terms of immutable verities combined to form Quinet's religion. To choose deliberately to make man's essential sinfulness an article of faith, to deny thus the efficacy of reason, to preach resignation, to bolster all of this with appeals to superstition and to ignorance was simply evil. Ignorance could justify such a faith. In the absence of ignorance only perversity or an interest in keeping society in obedience or in chains could explain adherence to it.

The belief that sanity is not statistical is based upon this faith in natural reason, and in the knowledge that environment can corrupt the reasoning capacity in most men. Quinet was fanatical in the conviction that truth had been revealed to him, but was not serene in this certainty. The prevalence of error in the world and its repeated victories over truth in France itself did not cause him to doubt. Instead his emotionalism and dogmatism were increased by these accidents of circumstance.

Quinet was proud of the unity of his whole thought, and not entirely without reason. Taine characterized the speech of the Revolution by writing that facts had no place in it:

Never facts; nothing but abstractions, a stringing together of sentences on nature, reason, the people, tyrants, liberty—giving the effect of so many inflated balloons crowding and bouncing one another fruit-lessly in space. If one did not know that it all culminated in practical and terrible results, one would believe himself before a diversion in logic. . . .[25]

This, he believed, was the "final formula and the last word" of the spirit of French classicism. The great virtue of the French, according to Mme de Staël, was the degree to which they could be expected to set about applying abstract truth in the material world. Two and two must always be four. In this, as in most things, Quinet belonged more to the seventeenth than to the eighteenth century.

Though he divorced himself permanently from the cosmopoli-tanism of Mme de Staël, otherwise he was more than true to her heritage. He learned the wisdom of intolerance; he might have dis-covered its justification in her views on religion. In the midst of the uproar and the passionate criticism which followed the publica-tion of *La Révolution,* Quinet gave evidence that this had not escaped him. He replied to a friend's comment regarding Mme de Staël: "Yes, I believe that *cette belle âme inspirée* is on my side in this thing, and that she looks down on Veytaux with one of her kind and indulgent glances."[26]

What must be kept constantly in mind is the place Quinet holds in the Revolutionary tradition. Even Hans Kohn, who is not a dedicated partisan, writes: "Michelet and Quinet were no longer there to witness it—the former had died in 1874, the latter in 1875 —but the light of the liberal and humanitarian tradition which they had so faithfully tended burned on. . . ."[27] In Quinet's case it is hardly possible to speak of genuine liberalism. Not only do his con-clusions prevent one from doing so; there is also the fundamentally important matter of his methods. A part of the liberal tradition is a belief in the practical wisdom of intellectual integrity and ruthless self-criticism. This is the theory. The fact, in so far as Quinet is concerned, is something else.

The Catholic Church with its evil doctrines seemed to Quinet to be the strongest force barring the dissemination of the Revolu-tionary faith among all classes of the French nation. He attempted to make history prove that tragedy was in store for France if this Church were not destroyed. The ordering of history to his purposes was part of his grand strategy, and serious historical comment is rarely to be expected from him. By common consent *La Révolution* reveals him at his best as a historian. Quinet's method for pursuing truth may be judged by observing him at work. The most indulgent critic could do no better than to choose these volumes, a history in which he also summed up his thought on a subject which had consumed his interest during most of his life.

Late in the year 1861, after a period of several weeks during which Quinet spoke repeatedly of the need to "uplift, enlighten, and rehabilitate" the people, he turned to the writing of *La Révolution.* Previously he had conceived a work which he thought to entitle "Épîtres au Peuple," modeled on Paul, but discarded the notion in favor of the study now in question.[28] Croce spoke as a Liberal in his statement that "true history always strikes a warlike note for the battles of life." But this cannot be made the sole criterion, if "true history" is to exist.

Mme Quinet contended that her husband did some preparatory work on *La Révolution* before 1857 while in Brussels. In December, 1861, with the histories of Blanc, Barante, Thiers, De Tocqueville, and Michelet as his guides and sources, Quinet took up the work in earnest. The manuscript was ready for the publisher in August, 1863, but the personal papers of the *conventionnel* Baudot came into Quinet's hands just as he was preparing to send it off to Paris. Fitting these papers into the scheme of his narrative took the author until January, 1864. The work did not go on sale in Paris until November, 1865. Quinet sold the manuscript outright for 15,000 francs, the highest monetary return he realized from a single work. Three editions sold out in eight weeks.[29]

A note to Michelet's history, at the end of the final volume, was the only comment Quinet made on any of the studies which preceded his own. Michelet, upon whose labors so much of Quinet's history was based, found this unforgivable. He wrote to Quinet that Thiers and Lamartine had done no research, that Blanc had been reduced to copying him while refuting him. He, and he alone, in a labor of seven years, "had exhumed the Revolution of the Archives." Michelet protested that he did not write to his friend in this fashion because of "stupid vanity," but to point out the surprising absence of proper credit to the sole person who had *travé les voies.*[30]

To this evidence of his friend's displeasure Quinet replied dishonestly. "Science" was a word he had used frequently in his lifetime, but he explained that, in this instance,

My practice was to follow somewhat the Cartesian method. I abstained from reading the works which had preceded me in the field. As for your admirable history, I feared it particularly. In rereading it I might well have become discouraged and discontented with my own.

Thus I abstained systematically from rereading a work which no one admires more than I do.[31]

Eight hundred pages on ten years of history, Quinet would have Michelet believe, had been written out of his head. This was near enough to the truth. Chronology and other "facts" might be found in the secondary accounts and the memoirs of a few of the participants. Around this framework Quinet fitted his preconceived message. The past, like other men's ideas, existed to be shaped to a particular end. Ruggiero wrote of the Liberal's concern that the rule of reason not degenerate into the rule of dogma, and of the necessity "to insure that the triumph of truth shall not close the road to the laborious process by which truth itself is reached." The laborious process, in so far as Quinet was concerned, was for the rest of humanity. He personally, with those who shared his convictions, knew truth, at least to the degree to which it had been revealed to the mind of man. The problem for the present was to raise the nation to the high plateau on which he and his circle stood. With this accomplished, the future might then be free.

The leading anticlericals of the Third French Republic were the disciples of Edgar Quinet. A religious reformation did not take place in France, but the dissemination of Quinet's anti-Catholic program assisted in making possible the republican majorities of the Third Republic. In May, 1877, Gambetta, quoting Peyrat, declared, "Le cléricalisme? voilà l'ennemi." Such a statement was then opportunistic; political, not religious. Radical republicans, emphasizing "defense of civil society against the clerical invasion," were defeating Gambetta's preferred candidates in elections. Gambetta chose the right slogan. For almost two generations of French politics the parties of the Left could be marshaled under the banner of anticlericalism. Combination after combination was formed in which the sole common principle was antagonism to the Catholic Church. Quinet's greatest importance lies in his formulation of the doctrines and the prejudices which aided in binding these men together.

Brisson, Méline, Combes, and Ferry are only a few of the more conspicuous leaders of the Third Republic who owed a deeper debt to Quinet. At the age of twenty Brisson, inspired to a more fervent anti-Catholicism by reading *Marnix,* addressed himself to the exile. Quinet answered: "You who are young, take the flame of life which is seized from our hands and carry it forward." He replied to a letter from Jules Méline: "Continue . . . you and your young friends. Be our hope and our consolation."[32] In 1853 Combes was preparing himself to become a seminary professor. Reading Quinet helped to change his mind.[33]

For Quinet did have a kind of religious influence. Dansette does not exaggerate when he writes that the educational program Quinet advocated after 1850 "became that of the Third Republic." In 1882 Jules Ferry left the office of Minister of Public Instruction. His bill, which made primary education free, compulsory, and secular, had become law that year. Vacating his office and assisting at the installation of his successor, Ferry picked up a volume by Quinet and remarked: "Celui-là, je l'emporte, c'est mon bréviaire."[34] Ferry left behind three particularly important administrative appointees: Ferdinand Buisson, Director of Primary Education; Jules Steeg, Inspector of Primary Education; and Félix Pécaut, Director of *l'École normale d'institutrices de Fontenay-aux-Roses.* Buisson remained at his post twenty years, Pécaut fifteen. Two of the three were former Protestant pastors; all three had known Quinet personally in Switzerland, and were his ardent partisans.

The 1882 education bill was a first step. The culmination came with the separation of Church and State in France. It is not sensible to state that Quinet contributed to making France "antireligious," even if, as is doubtful, it could be shown convincingly that France later became less or more religious than in his day. But there can be no doubt that the steps taken previous to World War I, in the direction, at least, of his minimum program, did little or nothing to achieve the result he expected from such a policy. The spirit in which this policy was carried out is suggested by the jeers which greeted Combes from the benches of the majority when he professed his *philosophie spiritualiste* during the final fight for separation of Church and State. "Point de salut en dehors du positivisme," was the cry of the anticlerical majority. A few carefully placed idealists of neo-Kantian variety at the head of the University system could not, and did not, create a world in their own image.

As important as Quinet's errors in interpreting the past was his blindness to the world of his own day. What has so appropriately been called the "generation of materialism" followed upon his death. Yet Quinet demanded a reformation of a kind that had never occurred. He appealed to the middle class to enrol in a crusade which demanded sacrifice and promised no material reward. In the end he asked for a dictatorship of religious idealists who were to come to power on a program which damned the material selfishness of the poor equally with that of the rich.

Quinet's final acceptance of intolerance was one of his most interesting aspects. Here he was truly prophetic: not because a dictatorship of idealistic, temporarily authoritarian liberals was ever more than a mad dream, but because he lost his liberal optimism in the face of experience. What seemed to be the firm establishment of democratic liberalism in western Europe came after his death, but Quinet foreshadowed a later awakening. He once stated, while declaring his willingness to give ground on all other points, that the essential necessity was freedom of thought. This was the base upon which his "modern spirit" rested. That freedom he sacrificed to Truth.

In discarding a basic principle Quinet did not desert his fundamental faith, and this is important. Man was good, only the Roman Church corrupted him. Proper environment need only be established and given time. All hope was not abandoned; but Edgar Quinet, in embracing the doctrine of intolerance, became a captive of a tradition, an example who lends support to his own overstated but sometimes penetrating analysis of the French experience.

Nineteenth-century France was exceedingly rich in men who missed greatness, but who were highly endowed with talent and intelligence. The work of such men remains significant for its intrinsic merit, and today has a real value beyond that which it possesses as source material which aids in understanding the spirit of the time and place in which it was produced. Renan, Proudhon, and De Tocqueville might be named to this group. Quinet falls short of such company. Yet in his influence upon the political aspects of French history he had a greater significance than any of these men. Eloquent and talented, he put his life into an attack upon the most powerful enemy in France of his own religious creed. The weapons he provided fell to more realistic men, men with political rather than religious ends in view.

Notes

Introduction

1. The most valuable critical evaluation of a rather extended period of Quinet's life is found in Gabriel Monod's masterful study, *La Vie et la Pensée de Jules Michelet* (2 vols.; Paris: Bibliothèque de l'École des Hautes Études, 1923). A discussion of Quinet's thought was interjected into this work only in so far as it related to Michelet, but the extensive consideration which Monod did give Quinet was based upon a more thorough investigation, and particularly a more complete command of the materials, than that to be found in any study devoted to Quinet himself. Monod concluded that Quinet, even in his own day, had a reputation inferior to his merit; and of course, his reputation was greater then than it has ever been since.

Excluding Richard Heath's curious *Edgar Quinet: His Early Life and Writings* (London: Trubner & Co., 1881), and Ernest Seillière's opprobrious *Edgar Quinet et le Mysticisme démocratique* (Paris: Société d'Économie Sociale, 1919), there are three important biographies. The first, Charles-Louis Chassin's *Edgar Quinet, sa Vie et son Oeuvre* (Paris: Pagnerre, 1859), was prepared to accompany the 1857 edition of Quinet's works. Chassin was a disciple. The work is given over largely to a discussion of each of the volumes which the biography was to supplement.

The second Mme Quinet published a two-volume biography of her husband some years after his death, *Edgar Quinet avant l'Exil* (Paris: Calmann Lévy, 1887); *Edgar Quinet depuis l'Exil* (Paris: Calmann Lévy, 1889). These volumes contain many inaccuracies, not a few of them deliberate, but are invaluable for the personal portrait of Quinet which does emerge. The distortions of the record are most flagrant with respect to details which have little to do with Quinet's opinions. A fair example of Mme Quinet's methods and her motivation is the attempt to hide the fact that Edgar received financial help from a young man of the working class (the relative of a former family servant) to publish his first literary effort. Rather than have this degrading circumstance live in history, Mme Quinet propagated the more romantic story of a young writer, cut off by an impatient father (another untruth), selling his meager furnishings in order to make his entrance into the literary world.

The most recent biography is that of Albert Valès, *Edgar Quinet, sa Vie et son Oeuvre* (Vienne: E. Aubinet Fils, 1936). But for minor additions and changes this work had been completed in manuscript before the first World War. Valès was long a close friend of Quinet's widow and gave her valuable assistance in the preparation of her husband's correspondence for publication. Manuscript material in Mme Quinet's possession passed into his hands upon her death, to be utilized by him in preparing a definitive life. Valès made a studious and conscientious effort to correct the errors in fact perpetuated by Mme Quinet, and to deal with his subject objectively. The degree to which he failed in the more ambitious project of dealing with Quinet's thought and its significance resulted largely from his apparent conviction that by projecting his own opinions, temperament, and virtues into the past was re-creating an authentic Edgar Quinet.

Chapter 1

1. Edgar Quinet, *Oeuvres complètes*, VII, *Les Tablettes du Juif errant* (Paris: Pagnerre, 1858).
2. Quinet, *1815 et 1840*, printed in *L'Enseignement du Peuple* (Paris: Germer-Baillière, n.d.), p. 205.
3. S. Charléty, *La Restauration: 1815-1830, Histoire de France contemporaine depuis la Révolution jusqu'à la Paix de 1919* (ed. Ernest Lavisse; Paris: Hachette, 1921), IV, 76.
4. Quinet, *Histoire de mes Idées* (7th ed.; Paris: Hachette, 1878), p. 200 and *Histoire de la Campagne de 1815* (Paris: Germer-Baillière, n.d.), p. 66.
5. Jacques Maritain, *Man and the State* (Chicago: University of Chicago Press, 1951), p. 37.
6. Henri Guillemin, "Introduction" to Lamennais, *Paroles d'un Croyant* (Paris: Les Classiques du XIXe, 1946), pp. 9-10.
7. Quinet, *Histoire de la Campagne de 1815*, p. 42.
8. Gabriel Monod, *op. cit.*, II, 89.
9. Roger Soltau, *French Political Thought in the Nineteenth Century* (New Haven: Yale University Press, 1931), p. xxiv.
10. Quinet, *O.C.*, IX, *Mes Vacances en Espagne* (Paris: Pagnerre, 1857), p. 249.
11. Quinet, *Histoire de mes Idées*, pp. 137-38; 165-66.
12. Lavisse, *op. cit.*, IV, 28.
13. Ernest Renan, *Souvenirs d'Enfance et de Jeunesse* (2nd ed.; Paris: Calmann Lévy, 1883), pp. 91-92.
14. H. A. L. Fisher, *Bonapartism: Six Lectures* (Oxford, 1914), p. 113.
15. Lavisse, *op. cit.*, IV, 175.
16. Quinet, *Histoire de mes Idées*, pp. 173-74.
17. Georges Weill, *Histoire du Parti Républicain en France: 1814-1870* (Paris: Alcan, 1928), p. 56 and pp. 196-97, discusses this entente, and the fact that many of the leaders of the party felt considerable reserve, not always publicly expressed, as to the wisdom of the policy.
18. Victor Hugo, *Histoire d'un Crime, Déposition d'un Témoin* (2 vols.; 31st ed.; Paris: Calmann Lévy, 1877), I, 265.
19. P. J. Proudhon, *La Révolution sociale démontrée par le Coup d'État du Deux Décembre* (Introduction and Notes by Édouard Dolléans and Georges Duveau; Paris: Marcel Rivière, 1936), p. 260.
20. Quinet, *Histoire de la Campagne de 1815*, p. 18.
21. Heinrich Heine, *Sämtliche Werke* (Leipzig: Meyers Klassiker-Ausgaben, n.d.), VI, 179-80. It may of course be argued that Lamartine is personally done an injustice here. Georg Brandes made a similar but more exaggerated defense of enthusiasm for the legendary Napoleon. See his *Hauptströmungen*

der Literatur des Neunzehnten Jahrhunderts (3 vols.; Berlin: Erich Reiss, 1924), III, 24.

22. Soltau, *op. cit.,* pp. 486-88 for this and the preceding quotation.
23. Louis Blanc, *Histoire de dix Ans, 1830-1840* (5 vols.; Paris: Pagnerre, 1849), I, 52.
24. Quinet, *Histoire de mes Idées,* pp. 75-76.

Chapter 2

1. Quinet, *Lettres à sa Mère* (2 vols.; Paris: Germer-Baillière, n.d.), I, 356.
2. See Mme de Staël, *De l'Allemagne* (Paris: Garnier, 1874), pp. 404-6, 424-25, and 448.
3. Carl Becker, "The Dilemma of Diderot," *Everyman His Own Historian* (New York: Scribners, 1935), p. 282. Pp. 274-82 discuss the problem.
4. See Lavisse, *op. cit.,* S. Charléty, *La Monarchie de Juillet (1830-1848),* V, 350.
5. Quinet, *L'Esprit Nouveau* (Paris: Germer-Baillière, n.d.), p. 337.
6. Victor Cousin, *Du Vrai, du Beau et du Bien* (2nd ed.; Paris: Didier, 1854), pp. 9-10.
7. Quinet, *Histoire de mes Idées,* p. 75.
8. Quinet, *Lettres à sa Mère,* I, 382.
9. François Chateaubriand, *OEuvres de Chateaubriand, Le Génie du Christianisme* (2 vols.; Paris: Dufour, Mulat et Boulanger, 1854), I, 101; II, 152.
10. Mme Quinet, *Edgar Quinet avant l'Exil,* p. 67. Oskar Wenderoth, *Der junge Quinet und seine Übersetzung von Herders "Ideen"; Ein Beitrag zur Geschichte der literarischen Wechselbeziehungen zwischen Frankreich und Deutschland* (Erlangan: 1906), p. 29.
11. *Ibid.,* pp. 25-27.
12. Paul Gautier, *Madame de Staël et Napoléon* (Paris: Plon-Nourrit, 1903), pp. 72-77. See also Mme de Staël, *Dix Années d'Exil; Fragmens d'un ouvrage inédit, composé dans les années 1810 à 1813* (Bruxelles: Louis Hauman, 1830), p. 41, where she criticizes those hostile to established religion.
13. Gautier, *op. cit.,* p. 198. *Corinne,* published in 1807, was Mme de Staël's most widely read novel. The work was named for its heroine.
14. See her introduction to the first edition of *De l'Allemagne* permitted in France, dated October 1, 1815.
15. Quinet, *Lettres à sa Mère,* I, 285, 288, and 292.
16. Gautier, *op. cit.,* p. 275, from H. F. Amiel, *Étude sur Mme de Staël* (1876).

Chapter 3

1. Johann Gottfried Herder, *Ideen zur Philosophie der Geschichte der Menschheit,* "Deutsche National-Litteratur" (3 vols.; ed., Eugen Kühnemann; Stuttgart, n.d.), II, 330.
2. Quinet, *Histoire de mes Idées,* pp. 200-201 and *Lettres à sa Mère,* I, 395-96.
3. Quinet, *Lettres à sa Mère,* I, 190.
4. Bibliothèque Nationale, Nouvelles acquisitions françaises 20781, "Corres-

pondance d'Edgar Quinet," XXI ("Premiers Essais de Quinet"), fols. 5-6.
5. Friedrick Meinecke, *Die Entstehung des Historismus* (2 vols.; München:
   R. Oldenbourg, 1936), II, 415-16.
6. Benjamin Constant, *De la Religion, considérée dans sa source, ses formes
   et ses développements* (5 vols.; Paris: 1824-31), I, 16.
7. J. Barthélemy Saint-Hilaire, *M. Victor Cousin: Sa Vie et sa Correspondance*
   (3 vols.; Paris: Felix Alcan, Hachette et Cie., 1895), II, 269-75. This
   writer overstates Cousin's Catholic sympathies, and certainly exaggerates
   what he feels was Constant's inability to see the practical political necessity
   of a religion for the people.
8. Pierre-Simon Ballanche, *Essais de Palingénésie social* (2 vols.; Paris: Jules
   Didot, 1827-29), I (Prolégomènes), 253-56.
9. *Ibid.*, I, 181 and Vicomte de Bonald, *Démonstration philosophique de
   principe constitutif de la société, suivie de Méditations politiques tirées de
   l'Évangile* (Paris: 1830), pp. 61-62.
10. Ballanche, *op. cit.*, I, 204.
11. *Ibid.*, I, 154; 159-60.
12. B.N., "Premiers Essais de Quinet," *loc. cit.*, fols. 256-61.
13. See my article, "Edgar Quinet and the First French Translation of Herder's
    Ideen zur Geschichte der Menschheit," *Romanic Review*, XLV (April,
    1954), 109-14, for a more detailed discussion of the translation and for
    corrections of Mme Quinet's account of Quinet's relations with Cousin.
14. Barthélemy Saint-Hilaire, *op. cit.*, II, 13; an 1825 letter to Lamennais.
15. George Boas, *French Philosophies of the Romantic Period* (Baltimore:
    Johns Hopkins Press, 1925), p. 198.
16. Cousin, *op. cit.*, pp. 428-29.
17. B.N., Nouv. acq. franç. 11831, "Journal Quinet," VII, 155. Monod, who
    was sharply critical of the manner in which Quinet turned against Cousin in
    1830, concluded that Cousin did not seem to have had any direct influence
    on either Quinet or Michelet (*op. cit.*, I, 71).
18. Quinet, *O.C.*, II, *Introduction à la Philosophie de l'Histoire de l'Humanité*
    (Paris: Pagnerre, 1857), 348-51. See pp. 354-66 for the quotations from
    this essay which follow.
19. Benedetto Croce, *History of Europe in the Nineteenth Century* (translated
    by Henry Furst; New York: Harcourt, Brace and Company, 1933), pp. 11
    and 86-87.
20. Meinecke, *op. cit.*, I, 104-5.
21. G. Vico, *The New Science of Giambattista Vico* (Thomas G. Bergin and
    Max H. Fisch, translators; Ithaca: Cornell University Press, 1948), p. 106.
22. *Ibid.*, pp. 57-58. My italics.
23. Vico, *The Autobiography of Giambattista Vico* (Max Fisch and Thomas
    Bergin, translators; Ithaca: Cornell University Press, 1944), p. 127.
24. Vico, *The New Science*, p. 313.
25. Herder, *op. cit.*, III, 487. See II, 323-24; III, 599, 637, and 641 for other
    examples of this characteristic optimism.
26. Meinecke, *op. cit.*, II, 458 and 469.
27. Herder, *op. cit.*, III, 626.
28. Quinet, *O.C.*, II *(Essai sur les Oeuvres de Herder)*, p. 426.
29. *Ibid.*, pp. 438-39.
30. *Ibid.*, pp. 415-16.

31. Quinet, *O.C.*, I, *De l'Origine des Dieux* (Paris: Pagnerre, 1857), 436-37.
32. Monod alone sensed this, and he wrote that although Quinet's 1829 voyage to Greece helped "free him" from German mysticism, as did his political and philosophical reaction against Germany in 1831, "the prose poem *D'Ahasvérus*," conceived since 1828, written in Italy in 1832, and published in 1833, "is again full of the philosophical mysticism of 1828" (*op. cit.*, II, 102-3). *D'Ahasvérus* clearly was an effort to fulfil the author's own prophecy.
33. Quinet, *O.C.*, I *(Le Génie des Religions)*, 5.
34. Vico, *The New Science*, pp. 382-83.
35. See Croce, *Die Philosophie Giambattista Vicos* (Tübingen: J. C. B. Mohr, 1927), pp. ix and 121 on the essential incompatibility of Vico's philosophy with Catholic dogma.
36. Charles-Louis Chassin, *op. cit.*, p. 106.
37. Heine, *op. cit.*, VI, 414.

Chapter 4

1. Soltau, *op. cit.*, p. 53.
2. Weill, *op. cit.*, p. 20.
3. Henry Michel, *L'Idée de l'État: Essai critique sur l'Histoire des théories sociales et politiques en France depuis la Révolution* (Paris: Hachette, 1896), p. 317.
4. See my article, "Edgar Quinet and the July Revolution," *The Historian* (Spring, 1955), pp. 199-200 for notes to this and the following paragraph.
5. Paul Thureau-Dangin, *Histoire de la Monarchie de Juillet* (7 vols.; Paris: E. Plon, Nourrit et Cie., 1884-92), I, 88.
6. Proudhon, *op. cit.*, pp. 57 and 165.
7. A. Debidour, *Histoire des rapports de l'Église et de l'État en France de 1789 à 1870* (Paris: Alcan, 1898), pp. i-ii.
8. Monod, *op. cit.*, II, 96.
9. Constant, *op. cit.*, I, xii, note 1.
10. Blanc, *op. cit.*, I, 134.
11. Weill, *Histoire du Parti Republicain*, p. 22. The affirmation of working-class well-being, even in a relative sense, is historically inaccurate. See Édouard Dolléans, *Histoire du Mouvement Ouvrier: 1830-1871 and 1871-1936* (2 vols.; 3rd ed.; Paris: Armand Colin, 1948), I, 28-29.
12. Quinet met Sainte-Beuve early in 1830 [Alfred Westphal, *Lettres inédites d'Edgar Quinet* (Lettre-Préface de M. Gabriel Monod; Paris: Stock, 1907), p. 29], and the latter attempted to enrol him in the Saint-Simonian movement (B.N., Nouv. acq. franç. 11833, "Journal Quinet," IX, 72).

Chapter 5

1. Barthélemy Saint-Hilaire, *op. cit.*, III, 387.
2. Monod, *op. cit.*, I, 245. Mme Quinet, *Cinquante ans d'Amitié: Michelet-Quinet (1826-1875)*, (2nd. ed.; Paris: Armand Colin, 1903), pp. 21-22, suppressed this passage.

3. Westphal, *op. cit.*, p. 13.
4. Barthélemy Saint-Hilaire, *op. cit.*, III, 120-21.
5. B.N., Nouv. acq. franç. 20799, "Correspondance d'Edgar Quinet," XIX, 181. See my "Edgar Quinet and the July Revolution," *loc. cit.*, pp. 203-14 for full documentation for the remaining pages of this chapter.
6. Sainte-Beuve wrote the unsigned review of Quinet's work which appeared in the October 12, 1830 *Globe*. See Sainte-Beuve, *Correspondance Générale* (Paris: Stock, 1935-), I, 170. In 1824 the *Globe* became the successor to *Archives philosophiques, politiques, et littéraires*, a journal directed by Royer-Collard, Guizot, Cousin, Villemain, and their group (see Boas, *op. cit.*, pp. 186-89 and 210). But in the fall of 1830 the *Globe* passed into the hands of the Saint-Simonians, and of course Guizot and Cousin ceased to participate in its activities.
7. See Jules Marsan, *La Bataille romantique* (Paris: Hachette, 1912), p. 293. Quinet, *Lettres à sa Mère*, II, 197 announces the project.
8. Quinet, *O.C.*, III, *Le Christianisme et la Révolution Française* (Paris: Pagnerre, 1857), 23.
9. Debidour, *op. cit.*, pp. 413-15.
10. Quinet, *O.C.*, IX *(Mes Vacances en Espagne)*, 139.
11. Proudhon, *op. cit.*, pp. 179-80.
12. L'Abbé Dupanloup, *De la Pacification Religieuse* (Paris: Jacques Lecoffre, 1845), p. 126.
13. Quinet, *Lettre à Sue*, in *Le Livre de l'Exilé* (Paris: Germer--Baillière, n.d.), p. 443.
14. Quinet, *O.C.*, VI, *Mélanges* (Paris: Pagnerre, 1857), 398.
15. Quinet, *O.C.*, VI *(Allemagne et Italie)*, 178-81 for the above two paragraphs.
16. Quinet, *La République: Conditions de la Régénération de la France* (Paris: Dentu, 1872), p. 141; and *L'Esprit Nouveau*, p. 331 for a like statement.
17. Blanc, *op. cit.*, II, 313 and 406.
18. The depiction of such scenes is a curious part of the "Journal Quinet." This was not a subject the second Mme Quinet would have been inclined to stress. See B.N., Nouv. acq. franç. 11829, "Journal Quinet," V, 38; and *ibid.*, 11833, "Journal Quinet," IX, 158, for typical examples of Quinet's preoccupation with the memory of the separation. The coolness which characterized Quinet's feelings toward his first wife during the last years of her life was quite marked, but "obsession" is not too strong a word to describe his later feelings.
19. B.N., Nouv. acq. franç. 20782, "Correspondance d'Edgar Quinet," II, 392.
20. In the 1857 and later editions of Quinet's works the volume *Allemagne et Italie* contains four articles, among others: "De la Philosophie dans ses Rapports avec l'Histoire politique" is dated November 1830 (*O.C.*, VI, 174-82); "Système politique de l'Allemagne" is dated October 1831 (*ibid.*, 142-58); "Avertissement à la Monarchie de 1830" is dated only "1830" (*ibid.*, 158-74); and "L'Allemagne et la Révolution" is also dated "1830" (*ibid.*, 135-42). The first was published by Buloz in December, 1831 under the title "De la Révolution et de la Philosophie." The last three originally appeared as the January, 1832 article and pamphlet, *L'Allemagne et la Révolution*. The 1857 and later editions of Quinet's works restore the 1832 *Revue* version with minor stylistic changes. See Paul Gautier, *Un Prophète: Edgar Quinet* (Édition nouvelle de ses articles sur l'Allemagne

d'après les textes originaux avec commentaire; Paris: Plon, 1917), pp. 69-71 and 90-91. The full pamphlet version is restored in this work. Gautier does not point out that Quinet obviously wished to have the world forget that he was so tardy in reacting against the July Monarchy, and pushed back some fourteen or more months, not only the date of original publication, but that of the actual writing of these essays. Marsan, in *La Bataille Romantique*, pp. 295-301, reproduces a number of Quinet's letters to Buloz protesting the editor's refusal to publish the articles in the form Quinet desired.

Chapter 6

1. Quinet's recollections of these incidents were recorded by the second Mme Quinet (B.N., Nouv. acq. franç. 11831, "Journal Quinet," VII, 323; and *ibid.*, 11833, "Journal Quinet," IX, 169). We are told of the injustice of Minna's ridiculous jealousy because Quinet paid attention to a woman who was "eccentric, ridiculous, fantastic and ugly." Fauriel honored Miss Clarke with a constant and patient devotion, comparable to that Ballanche paid Mme Récamier. Julius Mohl, the German orientalist, later married her. She was ten years Quinet's senior.

   The exact circumstances surrounding Quinet's separation from Minna in 1831 are obscure. His *Merlin l'Enchanteur* (2 vols.; Paris: 1860), II, 3-55, contains letters exchanged between the couple during his stay in Italy. But more revealing are those published by Ulrich Molsen in his *Philosophie und Dichtung bei Quinet* (Altona: 1913), pp. 73-77. Those of Minna's letters which have been preserved are in German, with a very few late exceptions, and date from 1828 to 1836 (B.N., Nouv. acq. franç. 20800, "Correspondance d'Edgar Quinet: Lettres de Minna Moré et d'Edgar Quinet," XX, 1-302). Quinet's letters to Minna (*ibid.*, ff. 303-97) date from November 1837 to October 1850.

2. Albert Valès, *op. cit.*, pp. 115-19.

3. See Mme Quinet, *Avant l'Exil*, p. 225. It has been suggested ["Notes et Documents," *Revue de Littérature comparée*, XVII (1937), 389] that Quinet was the French translator of Heine's poetry in the 1830's. This seems to me extremely unlikely.

4. This essay is included as an introduction in all subsequent editions of *Ahasvérus*, O.C., VII. Magnin was one of the friends who had attempted to dissuade Quinet from publishing his January, 1832 pamphlet attacking the government (B.N., Nouv. acq. franç. 20792, "Correspondance d'Edgar Quinet," XII, 124-26).

5. See Molsen, *op. cit.*, pp. 83-90; and Jean Boudout, "Faust et Ahasvérus," *Revue de Littérature comparée*, XVI (1936), 691-709. Two of Quinet's most important mentors, Mme de Staël and Benjamin Constant, had been unsympathetic to what they regarded as Goethe's ironic and negative incredulity. In 1836 Quinet himself wrote that "le manque de charité et d'entrailles fut le caractère constant de Goethe. Son système de neutralité permanente dégénérait avec l'âge en manie." This was henceforth typical of French comment. See Fernand Baldensperger, *Goethe en France: Étude de Littérature comparée* (Paris: Hachette, 1920), pp. 272-73, for

similar statements by Sainte-Beuve, Lamennais, Michelet, Chateaubriand, and Hugo.

6. *The Private Journal of Henri Frédéric Amiel* (Van Wyck Brooks and Charles Van Wyck Brooks, translators; New York: Macmillan, 1935), pp. 133-34 and 143-44.

7. Quinet, *O.C.*, VII *(Ahasvérus)*, pp. 227 and 289.

8. *Ibid.*, pp. 171-75.

9. Sainte-Beuve, *op. cit.*, I, 452; 531-33; 538-39.

10. Quinet, *O.C.*, VIII, *Napoléon* (Paris: Pagnerre, 1857). In all editions of Quinet's works after that of 1857 Mme Quinet suppressed *Napoléon*. Sainte-Beuve remarked that Quinet's 1836 work did not contribute to the Napoleonic legend, for the simple reason that it had not been read. See his *Portraits Contemporains* (5 vols.; Paris: Michel Lévy, 1869), II, 326. The critic prided himself that in 1836 he had viewed with reserve the effort to fashion the legend. But when he frankly accepted the Second Empire it was not he who suffered from the outcome. Quinet came to detest Sainte-Beuve, stating once that the French critic was *"un Grimm putréfié,* one of the most perverse souls on the face of the earth" (B.N., Nouv. acq. franç. 11831, "Journal Quinet," VII, 112).

11. Sainte-Beuve, *Portraits Contemporains,* II, 323.

12. Edmond Biré, *Victor Hugo après 1830* (2 vols.; Paris: Perrin et Cie., 1891), I, 53.

13. Marie Czapska, *La Vie de Mickiewicz* (Paris: Plon, 1931), pp. 11-12 and 127. Quinet met Mickiewicz in December, 1837 *(Lettres à sa Mère,* II, 289).

14. Quinet, *O.C.*, VIII *(Napoléon),* 291-92; 309-10.

15. B.N., Nouv. acq. franç. 20793, "Correspondance d'Edgar Quinet," XIII, 360-61.

16. B.N., Nouv. acq. franç. 20800, "Correspondance d'Edgar Quinet," XX, 309-10. This letter is dated October 23, 1837; another, dated October 9, 1837 *(ibid.,* 303), gives the same details as a letter dated "November" in Quinet, *Lettres à sa Mère,* II, 284. It would appear that Quinet moved to Paris in October, not in November as Mme Quinet related *(Cinquante ans d'Amitié,* p. 97).

17. Quinet, *O.C.*, VI *(Allemagne et Italie),* 327.

18. Czapska, *op. cit.*, pp. 179-80.

19. Ballanche, *op. cit.*, I, 88.

20. Quinet, *O.C.*, VIII *(Prométhée),* xii-xxi.

21. Buloz received the corrected proofs from Quinet in October. See Jules Marsan, *op. cit.*, pp. 309-10.

22. Gabriel Monod *(op. cit.*, I, 363) wrote that Salvandy, who admittedly was hostile to the advanced party during his second ministry (February 1, 1845 to February 24, 1848), was liberal during his first (March 15, 1837 to March 31, 1839). Monod was led to this conclusion by his thesis that Michelet belonged to the "advanced" party in 1838. Salvandy must be made "liberal" because he supported Michelet. During his first term Salvandy, like the government of which he was a part, sought clerical favor (see Thureau-Dangin, *op. cit.*, III, 434, for a Catholic-Royalist statement of the fact). Charléty wrote of Salvandy's 1845 appointment to replace Villemain that "his benevolence for the clergy and his indifference with regard to the University were well known" (E. Lavisse, *op. cit.*, V, 341). See also

Thureau-Dangin, *op. cit.*, V, 547. Mme Quinet fell into a more deliberate error: she had Villemain become Minister of Public Instruction in September of 1838, eight months before he did so in fact (Parant served from March 31, 1839 to May 12, 1839: Villemain replaced him on the latter date). She did this so that her husband would not seem to have been appointed by Salvandy, whose clericalism she justly saw no reason to doubt at any time of his career *(Cinquante ans d'Amitié*, p. 100).

23. See Quinet, *O.C.*, III, *Examen de la Vie de Jésus* (Paris: Pagnerre, 1857), 285-318.
24. Westphal, *op. cit.*, p. 45.
25. *Considérations philosophiques sur l'art* (Strasbourg: F. G. Levraut, 1839). Thèse de philosophie présentée à la Faculté des Lettres de l'Academie de Strasbourg, et soutenue publiquement le mercredi 23 janvier 1839, à 2 heurs après midi, pour obtenir le grade de docteur ès lettres (17 pages).
26. See Marsan, *op. cit.*, pp. 310-12 for the complete letter.
27. Quinet, *O.C.*, VI, *(Mélanges*, "le Champ de Bataille de Waterloo"), 389.
28. Quinet, *O.C.*, I, "Unité morale des Peuples modernes" (Paris: Pagnerre, 1857), 401.
29. Quinet, *O.C.*, I *(Le Génie des Religions)*, 7.
30. *Ibid.*, pp. 22-28.
31. Sainte-Beuve, *Correspondance Générale*, III, 279.
32. Ernest Dupuy, *Alfred de Vigny: ses Amitiés; son Rôle littéraire* (2 vols.; Paris: Société Française d'Imprimerie et de Librairie, 1910), II, 106-7 and 137.
33. B.N., Nouv. acq. franç. 20797, "Correspondance d'Edgar Quinet," XVII, 60.
34. B.N., Nouv. acq. franç. 20788, "Correspondance d'Edgar Quinet," VIII, 73. When Fauriel did choose to retire, Ozanam took his place at the Sorbonne, first, in 1841, as a substitute, and then, in 1844, as Fauriel's successor. Pierre Moreau, *Le Romantisme* (vol. VIII of *Histoire de la Littérature Française*, J. Calvet, ed.; 9 vols.; Paris: J. de Gigord, 1931-36), VIII, 315.
35. H. Monin, "Étude critique sur le texte des *Lettres d'Exil d'Edgar Quinet*, Madame Quinet, éditeur," *Revue d'Histoire littéraire de la France*, XVII (1910), 572-73.
36. Quinet, *Lettres à sa Mère*, II, 335.
37. Quinet, *1815 et 1840*, pp. 206-22.
38. Lavisse, *op. cit.*, V, 294-95.
39. Quinet, *1815 et 1840*, p. 193.
40. Quinet, *Avertissement au pays*, in *L'Enseignement du Peuple: Oeuvres Politiques avant l'Exil*, pp. 232-56.
41. Otto Pfleiderer, *The Philosophy of Religion on the Basis of its History* (Alexander Stewart and Allan Menzies, translators; 4 vols.; London: Williams and Norgate, 1886-88), I, 219.
42. Heinrich von Treitschke, *Politics* (Blanche Dugdale & Torben de Bille, translators; 2 vols.; introduction by Arthur James Balfour; New York: Macmillan, 1916), I, 122.

Chapter 7

1. Soltau, *op. cit.*, p. 76; Chassin, *op. cit.*, pp. 61-62; Monod, *op. cit.*, II, 99-101.

2. The short-lived ordinances of February, 1815, were never executed; but in August, 1815, the above *Conseil de l'Université* was replaced by a five-member *Commission de l'Instruction publique* and placed under the authority of the Minister of Interior. In July, 1820, this became the seven-member *Conseil royal de l'instruction publique.* One may not speak of a Minister of Public Instruction until 1821, when Corbière first sat in the cabinet as a Secretary of State because of his position as president of the *Conseil royal.* In August, 1824, the ministry of *Affaires ecclésiastiques et de l'instruction publique* was created, and first filled by Frayssinous. Upon the fall of the *ultra* Villèle government the two offices were separated. See Antoine Augustin Cournot, *Des institutions d'instruction publique en France* (Paris, 1864), pp. 470-75.

3. Adrian Dansette, *Histoire religieuse de la France contemporaine* (2 vols.; Paris: Flammarion, 1948-51), I, 203.

4. Lavisse, *op. cit.,* V, 327.

5. Thureau-Dangin, *op. cit.,* II, 66-67.

6. *Ibid.,* II, 332-33.

7. Heine, *op. cit.,* VI, 397.

Chapter 8

1. Thureau-Dangin, *op. cit.,* V, 504-5.

2. Henry Michel, "Edgar Quinet," *Cahiers de la Quinzaine* (July, 1903), pp. 18-19.

3. Soltau, *op. cit.,* pp. 117-18.

4. Dansette, *op. cit.,* I, 422.

5. Quinet, *Lettres à sa Mère,* II, 363-66. Two stenographers from the *Moniteur* took down each word.

6. Quinet, *O.C.,* IV (Paris: Pagnerre, 1857), 4. These remarks are from the 1857 introduction to the work. One may take lightly the claim to have searched the chronicles.

7. Sainte-Beuve, *Correspondance Générale,* V, 132. Sainte-Beuve nevertheless disapproved of the manner in which Quinet and Michelet carried on their fight (*ibid.,* V, 263). Years later Quinet reported that Sainte-Beuve was commissioned by Catholic friends at this time to ask him to cease his attacks upon the Church. The interview closed abruptly and a friendship of a dozen years was at an end (B.N., Nouv. acq. franç. 11832, "Journal Quinet," VIII, 105).

8. Quinet's social snobbery was pronounced. During his exile in Switzerland the maid he and Mme Quinet had employed for several years announced her intention to marry. Quinet regarded this as a disloyal and ungrateful act, and he regretted his past kindnesses to an inferior who now proved herself unappreciative. He remarked sharply to Mme Quinet that Rousseau "a perdu la noblesse de son esprit dans ce commerce de domestiques." B.N., Nouv. acq. franç. 11828, "Journal Quinet," IV, 25.

9. L. Schoumacker, *Erckmann-Chatrian: Étude biographique et critique d'après des documents inédits* (Strasbourg: Publications de la Faculté des Lettres de l'Université de Strasbourg, 1933), p. 33. Erckmann attended Quinet's lectures as a student (*ibid.,* p. 29).

10. Chassin, *op. cit.*, pp. 49-50. Monod suggested that Chassin grossly exaggerated these disorders, and that Mme Quinet only repeated Chassin (*op cit.*, II, 130-31). Admitting the likelihood of exaggeration, accounts like that of Erckmann support Chassin. Michelet was *"très sérieusement persuadé"* that a Jesuit plot was afoot to assassinate him on the opening day of his 1844 course, the first to follow the one devoted to the Jesuits. See *Correspondance du duc d'Aumale et de Cuvillier-Fleury* (2 vols.; Paris: 1910), I, 214. In May of 1843 Cuvillier-Fleury described disorders attending Quinet's course in terms which are quite compatible with Chassin's description. He wrote to the Duc d'Aumale: "J'étais là, voulant vous parler de toutes ces scènes comme témoin oculaire.... Quinet ... a été accueilli par des applaudissements frénétiques, mêlés de quelques sifflets que l'indignation générale a étouffés.... J'ai vu plusiers fois l'assistance tout près de se rouer sur les gens qui sifflaient. On criat 'A bas les Jésuites! ... Mort aux Chouans! ...' " (*ibid.*, I, 160-61). These remarks refer to the first two lectures.
11. Monod, *op. cit.*, II, 127.
12. Sainte-Beuve, *Correspondance Générale*, V, 202-3.
13. Quinet, *O.C.*, II (*Les Jésuites*), pp. xi-xiii and 121-22.
14. Ernest Troeltsch, *Protestantism and Progress: A Historical Study of the Relation of Protestantism to the Modern World* (New York: G. P. Putnam's Sons, 1912), p. 180.
15. Croce, *History of Europe in the Nineteenth Century*, p. 20.
16. H. Boehmer, *The Jesuits: An Historical Study* (Paul Zeller Strodach, translator; Philadelphia: Castle Press, 1928), pp. 98, 184.
17. Quinet, *O.C.*, II (*Les Jésuites*), pp. 87-107.
18. Preserved Smith, *The Age of the Reformation* (New York: Henry Holt and Co., 1920), p. 717.
19. Mme Quinet, *Avant l'Exil*, pp. 340-41. Monod (*op. cit.*, II, 165) repeated this.
20. Monod, *op. cit.*, II, 115.
21. B.N., Nouv. acq. franç. 20788, "Correspondance d'Edgar Quinet," VIII, 74.
22. B.N., Nouv. acq. franç. 20798, "Correspondance d'Edgar Quinet," XVIII, 299.
23. Quinet, *O.C.*, II (*L'Ultramontanisme*), pp. 130-31.
24. Monod, *op. cit.*, II, 232.
25. It should be noted, however, that although Quinet never attacked Christianity in print or in a public statement, in periods of depression during the years of exile in Switzerland, if at no other time, he did so privately. Reading Paul in 1861 he said to the second Mme Quinet, "What a slave doctrine! Bow down before all authorities, for all power comes from God. That is what Paul said to the people. Christ before him said: 'Render unto Caesar that which is Caesar's.' It is the religion of slaves." B.N., Nouv. acq. franç. 11826, "Journal Quinet," II, 194.
26. Carl Becker, *The Heavenly City of the Eighteenth Century Philosophers* (New Haven: Yale University Press, 1932).
27. Quinet, *O.C.*, II (*L'Ultramontanisme*), p. 249.
28. *Ibid.*, pp. 175-76.
29. *Ibid.*, pp. 211-22.
30. *Ibid.*, pp. 172-74.

31. *Ibid.*, pp. 200, 203.
32. *Ibid.*, pp. 272-73.
33. *Ibid.*, pp. 150-52.
34. Dupanloup, *op. cit.*, p. 231. Debate opened in the Chamber of Peers April 22, 1844, where the University defense was led by Cousin, and where the amended bill passed on May 24. Debate in the Chamber of Deputies began on July 13; Thiers was the leader of the fight against the bill in the lower house. See Thureau-Dangin, *op. cit.*, V, 533-48; Lavisse, *op. cit.*, V, 340-41; Debidour, *op. cit.*, p. 461.
35. Thureau-Dangin, *op. cit.*, V, 472.
36. Quinet, *O.C.*, III ("De la tactique parlementaire en matière de religion," *Le Christianisme et la Révolution française*), pp. 24-41.
37. Maritain, *Man and the State*, pp. 72-73, 75. My italics.
38. Heine, *op. cit.*, VI, 422-23. He generously, if not quite properly, excluded Quinet and Michelet from the charge.
39. Thureau-Dangin, *op. cit.*, V, 546-47. An irrational fear of Jesuit machinations was an important manifestation of Villemain's illness (Monod, *op. cit.*, II, 132).
40. Czapska, *op. cit.*, pp. 225-26.
41. Massari, who was present, reported these details to Sainte-Beuve. Years later Quinet recalled that the vote was seventeen to seven. See Sainte-Beuve, *Correspondance Générale*, VI, 194-95.
42. Chassin, *op. cit.*, pp. 56-58. See Mme Quinet *(Cinquante ans d'Amitié*, pp. 142-43) for Quinet's letter to Salvandy.
43. Monod, *op. cit.*, II, 169.
44. *O.C.*, III *(Le Christianisme et la Révolution française)*, 36-38.
45. *Ibid.*, pp. 48 and 88.
46. *Ibid*, p. 162.
47. Chassin, *op. cit.*, p. 56, and Mme Quinet, *Cinquante ans d'Amitié*, pp. 137-38.
48. Weill, *Histoire du Parti Républicain*, p. 214.
49. Chassin, *op. cit.*, pp. 58-60.
50. Quinet's April letter is printed in full at the end of *Cinquante ans d'Amitié*, pp. 367-70.
51. Quinet, *Le Livre de l'Exilé (Lettre sur la Situation Religieuse & Morale de l'Europe à Eugene Sue)*, pp. 505-6.

Chapter 9

1. Ernest Renan, *L'Avenir de la Science: Pensées de 1848* (25th ed.; Paris: Calmann Lévy, 1929), pp. 324-25 and 403.
2. Quinet, *O.C.*, IX *(Mes Vacances en Espagne)*, 213-14.
3. Quinet, *O.C.*, IV *(Les Révolutions d'Italie)*, 172-79. Only that part of this work which was completed before the February Revolution is under discussion here. At the last of these pages the February Revolution interrupted the printing of the first volume *(ibid.*, note 1, p. 179). This work found a wide audience in Italy, where three different translations were published. See L. Auvray, "Edgar Quinet e l'Italia," *Revue d'Histoire littéraire de la France*, XXVII (1920), 619.

4. Quinet, *L'Enseignement du Peuple (Discours prononcé au Collège de France)*, pp. 309-22.

5. Soltau, *op. cit.*, p. 90.

6. Lavisse, *op. cit.*, V, 376.

7. L. B. Namier, *1848: The Revolution of the Intellectuals* (vol. XXX of *The Proceedings of the British Academy;* London, 1944), p. 37.

8. H. Taine, *Le Régime Moderne* (vols. IX, X, XI of *Les Origines de la France Contemporaine)*, (Paris: Hachette, n.d.), XI, 308.

9. Debidour, *op. cit.*, p. 483.

10. See B.N., Nouv. acq. franç. 20800, "Correspondance d'Edgar Quinet," XX, 357-60.

11. Garnier-Pagès, *Histoire de la Révolution de 1848* (8 vols.; Paris: Pagnerre, 1861-62), VIII, 92.

12. See I. Tchernoff, *Le Parti républicain sous la Monarchie de Juillet: Formation et Évolution de la Doctrine républicaine* (Paris: A. Pedone, 1901), p. 452.

13. Lavisse, *op. cit.*, VI, Ch. Seignobos, *La Révolution de 1848–Le Second Empire: 1848-1859* (Paris: Hachette, 1921), 102.

14. In December, 1869, Quinet was shocked at a friend's article glorifying the June Days, that "war against the men of 1848" as Quinet still thought of them (B.N., Nouv. acq. franç. 11836, "Journal Quinet," XII, 97-98). He stressed the important role he believed Bonapartist agents played in the uprising, but if sincere he was mistaken; see Weill, *Histoire du Parti Républicain,* p. 226.

   Five existent brief notes dispatched from his headquarters to Minna during the insurrection strongly suggest that Quinet was carried away by the opportunity to play a "military" role. In one he expressed concern that rain might spoil his shako (B.N., Nouv. acq. franç. 20800, "Correspondance d'Edgar Quinet," XX, 361-68).

15. Debidour, *op. cit.*, p. 492.

16. David Owen Evans, *Social Romanticism in France, 1830-1848* (Oxford: Clarendon Press, 1951), pp. 76-77.

17. Weill, *Histoire du Parti Républicain*, p. 226, note 3.

18. Quinet, *L'Enseignement du Peuple*, p. 25.

19. Quinet, *Vie et Mort du Génie Grec* (Paris: Germer-Baillière, n.d.), "Appendix," p. 285.

20. Quinet, *L'Enseignement du Peuple*, pp. 15 and 144-45.

21. Jules Michelet, *Le Peuple* (Édition original, publiée avec notes et variantes par Lucien Refort; Paris: Marcel Didier, 1946), p. 3.

22. *Ibid.*, pp. 269-71.

23. Quinet, *L'Enseignement du Peuple*, p. 186.

24. *Ibid.*, pp. 19-26 and 69.

25. *Ibid.*, pp. 144 and 160-61.

26. Lavisse, *op. cit.*, VI, 141.

27. *Ibid.*, pp. 149-50.

28. Quinet, *La République*, p. 126.

29. Gustave Flaubert, *L'Éducation Sentimentale: Histoire d'un Jeune Homme* (Paris: Éditions de Cluny, 1939), p. 329.

30. Quinet, *L'Enseignement du Peuple (Discours prononcé au Collège de France)*, p. 311.

31. Quinet, *L'Enseignement du Peuple* (*L'État de Siège; La Croisade Autrichienne, Française, Napolitaine, Espagnole contre la République Romaine;* and *Révision);* the first two in 1849, the last in 1851.
32. The second Mme Quinet was a native of Rumania. Disturbed at the thought that future biographers might pry into her past, she wrote down the version of her life she desired history should perpetuate: Her real existence began on December 2, 1851. Life with "God on earth" effaced from her memory her previous existence, years which could be of no possible interest to posterity. She added that in 1836 a young girl hardly fifteen had been married to a "byzantine prince," twenty years old and "a little mad." Two years later, after the birth of a son, the girl had been abandoned by her husband. She lived under her father's roof, devoting herself to her son, until 1845, when she came to Paris so that her boy might be brought up "on the ideas of justice and truth." In 1852 the "widow" had only consented to live again out of pity for the poor proscript. "Voilà la vérité devant Dieu et devant les hommes" (B.N., Nouv. acq. franç. 11832, "Journal Quinet," VIII, 182.
33. Quinet, *O.C.,* IV *(Les Révolutions d'Italie),* 468; 523-26.
34. *Ibid.,* p. 528.
35. Croce, *History of Europe in the Nineteenth Century,* p. 203.

Chapter 10

1. Mme Quinet, in *Edgar Quinet depuis l'Exil* and in *Mémoires d'Exil* (2 vols.; Paris: Lacroix, Verboeckhoven et Cie., 1868-70), gives a detailed account of the uneventful years of exile.
2. Quinet, *O.C.,* IV *(Les Révolutions d'Italie),* 383.
3. *Ibid.,* p. 513.
4. Quinet, *O.C.,* V, *Marnix de Sainte-Aldegonde* (Paris: Pagnerre, 1857), 79-85.
5. *Ibid.,* pp. 72-76.
6. Croce, *History of Europe in the Nineteenth Century,* pp. 287-88.
7. Quinet, *Le Livre de l'Exilé (La Révolution Religieuse au dix-neuvième Siècle,* first published in 1857), p. 539.
8. *Ibid. (Lettre sur la Situation Religieuse & Morale de l'Europe à Eugene Sue,* first published in 1856), p. 451.
9. *Ibid. (La Révolution Religieuse),* pp. 524-33.
10. Guido de Ruggiero, *The History of European Liberalism* (translated by R. G. Collingwood; London: Oxford University Press, 1927), p. 182.
11. Quinet, *Le Livre de l'Exilé (La Révolution Religieuse),* p. 500, and *ibid. (Lettre à Sue),* p. 449.
12. Quinet, *La Révolution, précédée de la Critique de la Révolution* (3 vols.; 9th ed.; Paris: Germer-Baillière, n.d.), I, 17-24.
13. *Ibid.,* II, 343-47 and 392-98.
14. Valès, *op. cit.,* pp. 298-99.
15. Quinet, *La Révolution,* II, 257.
16. *Ibid.,* I, 7-11 and 41-48.
17. Quinet, *O.C.,* III *(Le Christianisme et la Révolution française),* 226-33.
18. Quinet, *La Révolution,* I, 172-201 and III, 327.

19. *Ibid.*, I, 235; III, 103 and 260-62.
20. *Ibid.*, I, 347.
21. *Ibid.*, II, 254 and III, 394.
22. *Ibid.*, II, 381-83.
23. *Ibid.*, III, 213 and 306.
24. Quinet, *O.C.*, III, *Philosophie de l'Histoire de France* (Paris: Pagnerre, 1857), 355-56.
25. *Ibid.*, pp. 364 and 410-16.
26. Quinet, *Le Livre de l'Exilé (La Révolution Religieuse)*, pp. 549-50.
27. Quinet, *La Révolution*, III, 432-33.
28. Quinet, *Le Livre de l'Exilé (La Révolution Religieuse)*, pp. 546-55.

Chapter 11

1. B.N., Nouv. acq. franç. 20802, "Correspondence d'Edgar Quinet," XXII, 344.
2. For these appeals, a number of which were in the nature of handbills, see Quinet, *Le Siège de Paris et la Défense nationale* (Paris: Lacroix, Verboeckhoven et Cie., 1871).
3. Jules Simon, *The Government of M. Thiers* (2 vols.; New York: Scribner's Sons, 1879), I, 168. Several others did speak against the treaty. See Deschanel, *Gambetta* (New York: Dodd, Mead and Company, 1920), p. 140.
4. Gabriel Hanotaux, *Contemporary France* (4 vols., New York: G. P. Putnam's Sons, 1905-12), I, 35.
5. Juliette Adam, *Mes Sentiments et Nos Idées avant 1870* (Paris: Alphonse Lemerre, 1905), pp. 47-48 and 103.
6. Juliette Adam, *Mes Angoisses et Nos Luttes, 1871-1873* (Paris: A. Lemerre, 1907), pp. 223-24.
7. Hanotaux, *op. cit.*, III, 148.
8. Deschanel, *op. cit.*, pp. 192-93; and Hanotaux, *op. cit.*, III, 188-94.
9. Juliette Adam, *Nos Amitiés Politiques avant l'Abandon de la Revanche* (Paris: Alphonse Lemerre, 1908), p. 90.
10. B.N., Nouv. acq. franç. 20202 bis, "Inventaire méthodique des Papiers Quinet," ff. 12-24.
11. Quinet, *Vie et Mort du Génie grec*, pp. 298 and 304.
12. T.-G. Djuvara, *Edgar Quinet: Philo-Roumain* (Paris: Belin, 1906), pp. 68-69.
13. Hanotaux, *op. cit.*, II, 717.
14. Joseph Reinach, *La vie politique de Leon Gambetta suivie d'autres essais sur Gambetta* (Paris: F. Alcan, 1918), p. 222.
15. J. P. T. Bury, *Gambetta and the National Defence* (London: Longmans, Green and Co., 1936), p. 270.
16. Chassin, *op. cit.*, pp. 30-31.
17. Quinet, *O.C.*, III *(La Christianisme et la Révolution française)*, 273. *O.C.*, II *(L'Ultramontanisme)*, 145. *O.C.*, IV *(Les Révolutions d'Italie)*, 69-70. B.N., Nouv. acq. franç. 11826, "Journal Quinet," II, 46-47, for these quotations.

18. B.N., Nouv. acq. franç. 11825, "Journal Quinet," I, 125; and *ibid.*, 11837, "Journal Quinet," XIII, 46.
19. Quinet's bitterest thoughts about France were never published. During the years of exile he frequently despaired. In 1867 he wrote to a friend: "Dieu merci, j'ai vu clairement depuis seize ans qu'il n'y a rien attendre de cette nation pourrie pour plusiers générations. On m'accusait d'être sévère, et toujours elle s'est trouvé au-dessous de mes mépris." Mme Quinet suppressed all such passages, or greatly modified them, when she edited her husband's *Lettres d'Exil* (4 vols.; Paris: Calmann Lévy, 1885-86). See H. Monin, *op. cit.*, XV, 484.
20. B.N., Nouv. acq. franç. 11825, "Journal Quinet," I, 5; *ibid.*, 11831, "Journal Quinet," VII, 300.
21. Jean-Jacques Kaspar, *La Révolution religieuse d'après Edgar Quinet* (Paris: Fischbacker, 1906).
22. B.N., Nouv. acq. franç. 11826, "Journal Quinet," II, 269.
23. *Ibid.*, 11829, "Journal Quinet," V, 229.
24. *Ibid.*, 11830, "Journal Quinet," VI, 200.
25. H. Taine, *Ancien Régime* (vols. I, II of *Les Origines de la France Contemporaine*), (Paris: Hachette, n.d.), I, 315.
26. Quinet, *Lettres d'Exil*, III, 76-77. Seillière, *op. cit.*, pp. 91-101 is correct in his statement that Quinet answered friends who were critical on that score by denying that he meant to preach intolerance; but that he took back nothing in replies to other friends who approved of this aspect of the work. Seillière's further contention, that Quinet was more violent on this subject privately than in print, is not borne out by the letters he cites, not even in the cases where his citations prove to be related to his argument. See Quinet, *Lettres d'Exil*, I, 149-54, for an 1854 letter to Mazzini, and *ibid.*, II, 249-51, for an 1862 letter to Bataillard, both of which suggest the wisdom of using force against the Catholic Church.
27. Hans Kohn, *Prophets and Peoples: Studies in Nineteenth Century Nationalism* (New York: Macmillan, 1946), p. 76.
28. See B.N., Nouv. acq. franç. 11826, "Journal Quinet," II, 194-264 (October-December 1861).
29. B.N., Nouv. acq. franç. 11826, "Journal Quinet," II, 279; *ibid.*, 11830, "Journal Quinet," VI, 6; *ibid.*, fol. 74; *ibid.*, 11831, "Journal Quinet," VII, 178; *ibid.*, 11832, "Journal Quinet," VIII, 12.
30. Mme Quinet, *Cinquante ans d'Amitié*, p. 321. In the seven subsequent editions of *La Révolution* during Quinet's lifetime he did nothing to meet Michelet's criticism. There were many other factors but none so important in the breakup of the Quinet-Michelet friendship as this. See H. Monin, "La rupture de Michelet et de Quinet," *Revue d'Histoire littéraire de la France*, XIX (1912), 818-41, for the definitive account of this much mooted point.
31. B.N., Nouv. acq. franç. 11835, "Journal Quinet," XI, 37-38. Mme Quinet suppressed this passage *(Cinquante ans d'Amitié*, pp. 322-24), although she printed the letter.
32. Quinet, *Lettres d'Exil*, I, 240; II, 171.
33. Yvon Lapaquellerie, *Emile Combes ou le surprenant roman d'un honnête homme* (Paris: Flammarion, 1929), pp. 38-40.
34. Henry Michel, "Edgar Quinet," pp. 25-26.

Bibliography

I. MANUSCRIPTS

Quinet, Edgar. "Carnets d'Edgar Quinet." Nouvelles acquisitions françaises 20690 à 20735, Bibliothèque Nationale, Paris.
————. "Correspondance d'Edgar Quinet," I-XXII. Nouvelles acquisitions françaises 20781 à 20802, Bibliothèque Nationale, Paris.
————. "Inventaire méthodique des Papiers Quinet." Nouvelles acquisitions françaises 20802 bis, Bibliothèque Nationale, Paris.
————. "Journal Quinet," I-XX (janvier 1861 à août 1874). Nouvelles acquisitions françaises 11825 à 11844, Bibliothèque Nationale, Paris.

II. QUINET'S WORKS

1. Collected Works

Quinet, Edgar. *Oeuvres Complètes,* Paris: Pagnerre, 1857-58.
Volume I: *Le Génie des Religions; De l'Origine des Dieux; De l'Unité morale des Peuples modernes.*
Volume II: *Essai sur les Oeuvres de Herder; Introduction à la Philosophie de l'Histoire de l'Humanité; Les Jésuites; L'Ultramontanisme.*
Volume III: *Le Christianisme et la Révolution française; Examen de la Vie de Jésus-Christ; Philosophie de l'Histoire de France.*
Volume IV: *Les Révolutions d'Italie.*
Volume V: *Marnix de Sainte-Aldegonde; La Grèce moderne et ses Rapports avec l'Antiquité.*
Volume VI: *Allemagne et Italie; Mélanges; Les Roumains.*
Volume VII: *Ahasvérus; Les Tablettes du Juif errant.*
Volume VIII: *Les Esclaves; Napoléon; Prométhée.*
Volume IX: *Des Epopées françaises inédites du XIIe Siècle; De l'Histoire de la Poésie; Mes Vacances en Espagne.*
*Volume X: *Avertissement au Pays; La France et la Sainte Alliance en Portugal; Histoire de mes Idées; Oeuvres diverses; 1815 et 1840.*

*References in the text to works which appear in this volume are to other editions.

191

2. Thesis

Considérations philosophiques sur l'Art. Thèse de philosophie présentée à la Faculté des Lettres de l'Academie de Strasbourg, et soutenue publiquement le mercredi 23 janvier 1839, à 2 heurs après midi, pour obtenir le grade de docteur ès lettres.

3. Post-1857 Works

La Création. 2 vols. Paris: Lacroix, Verboeckhoven et Cie., 1870.

L'Esprit nouveau. Paris: Germer-Baillière, n.d.

L'Enseignement du Peuple. Oeuvres politiques avant l'Exil (La Croisade autrichienne, française, napolitaine, espagnole contre la République roumaine. Discours prononcé au Collège de France. L'État de Siège. Révision. 1815 et 1840). Paris: Germer-Baillière, n.d.

Histoire de mes Idées. 7th ed. Paris: Hachette, 1878.

Histoire de la Campagne de 1815. Paris: Germer-Baillière, n.d.

Le Livre de l'Exilé (Lettre sur la Situation religieuse & morale de l'Europe à Eugene Sue. La Révolution religieuse au dix-neuvième siècle). Paris: Germer-Baillière, n.d.

Merlin l'Enchanteur. 2 vols. Paris: Michel Lévy, 1860.

La République: Conditions de la Régénération de la France. Paris: Dentu, 1872.

La Révolution, précédé de la Critique de la Révolution. 3 vols. 9th ed. Paris: Germer-Baillière, n.d.

Le Siège de Paris et la Défense nationale. Paris: Lacroix, Verboeckhoven et Cie., 1871.

Vie et Mort du Génie grec. Paris: Germer-Baillière, n.d.

4. Published Correspondence

Lettres d'Exil. 4 vols. Paris: Calmann Lévy, 1885-86.

Lettres à sa Mère. 2 vols. Paris: Germer-Baillière, n.d.

Westphal, Alfred (ed.). Lettre-Préface de Gabriel Monod. *Lettres inédites d'Edgar Quinet.* Paris: Stock, 1907.

III. BIOGRAPHICAL AND MONOGRAPHIC STUDIES DEVOTED TO QUINET

1. Biographies

Chassin, Charles-Louis. *Edgar Quinet: Sa Vie et son Oeuvre.* Paris: Pagnerre, 1859.

Heath, Richard. *Edgar Quinet: His Early Life and Writings.* London: Trübner & Co., 1881.

Quinet, Mme Edgar. *Cinquante Ans d'Amitié: Michelet-Quinet (1826-1875).* 2nd ed. Paris: Armand Colin, 1903.

————. *Edgar Quinet avant l'Exil.* Paris: Calmann Lévy, 1887.

————. *Edgar Quinet depuis l'Exil.* Paris: Calmann Lévy, 1889.

————. *Mémoires d'Exil.* 2 vols. Paris: Lacroix, Verboeckhoven & Cie., 1868-70.

Seillière, Ernest. *Edgar Quinet et le Mysticisme démocratique.* Paris: Société d'Économie Sociale, 1919.

Valès, Albert. *Edgar Quinet: Sa Vie et son Oeuvre.* Vienne: E. Aubinet Fils, 1936.

2. Monographs

Djuvara, T.-G. *Edgar Quinet: Philo-Roumain.* Paris: Belin, 1906.

Gautier, Paul. *Un Prophète: Edgar Quinet.* Édition nouvelle de ses articles sur l'Allemagne d'après les textes originaux avec commentaire. Paris: Plon, 1917.

Guerle, Edmond de. *Edgar Quinet.* Paris: Ch. Noblet, 1876.

Kaspar, Jean-Jacques. *La Révolution religieuse d'après Edgar Quinet.* Paris: Fischbacher, 1906.

Molsen, Ulrich. *Philosophie und Dichtung bei Quinet.* Altona, 1913.

Tronchon, Henri. *Le Jeune Edgar Quinet ou l'Aventure d'un Enthousiaste.* Paris: Publications de la Faculté des Lettres de Strasbourg, 1937.

Wenderoth, Oskar. *Der junge Quinet und seine Übersetzung von Herders "Ideen": Ein Beitrag zur Geschichte der literarischen Wechselbeziehungen zwischen Frankreich und Deutschland.* Erlangen, 1906.

3. Articles

Auvray, L. "*Edgar Quinet e l'Italia,*" *Revue d'Histoire littéraire de la France,* XXVII (1920), 618-20.

Baldensperger, F. "Quelques lettres inédites de romantiques français à Goethe," *Revue d'Histoire littéraire de la France,* XV (1908), 335-38.

Boudout, Jean. "Faust et Ahasvérus," *Revue de Littérature comparée,* XVI (1936), 691-709.

Michel, Henry. "Edgar Quinet," *Cahiers de la Quinzaine* (July, 1903), pp. 9-33.

Monin, H. "Étude critique sur le Texte des *Lettres d'Exil d'Edgar Quinet,*" *Revue d'Histoire littéraire de la France,* XIV (1907), 106-18 and 515-29.

———. *Ibid.,* XV (1908), 479-90.

———. *Ibid.,* XVII (1910), 545-80.

———. "La Rupture de Michelet et de Quinet," *ibid.,* XIX (1912), 818-41.

"Notes et Documents," *Revue de Littérature comparée,* XVII (1937), 389.

Powers, Richard H. "Edgar Quinet and the First French Translation of Herder's *Ideen zur Geschichte der Menschheit,*" *Romanic Review,* XLV (April, 1954), 109-14.

———. "Edgar Quinet and the July Revolution," *The Historian,* XVII (Spring, 1955), 191-214.

Rudler, G. "Deux lettres d'Edgar Quinet à B. Constant et une lettre sur Benjamin Constant," *Revue d'Histoire littéraire de la France,* XVIII (1911), 941-43.

IV. CONTEMPORARY WORKS

The Private Journal of Henri Frédéric Amiel. Translated by Van Wyck Brooks and Charles Van Wyck Brooks. New York: Macmillan, 1935.

Ballanche, P. S. *Essais de Palingénésie sociale.* 2 vols. (Vol. I, *Prolégomènes;* Vol. II, *Orphée).* Paris: Jules Didot, 1827.

Bonald, Vicomte Louis Gabriel Ambroise de. *De la Chrétienté et du Christianisme.* Paris: 1824.

———. *Démonstration philosophique du Principe constitutif de la Société, suivie de Méditations politiques tirées de l'Evangile.* Paris, 1830.

Chateaubriand, François René. *Le Génie du Christianisme.* 2 vols. Paris: Dufour, Mulat et Boulanger, 1854.

Constant, Benjamin. *De la Religion, considérée dans sa Source, ses Formes et ses Développements.* 5 vols. 1824-31.

Cousin, Victor. *Du Vrai, du Beau et du Bien.* 2nd ed. Paris: Didier, 1854.

Dupanloup, l'Abbé. *De la Pacification religieuse.* Paris: Pacques Lecoffre, 1845.

Goethe. *Goethes Werke: Festausgabe,* Vol. III. Leipzig: Meyers Klassiker-Ausgaben, 1926.

Heine, Heinrich. *Sämtliche Werke,* Vol. VI. Leipzig: Meyers Klassiker-Ausgaben, n.d.

Hugo, Victor. *Histoire d'un Crime: Déposition d'un Témoin.* 2 vols. 31st ed. Paris: Calmann Lévy, 1877.

Lamennais, F. R. *Paroles d'un Croyant.* Paris: Édition du livre Français, 1946.

Marx, Karl. *Le 18-Brumaire de Louis Bonaparte.* Paris: Éditions Sociales, 1949.

Michelet, Jules. *Le Peuple.* Édition originale, publiée avec notes et variantes par Lucien Refort. Paris: Marcel Didier, 1946.

Mill, John Stuart. *Autobiography of John Stuart Mill.* New York: Columbia University Press, 1924.

Montlosier, Comte de. *Mémoire à consulter sur un Système religieux et politique, tendant à renverser la Religion, la Société et le Throne.* 7th ed. Paris: Ambroise Dupont et Roret, 1826.

Proudhon, P.-J. *La Révolution sociale demontrée par le Coup d'État de Deux Décembre.* Introduction et notes de Édouard Dolléans et Georges Duveau. Paris: Marcel Rivière, 1936.

Renan, Ernest. *L'Avenir de la Science: Pensées de 1848.* 25th ed. Paris: Calmann Lévy, 1929.

————. *Vie de Jésus.* Paris: Calmann Lévy, 1949.

Sainte-Beuve, C.-A. *Causeries du Lundi.* 11 vols. Paris: Garnier, n.d.

————. *Portraits Contemporains.* 5 vols. Paris: Michel Lévy, 1869.

Staël, Mme de. *De l'Allemagne.* Nouvelle édition. Paris: Garnier, 1874.

————. *Considérations sur les principaux Événemens de la Révolution françoise.* 3 vols. 3rd ed. Paris: Delaunay, 1820.

————. *Dix Années d'Exil: Fragmens d'un Ouvrage inédit, composé dans les Années 1810 à 1813.* Bruxelles: Louis Hauman, 1830.

Taillandier, Saint-René. *Histoire de la Jeune Allemagne.* Paris: A. Franck, 1848.

V. Works Relating
to France from 1815 to 1875

1. Correspondence

Correspondance du duc d'Aumale et de Cuvillier-Fleury. 2 vols. Introduction par René Vallery-Radot. Paris: Plon, 1910.

Lamartine, Mme Valentine. *Lettres à Lamartine: 1818-1865.* Paris: Calmann Lévy, 1892.

Sainte-Beuve, C.-A. *Correspondance Générale.* Paris: Stock, 1935- .

2. Memoirs

Adam, Juliette. *Mes Angoisses et nos Luttes, 1871-1873.* Paris: A. Lemerre, 1907.

————. *Mes Sentiments et nos Idées avant 1870.* Paris: Alphonse Lemerre, 1905.

————. *Nos Amitiés politiques avant l'Abandon de la Revanche.* Paris: Alphonse Lemerre, 1908.

Barrot, Odillon. *Mémoires posthumes de Odillon Barrot.* 4 vols. Paris: Charpentier et Cie., 1875-76.

Guizot, F. P. G. *Mémoires pour Servir à l'Histoire de mon Temps.* 8 vols. Paris: Michel Lévy, 1859-67.

Renan, Ernest. *Souvenirs d'Enfance et de Jeunesse.* 2nd ed. Paris: Calmann Lévy, 1883.

Simon, Jules. *The Government of M. Thiers, from 8th February, 1871, to 24th May, 1873.* 2 vols. New York: Charles Scribner's Sons, 1879.

3. General Histories

Artz, Frederick B. *Reaction and Revolution, 1814-1832.* New York: Harper & Brothers, 1934.

————. *France under the Bourbon Restoration: 1814-1830.* Cambridge: Harvard University Press, 1931.

Blanc, Louis. *Histoire de dix Ans, 1830-1840.* 5 vols. Paris: Pagnerre, 1849.

Charléty, S. *La Restauration: 1815-1830 (Histoire de France contemporaine depuis la Révolution jusqu'à la Paix de 1919,* ed. Ernest Lavisse, Vol. IV). Paris: Hachette, 1921.

————. *La Monarchie de Juillet: 1830-1848 (Histoire de France contemporaine depuis la Révolution jusqu'à la Paix de 1919,* ed. Ernest Lavisse, Vol. V). Paris: Hachette, 1921.

Croce, Benedetto. *History of Europe in the Nineteenth Century.* Translated by Henry Furst. New York: Harcourt, Brace and Company, 1933.

Garnier-Pagès, E. J. L. *Histoire de la Révolution de 1848.* 8 vols. Paris: Pagnerre, 1861-62.

Hanotaux, Gabriel. *Contemporary France.* 4 vols. New York: G. P. Putnam's Sons, 1905-12.

Seignobos, Ch. *La Révolution de 1848—Le Second Empire: 1848-1859 (Histoire de France contemporaine depuis la Révolution jusqu'à la Paix de 1919,* ed. Ernest Lavisse, Vol. VI). Paris: Hachette, 1921.

————. *Le Déclin de l'Empire et l'Établissement de la 3e République: 1859-1875 (Histoire de France contemporaine depuis la Révolu-*

tion jusqu'à la Paix de 1919, ed. Ernest Lavisse, Vol. VII). Paris: Hachette, 1921.

Taine, H. *Le Régime Moderne (Les Origines de la France contemporaine,* Vols. IX, X, XI). Paris: Hachette, n.d.

Thureau-Dangin, Paul. *Histoire de la Monarchie de Juillet.* 7 vols. Paris: E. Plon, Nourrit et Cie., 1884-92.

4. Biographies

Barthélemy Saint-Hilaire, J. M. *Victor Cousin: Sa Vie et sa Correspondance.* 3 vols. Paris: Felix Alcan, Hachette et Cie., 1895.

Biré, Edmond. *Victor Hugo après 1830.* 2 vols. Paris: Perrin et Cie., 1891.

Czapska, Marie. *La Vie de Mickiewicz.* Paris: Plon, 1931.

Deschanel, Paul Eugene Louis. *Gambetta.* New York: Dodd, Mead & Co., 1920.

Dupuy, Ernest. *Alfred de Vigny: ses Amitiés; son Rôle Littéraire.* 2 vols. Paris: Société Française d'Imprimerie et de Librairie, 1910.

George, Albert J. *Pierre Simon Ballanche, Precursor of Romanticism.* Syracuse: Syracuse University Press, 1945.

Lapaquellerie, Yvon. *Émile Combes ou le surprenant Roman d'un honnête Homme.* Paris: Flammarion, 1929.

Lucas-Dubreton, J. *Lamartine.* Paris: Flammarion, 1951.

Monod, Gabriel. *La Vie et la Pensée de Jules Michelet.* 2 vols. Paris: Bibliothèque de l'École des Hautes Études, 1923.

Reinach, Joseph. *La Vie politique de Leon Gambetta suivie d'autres Essais sur Gambetta.* Paris: F. Alcan, 1918.

Schoumacker, L. *Erckmann-Chatrian: Étude biographique et critique d'après des Documents inédits.* Strasbourg: Publications de la Faculté des Lettres de l'Université de Strasbourg, 1933.

5. Monographs

Baldensperger, Fernand. *Goethe en France: Étude de Littérature comparée.* 2nd ed. Paris: Hachette, 1920.

Boas, George. *French Philosophies of the Romantic Period.* Baltimore: Johns Hopkins Press, 1925.

Brandes, Georg. *Hauptströmungen der Literatur des Neunzehnten Jahrhunderts.* 3 vols. Berlin: Erich Reiss, 1924.

Bury, J. P. T. *Gambetta and the National Defence.* London: Longmans, Green and Co., 1936.

Clement, N. H. *Romanticism in France.* New York: Modern Language Association of America, 1939.

Cournot, Antoine Augustin. *Des Institutions d'Instruction publique en France.* Paris: 1864.

Dansette, Adrian. *Histoire religieuse de la France contemporaine.* 2 vols. Paris: Flammarion, 1951.

Debidour, A. *Histoire des Rapports de l'Église et de l'État en France de 1789 à 1870.* Paris: Alcan, 1898.

Dolléans, Édouard. *Histoire du Mouvement Ouvrier: 1871-1936.* 2 vols. 3rd ed. Paris: Armand Colin, 1947-48.

Evans, David Owen. *Social Romanticism in France, 1830-1848.* Oxford: Clarendon Press, 1951.

Faguet, Émile. *Politiques et Moralistes du dix-neuvième Siècle.* 3 vols. Paris: Société française d'Imprimerie et de Librairie, 1891-1900.

Fisher, H. A. L. *Bonapartism: Six Lectures.* Oxford, 1914.

Gautier, Paul. *Madame de Staël et Napoléon.* Paris: Plon-Nourrit, 1903.

Gunn, H. Alexander. *Modern French Philosophy: A Study of the Development since Comte.* New York: Dodd, Mead and Co., 1922.

Haac, Oscar A. *Les Principes inspirateurs de Michelet.* Paris: Presses Universitaires de France, 1951.

Hayes, Carlton H. *France: A Nation of Patriots.* New York: Columbia University Press, 1930.

Herriot, Édouard. *Madame Récamier et ses Amis.* Paris: Payot, 1948.

Hunt, Herbert James. *The Epic in Nineteenth-Century France: A Study in Heroic and Humanitarian Poetry from Les Martyrs to Les Siècles Morts.* Oxford: Basil Blackwell, 1941.

Kohn, Hans. *Prophets and Peoples: Studies in Nineteenth Century Nationalism.* New York: Macmillan, 1946.

Lanson, Gustave. *Histoire de la Littérature française.* 12th ed. Paris: Hachette, 1912.

Leroy, Maxime. *Histoire des Idées sociales en France de Babeuf à Tocqueville.* 4th ed. Paris: Gallimard, 1950.

Michel, Henry. *L'Idée de l'État: Essai critique sur l'Histoire des Théories sociales et politiques en France depuis la Révolution.* Paris: Hachette, 1896.

Marsan, Jules. *La Bataille romantique.* Paris: Hachette, 1912.

Moreau, Pierre. *Le Romantisme (Histoire de la Littérature française,* ed. J. Calvet, Vol. VIII). Paris: J. de Gigord, 1931-36.

Namier, L. B. *1848: The Revolution of the Intellectuals (Proceedings of the British Academy,* Vol. XXX). London, 1944.

Pellissier, Georges. *Le Mouvement littéraire au XIXe Siècle.* 9th ed. Paris: Hachette, 1912.

Ruggiero, Guido de. *The History of European Liberalism.* Translated by R. G. Collingwood. London: Oxford University Press, 1927.

Schapiro, J. Salwyn. *Liberalism and the Challenge of Fascism: Social Forces in England and France (1815-1870).* New York: McGraw-Hill, 1949.

Shafer, Boyd C. *Nationalism: Myth and Reality.* New York: Harcourt, 1955.

Shine, Hill. *Carlyle and the Saint-Simonians: The Concept of Historical Periodicity.* Baltimore: Johns Hopkins Press, 1941.

Soltau, Roger. *French Political Thought in the Nineteenth Century.* New Haven: Yale University Press, 1931.

Tchernoff, I. *Le Parti républicain sous la Monarchie de Juillet: Formation et Évolution de la Doctrine républicaine.* Paris: A. Pedone, 1901.

Tronchon, Henri. *Romantisme et Préromantisme.* Paris: Publications de la Faculté des Lettres de Strasbourg, 1930.

Weill, Georges. *L'École Saint-Simonienne: son Histoire, son Influence jusqu'à nos Jours.* Paris: Alcan, 1896.

————. *Histoire du Parti républicain en France (1814-1870).* Paris: Alcan, 1928.

6. *Contemporary Fiction*

Flaubert, Gustave. *L'Éducation sentimentale: Histoire d'un jeune Homme.* Paris: Éditions de Cluny, 1939.

Musset, Alfred de. *La Confession d'un Enfant du Siècle.* Paris: Charpentier et Fasquelle, 1910.

Stendhal. *Le Rouge et le Noir, Chronique du XIXe Siècle,* ed. Henri Martineau. Paris: Garnier, 1950.

VI. THE ENLIGHTENMENT

Brandt, Richard B. *The Philosophy of Schleiermacher: The Development of His Theory of Scientific and Religious Knowledge.* New York: Harper & Bros., 1941.

Cassirer, Ernst. *Die Philosophie der Aufklärung.* Tübingen, 1932.

Croce, Benedetto. *Die Philosophie Giambattista Vicos.* Tübingen: J. C. B. Mohr, 1927.

Dorn, Walter L. *Competition for Empire: 1740-1763.* New York: Harper & Bros., 1940.

Herder, Johann Gottfreid. *God: Some Conversations.* Translated by Frederick H. Burkhardt. New York: Veritas Press, 1940.

————. *Ideen zur Philosophie der Geschichte der Menschheit* ("Deutsche National-Litteratur," ed. Eugen Kühnemann). Stuttgart, n.d.

Meinecke, Friedrick. *Die Entstehung des Historismus.* München und Berlin: R. Oldenbourg, 1936.

Pfleiderer, Otto. *The Philosophy of Religion on the Basis of Its History.* Translated by Alexander Stewart and Allan Menzies. 4 vols. London: Williams and Norgate, 1886-88.

Robertson, J. G. *Studies in the Genesis of Romantic Theory in the Eighteenth Century.* Cambridge University Press, 1923.

Schleiermacher, Friedrich. *The Christian Faith,* eds. H. R. Mackintosh and J. S. Stewart. Edinburgh: T. and T. Clark, 1928.

Vico, G. *The Autobiography of Giambattista Vico.* Translated by Max Fisch and Thomas Bergin. Ithaca: Cornell University Press, 1944.

————. *The New Science of Giambattista Vico.* Translated by Thomas G. Bergin and Max H. Fisch. Ithaca: Cornell University Press, 1948.

VII. MISCELLANEOUS

Becker, Carl. *Everyman His Own Historian.* New York: Scribners, 1935.

————. *The Heavenly City of the Eighteenth Century Philosophers.* New Haven: Yale University Press, 1932.

Boehmer, Heinrich. *The Jesuits: An Historical Study.* Translated by P. Z. Strodach. Philadelphia: The Castle Press, 1928.

Curtius, Ernst Robert. *Frankreich: Die Französische Kultur; eine Einfuhrung.* Berlin: Deutsche Verlags-Anstalt, 1931.

Fauvet, Jacques. *Les Forces Politiques en France.* Paris: Éditions "Le Monde," 1951.

Lovejoy, Arthur O. *The Great Chain of Being: A Study of the History of an Idea.* Cambridge: Harvard University Press, 1950.

Maritain, Jacques. *Man and the State.* Chicago: University of Chicago Press, 1951.

————. *Three Reformers: Luther—Descartes—Rousseau.* New York. Charles Scribner's Sons, n.d.

Ortega y Gasset, José. *The Revolt of the Masses.* New York: W. W. Norton, 1932.

Pariset, G. *La Révolution: 1792-1799. (Histoire de France contemporaine depuis la Révolution jusqu'à la Paix de 1919,* ed. Ernest Lavisse, Vol. II). Paris: Hachette, 1921.

Rousseau, J.-J. *Émile ou de l'Éducation.* Introduction par Françoise et Pierre Richard. Paris: Garnier, 1951.

Saint-Leger, A. de., Rebelliau, A., and Sagnac, P. *Louis XIV. La Fin du Règne: 1685-1715 (Histoire de France depuis les origines jusqu'à la Révolution,* ed. Ernest Lavisse, Vol. VIII, Part 1). Paris: Hachette, 1911.

Smith, Preserved. *The Age of the Reformation.* New York: Henry Holt and Co., 1920.

Treitschke, Heinrich von. *Politics.* Translated by Blanche Dugdale and Torben de Bille. Introduction by Arthur James Balfour. 2 vols. New York: Macmillan, 1916.

Troeltsch, Ernst. *Protestantism and Progress: A Historical Study of the Relation of Protestantism to the Modern World.* Translated by W. Montgomery. London: Williams & Norgate, 1912.

Index